The Trial
of the Poet

The Trial
of the Poet

AN INTERPRETATION
OF THE FIRST EDITION OF
Leaves of Grass

by
Ivan Marki

NEW YORK
COLUMBIA UNIVERSITY PRESS
1976

The Andrew W. Mellon Foundation, through a special grant,
has assisted the Press in publishing this volume.

Library of Congress Cataloging in Publication Data

Marki, Ivan.
  The trial of the poet.

  Bibliography: p.
  Includes index.
  1. Whitman, Walt, 1819–1892.   Leaves of grass.
I. Title.
PS3238.M27   811'.3   76-18792
ISBN 0-231-03984-0

Columbia University Press
New York—Guildford, Surrey

For Jeanne

CONTENTS

CONTENTS

PART THREE: THE OTHER POEMS

PREFACE

This study offers a critical explication of the text of the first edition of *Leaves of Grass*—the thin quarto which pious tradition insists was published on the Fourth of July in 1855. It astounded a few people like Emerson, outraged a few others like Whittier, and then, having yielded the barest encouragement to its author, disappeared from view, to remain for nearly a century "the buried masterpiece of American writing." When Malcolm Cowley unearthed it with that memorable phrase in the introduction to his excellent modern edition of the text—*Walt Whitman's Leaves of Grass; The First (1855) Edition* (New York: The Viking Press, 1959)—he also made "some unqualified statements . . . of simple truths that should have been recognized long ago," perhaps the simplest among them being "that the long opening poem . . . is Whitman's greatest work . . . and one of the great poems of modern times" and "that the first edition is a unified work" (p. x). It is the ambition of this study to add to the substance of Cowley's inspiring assertions by allowing analysis to do its job of "[improving] our intuition of any complex whole" (W. K. Wimsatt, Jr., "Explication as Criticism," in *Explication as Criticism*, ed. W. K. Wimsatt, Jr. [New York: Columbia University Press, 1963], p. 23).

PREFACE

The argument is organized into three phases, after the division into which Whitman's own book seems to fall naturally. Coleridge once complained that often "what is charged to the *author,* belongs to the *man*" (*Biographia Literaria,* ed. J. Shawcross [1907; rpt. London: Oxford University Press, 1965], I, 24). Whitman's predicament, it seems, was twice as difficult: before "Walt" could become "the greatest poet," "Walter" had to find "Walt" in himself. After an introduction in which the critical perspectives of the discussion are elaborated and the pertinent facts of the book's history and appearance reviewed, four chapters trace the manner in which the creative personality capable of becoming the "I" of the poems emerges from the essay opening the volume. The next four chapters deal with Whitman's greatest achievement: the first, long poem, which creates the poet out of the man encountered in the essay. Finally, the concluding chapter assesses the book as a whole through a survey of its "other" poems.

I want to acknowledge my debt of gratitude to the many people who have helped me in the preparation of this study. I wish to thank the following: George Stade, for his tact and patience in reading the entire manuscript and for his excellent advice; Michael Rosenthal; Carl F. Hovde; Lewis Leary, under whose guidance my work on Whitman began, for his support and encouragement of the first, very tentative outlines of this study; Owen Barfield, for some instructive conversations on Coleridge, Whitman, and organicism; my colleagues, past and present, in the Department of English at Hamilton College, particularly Dwight N. Lindley, Frederick Wagner, and, for his careful reading of chapter 5, Ronald Wendling; Russell Blackwood, of the Department of Philosophy at Hamilton, for allowing me to test on him the reasons for my reluctance to regard Whitman as a mystic; and Stephen G. Kurtz, Principal of Phillips Exeter Academy and formerly Dean of Hamilton College, for his friendship and encouragement.

Most of my research was done at the Libraries of Columbia University, but it also led me to the New York Public Library and, for a look at O. S. Fowler's silly book on "amativeness," to the Library of Congress. I am indebted to the Berg Collection of the New York Public Library for permission to read through the Whitman holographs that might have proved relevant to my subject and to the Oscar Lion Collection of the New York Public Library for permission to examine Whitman's own paperbound copy of the first edition. For courtesies and hospitality extended over several summers I am grateful to the Library of Eckerd College (founded as Florida Presbyterian College). That new developments in Whitman criticism and scholarship have not left me behind during the long years of writing is due, to an extent I deeply appreciate, to the Hamilton College Library, particularly to the helpfulness and efficiency of its Interlibrary Loan staff.

I regret that my argument could not draw on Stephen A. Black's *Whitman's Journeys into Chaos: A Psychoanalytic Study of the Poetic Process* (Princeton: Princeton University Press, 1975). The manuscript of my study had been sent to the printer before Professor Black's book was published.

I am grateful to the Woodrow Wilson Foundation for a Dissertation Fellowship in 1964/65, which enabled me to begin this study, to Hamilton College for the financial assistance which enabled me to complete it, and to the Mellon Foundation for the funds which made its publication possible.

I also wish to thank William F. Bernhardt and David Diefendorf, of Columbia University Press, for editing the manuscript.

Without my wife's patient devotion and good-humored goading, this book would have taken even longer to write than it has; my special gratitude to her goes without saying, but I am happy and eager to say it anyway.

ABBREVIATIONS

Centenary *The Complete Works of Ralph Waldo Emerson*, ed. E. W. Emerson, 12 volumes (Boston: Houghton Mifflin, 1903).

Corr Walt Whitman, *The Correspondence*, ed. Edwin H. Miller, 5 volumes.
> Vol. I, 1846–1867 (New York: New York University Press, 1961);
> Vol. II, 1868–1875 (New York: New York University Press, 1961).

Cowley *Walt Whitman's Leaves of Grass: The First (1855) Edition*, ed. Malcolm Cowley (New York: The Viking Press, 1959).

CRE Walt Whitman, *Leaves of Grass: Comprehensive Reader's Edition*, ed. Harold W. Blodgett and Sculley Bradley (New York: New York University Press, 1965).

Early Walt Whitman, *The Early Poems and the Fiction*, ed. Thomas L. Brasher (New York: New York University Press, 1963).

Facs Walt Whitman, *Leaves of Grass: Facsimile of the 1855 Edition*, ed. Clifton Joseph Furness; Facsimile

Text Society, Publication No. 47 (New York: Columbia University Press, 1939).

Handbook   Gay Wilson Allen, *Walt Whitman Handbook* (Chicago: Packard and Co., 1946).

Naissance   Jean Catel, *Walt Whitman: La Naissance du Poète* (Paris: Rieder, 1929).

PW 1892   Walt Whitman, *Prose Works 1892,* ed. Floyd Stovall, 2 volumes.

> Vol. I, *Specimen Days* (New York: New York University Press, 1963);
>
> Vol. II, *Collect and Other Prose* (New York: New York University Press, 1963).

Revisions   Sister Mary William Brady, *Whitman's Revisions of the "Song of Myself"* (Diss., University of Chicago, 1947).

Singer   Gay Wilson Allen, *The Solitary Singer: A Critical Biography of Walt Whitman* (New York: Grove Press, 1955).

UPP   *The Uncollected Poetry and Prose of Walt Whitman,* ed. Emory Holloway, 2 volumes (Garden City, N.Y.: Doubleday, Page and Co., 1921).

WWC   Horace Traubel, *With Walt Whitman in Camden,* 5 volumes.

> Vol. I, (Boston: Small, Maynard, and Co., 1906);
>
> Vol. II, (New York: D. Appleton and Co., 1908);
>
> Vol. III, (New York: M. Kennedy, 1914);
>
> Vol. IV, ed. Sculley Bardley (Philadelphia: University of Pennsylvania Press, 1953);
>
> Vol. V, ed. Gertrude Traubel (Carbondale, Ill.: Southern Illinois University Press, 1964).

Workshop   *Walt Whitman's Workshop: A Collection of Unpublished Manuscripts,* ed. C. J. Furness (Cambridge, Mass.: Harvard University Press, 1928).

NOTE ON QUOTATIONS

References to the first edition of *Leaves of Grass* are indicated in parentheses within the text. The *Facs* text has been used throughout; however, for easier reference, individual lines from the poems have been identified by the numbering they have in *Cowley*. Lower case Roman numerals refer to the Preface by page; Arabic numerals without further identification refer to line numbers in the first poem ("Song of Myself"); line references to the other poems in the volume are preceded by the title they bear in *Cowley*. Also, to avoid confusion with Whitman's use of four and sometimes two points of suspension, ellipses not his own are enclosed in square brackets, thus: [. . .].

The system is much less complicated than its description.

Unless otherwise indicated, passages from foreign languages have been translated by me.

The Trial
of the Poet

INTRODUCTION

Walt Whitman has remained unfinished business for Americans to this day. More than a century has passed since he declared, more in impatience than in self-confidence, that "the direct trial of him who would be the greatest poet is today" (xi), yet it is still not clear whether the country for which he wrote has, in fact, "[absorbed] him as affectionately as he has absorbed it" (xii). His "presence" has, obviously, not "conquered" as completely and irresistibly as he said "the presence of the greatest poet" (v) would, nor has he receded into the ignominy and ridicule that some of his first readers prophesied for him. He is "around, tenacious, acquisitive, tireless . . . . and can never be shaken away" (139): just when he seems to have been permanently fixed, as "good gray poet" or "the bard of democracy," an innocuous object of obligatory national pride, another Whitman revival gets under way, and the trial of the poet continues.

Part of the reason for this stubborn fascination with Whitman is, no doubt, in the peculiar elusiveness of his work. "To elaborate is no avail" (40), he warned, yet since the time his advice was first heard many have found it impossible to follow, for his book engages the intellect as powerfully as it does the feelings, just as he knew it would: "My words itch at your ears till

1

you understand them" (1242). The head keeps trying to catch up with the heart's often deceptively easy and immediate under-standing, and in the face of long and rather bitter experience the illusion persists that full comprehension is within arm's reach and takes just one more effort to attain. The "poet of common-sense and of the demonstrable" (466), who boasts that he "per-mit[s Nature] to speak at every hazard," [1] proves, in the end, that he was also telling the truth when he admitted that "there is something in [his] nature *furtive* like an old hen!" [2]

Much more important, however, than the various puzzles in Whitman's text is the problem of his statement taken as a whole. The response to his work has been dominated from the first by the indistinct yet inescapable sense that what he does has pro-found relevance to what Americans are all about. "That he was an American," wrote Charles Eliot Norton about the poet of *Leaves of Grass* in 1855, "we knew before, for, aside from America, there is no quarter of the universe where such a pro-duction could have had a genesis," [3] and a century later Randall Jarrell echoes him: " 'How very American! If [Whitman] and his country had not existed, it would have been impossible to imag-ine him.' " [4] This persistent conviction is the force that has not allowed opinions to settle about *Leaves of Grass*, because it means not only that by understanding Whitman Americans un-derstand themselves but that they understand themselves only so far as they understand Whitman. For this reason, the famous "pact" Ezra Pound wrote of must be kept under permanent re-view. Since the day it appeared, *Leaves of Grass* has been felt to be the classic test of national self-recognition in all American po-etry. To follow up this intuitive response analytically and to artic-ulate the sense in which the poet's achievement of personal selfhood also implies a proposition of collective identity is the continual challenge at the heart of all critical concern with Whit-man.

The pages that follow attempt to contribute toward meeting that challenge by offering a detailed interpretation of the first *Leaves of Grass*. The book's importance in assessing Whitman's

INTRODUCTION

life's work had been widely recognized even before Malcolm Cowley declared that it was "the buried masterpiece of American writing." [5] The Whitman whom the world has not quite been able to get out of its mind appears in full strength and purest form in the first edition; the later editions may reinforce and, particularly in 1860, even enhance his stature as a poet, but his impact as "a figure in the culture" [6] is softened with every reappearance. Also, in no subsequent edition is integrity of vision and structure realized as successfully as in the first, and the text of the two most important poems in it—the ones that eventually became "Song of Myself" and "The Sleepers"—is clearly superior to all later revisions. There are, of course, considerably less impressive poems in the volume as well. The 1855 version of the Deathbed Edition's "I Sing the Body Electric" or "A Song for Occupations," for example, profited by virtually every correction and emendation Whitman could make in it over the years, and his decision to omit from *Leaves of Grass* the poem which concluded the first edition came none too soon in 1881. [7] Two others ("Europe: the 72d and 73d Years of These States" and "A Boston Ballad" are the titles they finally received) definitely antedate the rest of the poems, [8] and the reason why Whitman included these very indifferent pieces in *Leaves of Grass* at all is rather hard to see, unless it was to swell the bulk, though decidedly not the substance, of his volume. Thus, "buried masterpiece" though the first *Leaves* may be, it is by no means flawless. Of course, attempts to rank the various editions seem really beside the point. The present study, in any case, was inspired by the many singular virtues of the edition of 1855, but it is undertaken to elucidate the book's significance, not to "champion its cause."

Although the first edition has not been examined in a book-length study before, it has been dealt with on a smaller scale in a number of articles or within summary assessments of Whitman's accomplishment. For all their brevity, some of these, particularly Cowley's introduction to his edition of the 1855 text and Gay Wilson Allen's commentary in his admirable biography of Whitman, sketch out with remarkable accuracy perspectives from

3

which the volume can be viewed as a single, complete work of art in its own right.[9] For the other treatments, however, the useful significance of the book is usually the historical, and they discuss it primarily in the context of Whitman's development as a poet, some of them leading up to it, like Jean Catel's biographical study, some others taking off from it, like Roger Asselineau's history of Whitman's career.[10] But even if the first edition as a whole has not received all the critical attention it deserves, some of its contents most definitely have. Of its major portions only the preface can be said to have suffered undue neglect; most of the poems have been—in their final version, of course—quite often discussed, and "Song of Myself" and "The Sleepers" have provoked voluminous commentary and some of the most inventive and penetrating observations on Whitman's art. As a matter of fact, the variety, thoroughness, and sophistication that the tradition of reading these two poems has acquired over more than a century grant latter-day studies—the present one among them—the luxury of not starting to discuss them all over again from naive extremes but often merely dotting the i's that earlier labor has written. This may be the first detailed interpretation of the first edition, but much of the ground it has to cover has been broken before.

The logical point of departure in analyzing the first *Leaves* was indicated by Emerson: "for such a start," there must have been "a long foreground somewhere." [11] The hint has been taken up by several scholars since, and by now that "long foreground," the thirty-six years of Whitman's life until the publication of *Leaves of Grass,* has been explored with greater thoroughness and precision than one might have thought possible at first.[12] The more details are uncovered, however, the greater the mystery they should be shedding light on. It may have seemed a logical first step, but the study of the volume's origins has proved unable so far to answer the question that prompted it and is unlikely to do so in the future. Sometime in the late 1840's a thoroughly undistinguished, indolent, and no longer very young newspaperman began to jot down some very

4

private speculations, in which a much delayed personal identity crisis is fitfully intermingled with the concerns and occasionally the idiom of the chronic crisis of national identity. He is cautious at first:

> The truths I tell to you or to any other may not be plain to you, because I do not translate them fully from my idiom into yours.—If I could do so, and do it well, they would be as apparent to you as they are to me; for they are truths.—No two have exactly the same language, and the great translator and joiner of the whole is the poet.

But then, in the same notebook, after some blank pages, he erupts with a litany of assertions, feverishly repeating: "I am the poet"—"of slaves, and of the masters of slaves," "of Strength and Hope," "of reality," "of little things and of babes," "of Equality," and at last starkly, without modifiers: "I am the Poet." [13] What brought on this sudden, devastating self-confidence? And, perhaps more important, what could make it recede again? These lines, according to Holloway, were most probably written not later than 1849; [14] after five years, Whitman was still not always sure that he was, indeed, "the Poet." In another notebook he wrote of a shipwreck that had occurred in December 1853; [15] the "Poet's" reaction is first described in the third person—"All this he drinks in his soul, and it becomes his"—and only then emended to read: "All this I swallow in my soul, and it becomes mine, and I like it well." [16] Not a single item in the wealth of biographical details brought to light so far can explain either the causes that led Whitman to view himself in these perspectives or his vacillations and diffidence about accepting what he saw; least of all can it explain his decision in the end to submit his tentative, insecure poet-self to "trial" (xi) by publishing Leaves of Grass. The "long foreground" has kept its secret almost as if it consisted only of those few blank pages which precede Whitman's first extant attempts in his characteristic verse. The manuscript of the poems in the first edition might be, of course, much more revealing, if it had survived, but

INTRODUCTION

Whitman, who later preferred living knee-deep in paper to throwing even his most trivial jottings away, claimed not to have cared enough about it at the time to retrieve it from the printer. In 1888 he remarked to Traubel:

> You have asked me questions about the manuscript of the first edition. It was burned. Rome [i.e., Andrew or James Rome, the book's printers [17]] kept it several years, but one day, by accident, it got away from us entirely—was used to kindle the fire or to feed the rag man.[18]

Thus, any effort to interpret the first edition has no alternative but to rely on what the text is in and by itself. The emphasis in this study on structural analysis and on explication is, therefore, not just a matter of critical temperament and inclination (although it is that, too, of course) but of necessity as well. It behooves explications to apologize for themselves in these days of loud reaction against the excesses of New Criticism, but they have no reason to doubt their essential usefulness to the study of literature. "Such jobs still need doing," allows even Roy Harvey Pearce, eager as he is to instruct the critic to find the proper "relevance" of his work in "historicism." [19] In any case, no good explication can be all explication. Possibilities of interpreting the poems in the context of literary or cultural history are not ignored in this study, but it has been undertaken not so much to follow up such possibilities as to make the text of the first edition more accessible than it seems to have been so far to those critics who wish to follow them up. This approach may be New Critical, but only in a very pragmatic way. In fact, it seems only common sense rather than New Criticism to attempt to ask all the questions one finds pertinent to the poem's meaning and to use all the evidence one finds pertinent to answering them. The pages that follow are bound by little else beyond this rule of thumb.

The immediate circumstances of the book's publication as well as the first impression that its visual and physical character may have made on the contemporary reader have been often discussed and need no elaborate recapitulation. Tradition holds that *Leaves of Grass* was put on sale in New York on July 4, 1855, but a number of scholars have shown that July 5 is a much more likely date.[20] About eight hundred copies were bound and sheets for many more printed; between July 1855 and August 1856 the edition saw four issues altogether—two in hard cover, each of them followed by a paperbound version. The printing was done by the brothers Andrew and James Rome, of Brooklyn, and Fowler and Wells, "Phrenologists and Publishers," were in charge of the book's distribution.[21] At various times Whitman claimed both that the first *Leaves of Grass* sold very well and that it sold not at all: the latter claim, though probably exaggerated, seems closer to the truth.[22] Several complimentary copies were also sent out, and one of these—a cheaper, paperbound copy [23]—aroused Emerson's curiosity. The rest is literary history.

The looks of the volume have always aroused considerable commentary. The book probably appears odder today than on the day it was published, but even if its decorations fall within the age's conventions of taste, it is obviously laid out in a fashion contrived to give pause. The quarto size strikes one as rather exaggerated for such a skimpy book, and the binding arrests the eye with the quaint title's curious design, which makes *Leaves of Grass* look like weeds of gold, and with the "now-you-see-it-now-you-don't" foliage embossed on the green hard covers. The author's name is missing so conspicuously that by the time one turns to the acknowledgment of legal ownership by "Walter Whitman" on the inside of the title-page, the name seems to belong to someone connected at best only technically with the volume.

The strange, unidiomatic title itself has been frequently discussed. It "probably grew out of a general trend of the times," C. J. Furness noted, adding that the direct inspiration for it most likely came through the popularity, during the years just before 1855, of the *Leaves* from the *Portfolios* of Whitman's friend Mrs. Sara Payson Willis Parton, who wrote under the penname of Fanny Fern. Furness also conjectured very persuasively that

Whitman's metaphor was also punning in current printer's slang, in which " 'grass' . . . means a person who does casual work around the shop, and applies as well to the work such a person does," so that "leaves" of "grass" could also mean "printed sheets of poetic composition probably regarded by the shop as effusions of dubious merit." [24] At the same time, as Joseph Jay Rubin observes, "grass" recalls the biblical image: "All flesh is grass . . . surely the people is grass." [25] Along with these inventive suggestions, however, one must also remember that, so far as Whitman had a consistent theory of art, that theory, as the preface to the first edition demonstrates, was a version of organicism, and in the literature of organicism vegetable growth is the master-analogy and "leaves" the favorite metaphor. For example, Goethe, notes Owen Barfield, "found that the leaf of a plant expressed its essential nature as plant, while the blossom and the root could be considered as metamorphoses of the leaf." [26] It is not entirely impossible that it was Goethe's formulation, given in a somewhat more complex and detailed manner in his botanical writings,[27] that trickled down to Whitman, since Emerson made a note of it in his journals decades before,[28] then incorporated his note into one of his lectures, which he delivered on a number of occasions; [29] Whitman, who is said to have heard Emerson for the first time in 1842,[30] may have attended one of these lectures. This sort of guessing, of course, cannot be anything but idle, in the end. The metaphor, at any rate, had become quite hackneyed by the time the irrepressible Fanny Fern got hold of it, and it is pointless to speculate just which one of the literally scores of potential examples[31] Whitman followed in choosing his title. Obviously, his choice itself can hardly be called original; what he developed from it is another matter.

The striking portrait facing the title-page is another noteworthy item. It impresses the onlooker as a kind of self-portrait—not the artist's vision of a model but the model's vision of himself. According to Samuel Hollyer, who engraved the portrait in the spring of 1855 after a daguerreotype taken "on a hot day in July, 1854," [32] Whitman did, as a matter of fact, ask for "one or two trifling alterations" on the picture's first version.[33] Just what those adjustments were it is impossible to tell now, but the story confirms the impression that Whitman had the picture prepared and possibly even struck his pose for the daguerreotype with a specific purpose for the book's design in mind. The self-consciously negligent pose and the informal clothing reminded Cowley "of a devil-may-care American workingman, one who might be taken for a somewhat idealized figure in almost any crowd." [34] One is also reminded of an anecdote Perry Miller has recorded about Evert Duyckinck and Charles Frederick Briggs. Duyckinck visited "Harry Franco" on Staten Island unexpectedly in 1843 and found him "without shoes, stockings, neckerchief, coat, or suspenders," that is, looking very much like the man on the frontispiece of the first *Leaves of Grass*. Briggs' attire meant not only that he was no gentleman but that he was, in his shocked visitor's words, "as nearly in a state of nudity as decency permitted." [35]

Duyckinck may have been perhaps a touch too squeamish, but his response probably reflects the standards and expectations of his contemporaries closely enough, nor are those standards likely to have changed much during the twelve years between 1843 and 1855. Whitman, therefore, had to know that the man on the frontispiece of his book was, for all social intents and purposes, virtually naked. The "hankering, gross, mystical, nude" (388) poet felt in his senses and his imagination alike that nudity was truth made visible, and he went to the woods to become "naked" because it meant being "undisguised" (11); he gave the irresistible command, "Undrape . . . " (137), to all while "worshipping" the "spread of [his] body" (530), because he believed with Diogenes Teufelsdröckh that

> there is something great in the moment when a man first strips himself of adventitious wrappages; and sees indeed that he is naked, and, as Swift has it, 'a forked straddling animal with bandy legs'; yet also a Spirit, and unutterable Mystery of Mysteries. [36]

It seems neither impossible nor improbable, then, that he would begin his performance by revealing himself not in a name or a mere likeness of features but in the pose and condition representing his self's truth as in his aspirations he conceived of it. Through the portrait he steps forth "as nearly in a state of nudity as decency permits," to come naked into the book in which he is willing himself to life, in which he is born.

Thus, even before he was admitted to the text itself, the reader who happened to pick up Whitman's slim volume in July 1855 was put on notice by an elaborate and purposeful layout that traditional or conventional expectations were not going to be of much use to him if he chose to read it. As he turned the page to the opening essay, he was free to remember all that he had read before, but he would have been ill-advised to start reading with any preconceived notion at all about what he should find this time. The warning was worth heeding then, and it is worth heeding today.

Part One

THE PREFACE

Chapter One

WHAT'S IN A TITLE?

I

In a volume meticulously designed to engage the reader's attention through a calculated visual effect, the ten pages of the Preface to the first edition of *Leaves of Grass* practically beg to be skipped over. With their double columns of thickly-set small type they look as if their sole function were to make plainly visible the difference between themselves and the pages that follow and foil with the uninviting format of their prose what otherwise might not necessarily have been taken for poetry. A simple glance at those pages easily confirms Bliss Perry's suspicion, that the book's first readers probably did skip them over, although had they but looked they would have found their efforts abundantly rewarded.[1]

Whitman himself seems to have shared, oddly enough, his first readers' presumable attitude toward the essay. In 1870, in a letter to Peter Dixon, one of his self-appointed disciples, he wrote:

> My prose preface to first Leaves of Grass . . . was written hastily while the first edition was being printed in 1855—I do not consider it of permanent value.[2]

13

The context might mitigate somewhat the curt finality of the statement, since the whole letter suggests a certain coolness toward Dixon, but some other remarks, made three years earlier, in the course of the correspondence preceding the first English edition of his work, would seem to prove beyond any doubt that, for a while at least, Whitman for some reason did not take very great pride in his essay. "It is a question with me," he wrote in a letter to Moncure Conway, "whether the introductory essay or prose preface to the first edition is worth printing.[3] He confirmed his opinion by the offhand manner in which shortly afterwards he authorized William Rossetti, the editor of the projected volume of selections, "to change certain words in the Preface to the first edition of poems, etc. . . . ," while politely but forcefully insisting on his exclusive right to do so in the poems.[4] Obviously, Whitman no longer felt about the Preface that "who touches this touches a man," and this apparent repudiation has been often taken for "another example of his inability to recognize his own greatest achievements." [5]

This opinion is given further support by the poet himself, who in his declining years persisted in deprecating the worth of his essay, despite occasional second thoughts.[6] Before concluding, however, that Whitman could write only by ear, and his ear, apparently, was not always infallible, one should consider also the evidence of his steady preoccupation with this piece.[7] He continued to elaborate the notions and pronouncements of his essay in his poetry for nearly eleven years, transposing from it whole passages or single lines and phrases, as the case might be, unchanged or with the slightest alterations, into poems which were incorporated by him in what he considered the definitive version of his volume. "No one of [the Preface's] twenty-eight paragraphs was wholly neglected," writes Willie T. Weathers, and twenty-four of the twenty-eight were extensively used; in other words, according to his count, out of the 789 lines of the Preface, 347 are, one way or another, reproduced in poetic lines—an astonishing reliance on composition claimed to be unfinished and insignificant.[8] Weathers concludes, "that it was

only the prefatorial form which the poet considered of no permanent value," [9] but one may well wonder if even this conclusion does complete justice to the essay or to Whitman's competence in assessing his own performance.

II

The first reviewer of *Leaves of Grass,* Charles A. Dana, took it for
granted that the long essay preceding the poems was a "preface," that the preface contained "the poetic theory of our name-
less bard" and was meant "to enlighten our benighted minds as
to the true function of the American poet," and, finally, that the
poems were "doubtless intended as an illustration of the natural
poet." [10] Thus, the view that the poet announced his program
and theory in the preface and tried to implement them in his
poems is among the oldest traditions of Whitman criticism. The
argument of the essay, according to this theory and in the words
of Willie T. Weathers, can be summarized as follows:

> Within the frame of an introductory statement of America's need
> and a concluding prediction that she will immediately recognize
> her own when he appears, is inclosed a discussion of his necessary
> qualifications and of the form and subject matter which he must
> use: the ideal man in his physical and mental heredity, the ideal
> American in what he has absorbed from his environment, and a
> poet endowed with superlative spiritual vision and the originality to
> abandon poetic conventions for new and indigenous forms, he
> must use a twofold subject matter, that furnished by the nation and
> her individual citizens and that furnished by cosmic Nature as a
> book in which to read the secrets of Being. [11]

Even a cursory acquaintance with the essay would be
enough, however, to suggest that this account misses the mark
in some very important respects. Weathers' summary is rendered inaccurate above all by its very lucidity, since it furnishes
logical connections and categories which are simply not to be
found in the piece. The distinction between what "the greatest
poet," as Whitman put it, should be and what he should do can-

not be deduced from the text, only speculated upon, and the clear-cut separation of the subject matter into two different classes oversimplifies Whitman's argument. Nor does this summary take into account the work's most remarkable features, its unique manner and style, "aquiver with lyricism," [12] captivating and baffling at the same time, with the "beautiful suggestiveness" and "the jocund spirit of the morning" that, for example, Emory Holloway found in it.[13] It has been noted that Whitman could, on occasion, "edit the life out of his material": [14] critics attempting to summarize his introductory essay as a poetic theory and program usually wind up, despite their best intentions, doing the job for him. What is left, then, is often a neat little theory and program, but it is neither particularly original nor inspiring, and totally incapable of justifying the fascination that the Preface, as the essay soon came to be known, has exercised upon its readers virtually from its first appearance.[15]

Of course, Whitman left his essay untitled, and perhaps it would have been better if it had remained so. But references to the Preface started to appear in the first reviews, indirectly imposing demands on the piece it was not meant to meet and confusing the readers who were impressed by it but could not tell why. The title Whitman never gave his essay epitomizes the misconception that the piece is a reasoned elaboration of a poetic theory. By now the misleading label has stuck, and it would be pedantry to call the essay anything else today, but in 1855 Charles A. Dana could not call it a preface without linking it to another famous essay known by the same title: the one Wordsworth wrote to introduce the second edition of *Lyrical Ballads*, in 1800. By the mid-fifties, Wordsworth was, naturally, widely known and highly esteemed in the United States, and the special attention directed at his life's work after his death in 1850 had not yet faded; the attempt to draw an analogy between the two pieces had to be obvious to all. That title meant inviting comparison with an essay whose author, although prudently claiming to write "a few words of introduction" and not "a systematic defence of the theory upon which the Poems were written," nevertheless set out "to state what [he has] proposed to [himself] to perform; and also (as far as the limits of a preface permit) to explain some of the chief reasons which have determined [him] in the choice of [his] purpose." [16] Since Wordsworth's Preface is a poetic program, first of all, and only the outline of a poetic theory, Whitman's should follow the same pattern and fulfill the same function of explanation if a comparison is to be meaningful at all. There is virtually no evidence to indicate that Whitman ever intended to accept such constrictions for his essay.

There are, to be sure, several points of similarity between the works of the two poets, and some of the most pronounced of these are in the Prefaces.[17] Although it is an open question whether Whitman ever read Wordsworth's Preface, he was no doubt influenced by some of the contemporary reviews and assessments of Wordsworth's poetry, which abound in sentences such as the following, practically inviting the critic to jump to conclusions:

When [Wordsworth] discovered that the regularly constituted arbiters of public opinion on matters of taste were indisposed to do him justice, he took the task upon himself, and his prefaces glorified his own powers and works in a spirit of unhesitating self-reliance.[18]

This sentence prompted Asselineau to conjecture—stating directly what Dana implied—that "this is perhaps the reason that [Whitman] himself introduced the first edition of his *Leaves of Grass* with a preface in which he announced his intentions." [19] But, impressive as such correspondences may be, they do not warrant the conclusion that the two essays are analogous in purpose or method. Whitman's preface announces no intentions and is carefully kept not only anonymous but impersonal as well—at least grammatically.

Were it not for the complications that being drawn into the enormous shadow of the Preface to *Lyrical Ballads* induces, this pedantic concern over an otherwise very logical and convenient title might seem a waste of time. But Whitman himself, apparently, would not have thought so. "Caution," he said, "seldom goes far enough" (ix), and as long as doing so made any sense he steered consistently clear of the title that was placing a burden of ill-suited demands on his essay. C. J. Furness' research supplies an interesting example of this caution.[20] For reasons of his own, Whitman discarded his essay as the opening piece of his volume after 1855 and cast about for a new introduction. As Furness puts it, unhampered by issues tradition has more or less decided for scholarship, "[Whitman] appears to have worried the bone of a suitable preface-idea for *Leaves of Grass* intermittently from beginning to end of his career, without ever arriving at any solution wholly satisfactory to him." [21] Among the several manuscript attempts written between 1855 and 1870 and carefully pinned into the poet's own paperbound copy of the first edition, lost sometime in 1871 and not recovered until after his death, there is not a single one called by the name freely used by friend and foe alike since 1855. The tentative titles include "Introduction," "Introductory Notice," "Advertisement," "Notice," and combinations of these. There is even a portentous "Inscription to the Reader at the entrance of Leaves of Grass," and there is an untitled appraisal of the poet's own achievement, but no Preface.[22] Only in 1867 does Whitman begin to become reconciled to the title, by which time its use has become general, and, besides, the essay had apparently rendered all the services it was expected to. In a letter to Moncure Conway he refers, with obvious reluctance, to "the introductory essay or prose preface to the first edition," [23] and from then on he goes along with everybody else and speaks of the Preface.

If the title traditionally assigned to the essay sounds as if it had been borrowed from Wordsworth's Preface, so do the purposes and functions attributed to it. The Preface is supposed to be the poet's program and a key to the appreciation of the poems.[24] It is true enough, as Perry declared, that, "*Leaves of Grass* will not be understood without it," [25] but not because it is a gloss or a commentary on the text, or because "Whitman put into [it] the basic ideas which were to be the stock in trade of all his poetry." [26] Without some added distinctions and modifications, such claims can only be misleading, since, put in this manner, they are by and large unfulfilled in the essay. Anxious as he was to reach as wide an audience as possible, to be "absorbed" by his country, Whitman was nevertheless the first one to acknowledge that efforts at direct explanation could never lead to the kind of reception his poems needed to become realized at all. "It will always remain . . . impossible," he wrote in 1872, in one of his notorious self-reviews, "to clearly or fully state either the theory of Walt Whitman's composition or describe his poem, its results. They may be absorbed out of themselves, but only after many perusals." [27]

These words are not a mere admission of failure after long and futile experimentation but the reaffirmation of the poet's original intentions, as Whitman's conception of the task that an introduction to his volume should perform indicates. In one of his own reviews of the first *Leaves* he remarked that, "in the scheme this man has built for himself, the writing of poems is but a proportionate part of the whole." [28] The remark implies, among other things, his awareness that while it was useless to try to explain them, his poems were nevertheless too new, too strange to stand by themselves, and to release their full energy he had to place them in the right context. That he often thought of accomplishing this task by public lecturing and by collecting these lectures into "a companion volume to *Leaves of Grass*, to take the place of a preface" [29] is a powerful clue to what, in his estimation, this right context would be.

III

In the eighteen-thirties and forties, Matthiessen writes,

> when the vogue of the modern newspaper had not yet quite begun and libraries were relatively scarce, public addresses were still the chief means of popular education . . . [and] provided also one of the few sources of general diversion. . . . [30]

19

To illustrate the degree to which this particular form of expression has pervaded American life, he quotes Tocqueville:

> An American cannot converse, but he can discuss; and his talk falls into a dissertation. He speaks to you as if he was addressing a meeting; and if he should chance to become warm in the discussion, he will say 'Gentlemen' to the person with whom he is conversing.[31]

It was during this period that Whitman first thought of making a career of public lecturing, and he did not abandon the idea until long after his poems had made him "become a fixed fact."[32] These plans were particularly alive in the years surrounding the publication of the first *Leaves*. The idea of compiling a companion volume of lectures for the poems dates from 1858,[33] and Traubel testifies that the majority of the notes originally meant for a lecture and collected by him in *An American Primer* were "scribbled on sheets of various tints improvised from the paper covers used on the unbound copies of the 1855 edition," although Whitman had already written "at this *Primer* in the early fifties."[34]

Traubel's suggestion that by lecturing Whitman merely intended to get off "his financial uppers" (he got on them "every now and then")[35] is attractively simple but hardly sufficient to account for these ambitions. Whitman's preoccupation with eloquence was far too persistent, his theory of it far too individual and perceptive to have been the incidental outcome of impatient exertions to gain him bread and butter. If his ambition was rather conventional, his way of realizing it was not, in an age that held Mill's familiar distinctions ("eloquence is *heard*; poetry is *overheard*") accurate as well as sufficient.

Apparently, he often considered his oratorical intentions didactic, and he usually referred to his lectures as "lessons."[36] But the "lessons" he was teaching were not mere affairs of the intellect, for those he apparently found simply tiresome: "Do not attempt to put *too much* in one Lecture nor make it too complicated," he wrote, and "all [must be] carefully kept down

so that the *strong colors, lights* and *lines of the Lecture* mark
. . . *one simple leading idea or theory.*" [37] Another fragment
reveals the conviction that could prompt such advice:

> The test of the goodness or truth of anything is the soul itself—
> whatever does good to the soul, soothes, refreshes, cheers, in-
> spirits, consoles, & &c—that is so, easy enough.—But doctrines,
> sermons, logic? [38]

The purely rational played a naturally important but strictly subordinate role in what Whitman conceived of as his total argument. Thus, he wrote,

> A Lesson must be supplied, braced, fortified at all points. It must
> have its facts, statistics, materialism, its relations to the physical
> state of man, nations, the body, and so forth, and to moneymaking
> and well being. It must have its intellectual completeness, its
> beauty, its reasoning to convince, its proofs, and so forth.

but to render all this "supporting evidence" irresistible, "it must
have its reference to the spiritual, the mystic in man, that which
knows without proof, and is beyond materialism." [39]

Among his notes on oratory there are some hints about his
idea of how this ultimate step was to be achieved. They bear out
his assertion, made late in his life, that he had "never given any
study merely to expression" and "never fooled with technique
more than enough to provide for simply getting through": [40]
they show him more concerned with the effect the speaker
could have on his listeners than with the "expression or utterance" of what he had to communicate. He declares:

> Keep steadily understood, with respect to the effects and fascina-
> tion of *Elocution* (so broad, so spacious, and vital that although the
> Lectures may be printed and sold at the end of every performance,
> nothing can make up for that *irresistible attraction and robust* living
> treat of the lecture, by me,—[41]

One discerns the same stress in his description of the Orator
mounting his platform: "Suddenly the countenance illumined,

the breast expanded, the nostrils and the mouth electric and quivering, the attitude imperious and erect—a God stands before you." [42] The "transfiguration" occurs before a word is uttered: the Orator himself is "getting through" before his feelings.

Whitman, then, wants to create a rhetorical effect which is essentially anterior to rational discourse and not to be contained by Mill's categories of persuasion. His ambition is explained by his particular sensitivity to the sensuous power of the individual word and by what Allen describes as the poet's curious talent of "not only [feeling] but [thinking] sensuously:" [43]

> The subtle charm of the beautiful pronunciation is not in dictionaries, grammars, marks of accent, formulas of language, or in any laws or rules. The charm of the beautiful pronunciation of all words, of all tongues, is perfect flexible vocal organs, and in a developed harmonious soul.—All words, spoken from these, have deeper sweeter sounds, new meanings, impossible on any less terms. —Such meanings, such sounds, continually wait in every word that exists. . . .[44]

As Catel comments: "Whitman has sensations rather than thoughts; the word for him rests on the periphery, ready to renew itself with its special halo of secondary perceptions. . . . [It is for him] a reserve of energy and not an element of grammar." [45] While these remarks tend to be more relevant to poetry than to oratory or prose and lead to the question, often raised and sometimes brilliantly discussed,[46] of what difference, if any, there is between Whitman's conceptions of poetry and rhetoric, they are also clearly applicable to his understanding of the possibilities of oratory.

To that understanding, evidently, even such a loose phrase as Mill's "feeling pouring itself out" was far too explicit and neatly defined. Thus, if Whitman thought that he could arrive at the right context for his poems through the effects his oratory could create, that context, whatever else it may have been, was certainly *not* an analytical scaffolding of ideas and insights structured and made coherent by a disembodied intellect; in other words, it was nothing of the sort implied by the assumption that Whitman's essay is—like Wordsworth's Preface, for example—simply the poet's reasoned explanation of his purpose and method.

This much is suggested by Furness as he speaks of Whitman's conviction that

> the proper feeling for his poems' right reception could be more effectively kindled by the living spoken word and personal presence of the author, than aroused by the finest phrasing of the thought possible to set down on paper in cold print.[47]

This description, however, assumes an audience made up of several people, whereas the characteristic grammatical number in all of Whitman's writing is the dual: in the end, it is always directed at "a single, separate person," even while he is "enmasse." Whitman aimed at individual contact: his injunction that

> . . . This is no book,
> Who touches this touches a man,[48]

is one man's outcry to be heard and understood by another, a "camerado." Many poets have, of course, envisioned an audience of one, but few poets adhered to this perspective as exclusively as Whitman, who rarely addressed a group in his poems or allowed himself to be "overheard" by one. He did, indeed, "ordinarily [assume] that in his songs he was talking to everybody . . . to all the common people of these States," as Matthiessen observed, but he was not preparing to move crowds, large or small. There is a suggestion of failure in Matthiessen's conclusion that, "in [Whitman's] best poetry his favorite oratorical figures, the questions and exclamations, the apostrophes and parenthetical asides, have all become personal: they imply the presence not of many but of one," [49] but the poet's notes indicate that he never aimed at anything else even in his lectures. He writes,

Talk directly to the hearer or hearers [a revealing afterthought of caution, significantly analogous with his habitual addition of 'or woman' each time he writes 'man']: [50]—You so and so.—Why should I be so tender with you?—Have you not, etc., etc. . . . Why not mention myself by name Walt Whitman in my speeches? [51]

Quite clearly, then, by striving toward what he called a "vocal style" Whitman wanted to endow the relative abstraction of verbal communication with the immediacy of palpable contact intensified by a sense of intimacy. In the lecture hall, his aim would have been to make each listener feel that the words were being addressed to him alone; in his printed efforts of what he considered oratory, that is, his various introductions and among them the 1855 Preface, he sought to empower his text with the singular force of the word spoken in confidence.[52]

IV

This conclusion is corroborated by the characteristic manner in which the poetic address finds its ultimate direction in the sequence of poems which finally, in the Deathbed Edition, came to fulfill the function of introducing *Leaves of Grass*. In "Inscriptions," [53] the classicizing, elevated tone struck in the first three pieces by a Whitman self-consciously posing as the inspired poet allowing himself to be "overheard" soon begins to alternate with various manners of personification and apostrophe. In these short poems of dedication the poet seems to be seeking to define an audience, besides announcing themes and establishing symbols.[54] The central drift of this search is from the abstract and the indistinct toward the specific and personal, from the collective toward the individual, from the plural toward the singular; it begins by addressing the book and foreign lands, and it concludes by discovering "You":

> . . . Why should you not speak to me,
> And why should I not speak to you? [55]

WHAT'S IN A TITLE?

The same stages of orientation are found in "Starting from Paumanok." [56] Striking up "solitary," in a meditative-lyric stance, the poet practically conjures up an audience for himself with a kind of incantatory magic. After the soliloquy of Section I, suddenly an undefined interlocutor appears in Section II ("See revolving the globe, / . . . See vast trackless spaces . . .), to whom the poet points out his "audience interminable" (30). This audience, which duly replaces the interlocutor in Section III, is distinct only by its vastness and shifts constantly amid categories of kind, number, and time:

> Americanos! conquerors! marches humanitarian!
> Foremost! century marches! Libertad! masses!
> For you a programme of chants.
>
> (37–39)

America is personified and addressed next in Section IV; then, in Section V exponents and embodiments of the past are acknowledged and greeted in preparation for the entrance of "the satisfier . . . my mistress the soul" (67–68), whereupon the poem modulates to soliloquy again, through Sections VI and VII. With the strident assertions toward the end of Section VII, the solitary meditation begins to change back into direct address, and in Section VIII the true interlocutor is discovered: "What are you doing young man?" (114). This young man, the "camerado" and "dear son" of the poet, is the first version of the one at whom Whitman's last, exultant apostrophe is directed: "O you and me at last, and us two only" (266); although this interlocutor undergoes various transformations before he is given his final identity, from here on the tone of the poem remains that of an intimate dialogue.

With the last line of "Starting from Paumanok," the same point has been reached in the last *Leaves* as at the conclusion of the Preface to the 1855 edition. "Song of Myself" follows, the first poem in the first *Leaves*, severally metamorphosed. By reducing the various objects—living and lifeless—of his apostrophes into a "single, separate" listener, the poet has created the atmosphere of intimacy as well as the audience that he insisted was indispensable to the proper appreciation of his poems.

One may well argue that this effect is not wholly realized through these sequences; nevertheless, the poet's intent is unmistakable in them. Whitman's arrangement of the introductory poems to his last volume displays essentially the same creative method that was implied by his earlier conviction that the context suitable for his poems could only be established by as close a written approximation as possible of a "lesson," that is, of a lecture-oration in the "vocal style" based on the principles laid out in his notes on oratory. In both cases, the analysis leads to the same conclusion: Whitman conceived of the context which could release his poems in their full power as the listener's intimate experience of the poet's person. It follows from this conclusion that, as indicated earlier, the Preface could not be merely a rational exposition of poetic theories and purposes; it also follows quite clearly that, to repeat Perry once again, without the Preface, *Leaves of Grass,* especially in its first edition, cannot be understood. Whitman, of course, knew very well what he was talking about when he insisted in that anonymous review of the first edition that writing poems was only part of his scheme: another integral, organic part of it was the writing of a cunningly devised essay making the poems possible. The Preface creates the conditions indispensable to the understanding of the volume, but it cannot explain anything, since it is a part of what needs to be explained.

Chapter Two

THE "CURIOUS TRIPLICATE PROCESS"—IN THEORY

I

As one begins to read the Preface, it becomes soon obvious and at first quite confusing that Whitman uses apparently familiar techniques of expression while subverting the critical premises traditionally applicable to them; or, to oversimplify a little, his rhetorical devices bring forth a text that does not yield to rhetorical analysis.[1] A comparison of Whitman's opening paragraph with one by Emerson, whom he is often said to be imitating, might serve as an illustration. Here is a well-known passage from "Compensation":

> The world globes itself in a drop of dew. The microscope cannot find the animalcule which is less perfect for being little. Eyes, ears, taste, smell, motion, resistance, appetite, and organs of reproduction that take hold on eternity,—all find room to consist in the small creature. So do we put our life into every act. The true doctrine of omnipresence is that God reappears with all his parts in every moss and cobweb. The value of the universe contrives to throw itself into every point. If the good is there, so is the evil; if the affinity, so the repulsion; if the force, so the limitation.[2]

If there is obscurity here, it is in the thought itself, not in the manner. Although the subject matter is complex and the voice is not without inflections that his critics like to call "oracular," Emerson stays well within the limits of conventional diction and syntax as well as of the rhetorical tradition which is at the roots of his style. Even in such "slippery" words as "life" or "value" the outlines of the conventional significance remain recognizable, although their context reveals startling new connotations in them. The light of the traditional mode dispels the obscurity in a phrase like "we put our life into every act" or in a metaphor like "the world globes itself in a drop of dew," the scientific and religious references are apt and effective because they are eminently accessible, and the argument itself unfolds in an orderly progression of careful reasoning: Emerson's assumptions may make philosophers impatient and logicians smile, but his presentation makes perfectly good conventional sense.

These lines are placed in curious perspective by one of Emerson's own insights in "Self-Reliance," which, incidentally, defines with remarkable accuracy Whitman's situation both as source of strength and as predicament:

> When good is near you, when you have life in yourself, it is not by any known or accustomed way; you shall not discern the footprints of any other; you shall not see the face of man; you shall not hear any name;—the way, the thought, the good, shall be wholly strange and new.[3]

Emerson's theory, however, contradicts his practice here. His "thoughts" may be "wholly strange and new"; his "way" is not. Whitman's way, on the other hand, is new, as the following lines demonstrate:

> America does not repel the past or what it has produced under its forms or amid other politics or the idea of castes or the old religions . . . . accepts the lesson with calmness . . . is not so impatient as has been supposed that the slough still sticks to opinions and manners and literature while the life which served its requirements has passed into the new life of the new forms . . . perceives

28

that the corpse is slowly borne from the eating and sleeping rooms of the house . . . perceives that it waits a little while in the door . . . that it was fittest for its days . . . that its action has descended to the stalwart and well-shaped heir who approaches . . . and that he shall be fittest for his days. (iii)

This long, rambling sentence disguised as a paragraph advances no recognizable argument beyond the statement in the first line that "America does not repel the past," and that statement in itself is either nonsensical, or trite, or ridiculous, as long as it is taken in the same direct, conventional sense as Emerson's words had to be. As a geographical concept, America can no more repel the past than accept it. If the name denotes a cultural concept, the oversimplification borders on the inane and becomes practically meaningless (or about as "meaningful" as some parallel claim that "Europe does not repel the future" would be). At best, the hopelessly impaired sense of proportion in the phrase makes for the same kind of unwitting comedy that people found in Margaret Fuller's generous concession to "accept the universe." And there are other words besides "America"—"action," for example, or "forms," or "fittest,"—that make no sense in the context of the paragraph as long as their traditional significance alone is assumed. The strange sequence itself of images—a kind of personification for which a traditional "America" is an altogether inappropriate subject—embodies no logical argument; in fact, it "embodies" nothing beyond itself; it is not, as Emerson would have it, an analogy of anything and, again, makes no conventional "sense."

And yet, the passage cannot be simply dismissed, since the trite "argument" of the first line is soon overshadowed by another kind of appeal, which derives its insistent power from the presentation itself. The sentence most palpably has meaning, even if its significance is not immediately obvious.

The rambling form—a concatenation, really, of subordinate clauses dependent on elements of a compound predicate, the last of which, "perceives," becomes the basis of a secondary series of subordination—creates an impression (with deliberate

29

art, as one begins soon to suspect) of a spontaneous voice, a person seeking the right expression, sorting out the most precise image for his thought. The reader—listener, rather,—responds to this voice long before what it says is understood, let alone accepted or rejected. The apparently artless, tentative formulation itself fuses rhetoric with organicism as the sentence grows from the seed of the single word "America" through images in which contrasts in space—movement and stasis—are used to develop contrasts in time: old and new forms, death and life, time and timelessness. The progression of these contrasts has the persuasive force of spontaneous association. The evolution of the images of motion begins with the past moving into "the new life of the new forms," continues with the corpse carried through the door out of the house, and concludes with the corpse's "action" shifting to "the stalwart and wellshaped heir."

The culmination of this sequence and the pivotal point of the sentence is in the pause as the corpse "waits a little while in the door." In this image the frozen moment defies time, and the pause arrests motion without essentially interrupting the movement; thus, a borderline, a moment of balance and resolution is reached between the opposites. Through this moment and gesture, the limitations of both space and time are shaken off. The particular syntax thus points up the equilibrium which defines the subject of the sentence, "America": perceiving and participating at the same time, "both in and out of the game," "America" itself is planted on the same borderline and made up of the same balance and resolution.

In this one long sentence of inception Whitman does not so much begin an argument as sets a whole machinery of meaning in motion. He elicits the proper mode of understanding his idiom by rendering all others irrelevant, establishes the voice which will be developed into a central instrument of the scheme of the whole book, and, by exposing his listener to a "grammar of images," introduces, in the images themselves, versions of what later emerge as some of his most significant preoccupations. Above all, by resolving every suggestion, logical as well as metaphorical, into "America," he announces one of the two major themes of his discourse without defining it in any but the most provisional sense beyond rejecting the word's conventional meaning.

II

Once the lesson of the first paragraph is absorbed, the second one will no longer surprise the reader, although his bafflement is most likely to continue. Here again, the first statement turns out to be the most important: "The Americans of all nations at any time upon the earth have probably the fullest poetical nature. The United States themselves are essentially the greatest poem" (iii). In conventional terms these claims do not make any more sense, either logically or figuratively, than America's tolerance of the past did, but that is no longer a difficulty. It is worthy of note, however, that Whitman distinguishes here between "America" and the United States and that no allusion to verse and genre can explain the references to "poem" and "poetical nature." As in the case of the key term of the first sentence, one will have to settle again for some rudimentary process of elimination and stay content, at least for the time being, with knowing what the phrases do *not* mean. This apparently extravagant assertion about the "poetical nature" of "Americans" introduces the other major theme of the essay: "the poet." This theme is reinforced a few lines further on in the call for the "gigantic and generous treatment worthy" of the "unrhymed" and as yet unrealized "poetry" latent in "the genius of the United States" (iii).

The whole essay achieves significance through elaborating these two themes, "America" and "the poet," although it is not primarily an elucidation of them; to show *what* they mean is not its purpose, but it achieves its purpose by showing *how* they mean. The two themes also serve as the essay's main structural device, since the alternation of the stress between them organizes it into five large, "well entretied" yet clearly distinguishable movements. The statement that "their presidents shall not be their common referee so much as their poets shall" (iii) concludes the first of these movements; the second is concluded with "the greatest poet has lain close betwixt both and they are vital in his style and thoughts" (vi); the third with "to be is just as great as to perceive or tell" (viii); the fourth with "in his spirit in any emergency whatever [that person] neither hurries or avoids death" (xi); and the fifth and last movement rounds out the essay.

The first movement consists of a deceptively unsophisticated discussion of "America" as not only the most propitious but a practically indispensable condition for the appearance of "the poet." The strange and powerful metaphor of the opening paragraph is reduced in swift gradation from suggestive obscurity to obscure bombast in the next. "Something in the doings of man that corresponds with the broadcast doings of the day and night" (iii) is fetching enough for all its apparent awkwardness, but "the performance disdaining the trivial unapproached in the tremendous audacity of its crowds and groupings and the push of its perspective spreads with crampless and flowing breadth and showers its prolific and splendid extravagance" (iii) is extravagance of a singularly unsplendid kind, painfully reminiscent of the effusions of a Cornelius Mathews compounded with the graceless syntax, "lush emotion, and swooning patriotism" [4] of a Walter Whitman thirteen years younger.

Much of the same follows. Indeed, the first two pages of the essay may well strike one at first as a poor imitation, in argument and manner alike, of the manifestoes of shrill patriotism that cluttered up the "literary scene" of New York in the 1830s and 40s. The "thesis" of these manifestoes, as Perry Miller describes it, "was that we should automatically create a big literature because we were a big country; inevitably," Miller adds, "bigness became a catalogue of mountains and rivers, always including Niagara Falls." [5] By claiming that, "of all nations the United States with veins full of poetic stuff most needs poets and will doubtless have the greatest and use them the greatest," Whitman's conclusion seems to be merely following this pattern. His argumentation itself is equally unoriginal. After expounding American manners ("hospitality," "deathless attachment to freedom," "picturesque looseness of . . . carriage," "self-esteem and wonderful sympathy" [iii]) and extolling American history ("As if the opening of the western continent by discovery and what has transpired since in North and South America were less than the small theatre of the antique or the aimless sleepwalking of the middle ages!" [iii]), he winds up—like his elders, "inevitably," it seems—waxing ecstatic over American geography:

> Mississippi with annual freshets and changing chutes, Missouri and Columbia and Ohio and Saint Lawrence with the falls and beautiful masculine Hudson, do not embouchure where they spend themselves more than they embouchure into [the bard of America]. (iv)

There is, however, more to arrest one's attention in this movement than the unobtrusive way in which the obligatory obeisance to Niagara Falls is made. For an altogether slavish imitation of the pattern of nationalistic turgidity, these pages contain an excess of stylistic idiosyncrasies. The first and possibly oddest among these is the usage of "full" in a sense of "completed" or "wholly realized," rather than "replenished" or "filled." "The fullest poetical nature" of the nation is first explained by the "ampler largeness" of its history, then reasserted as its "pride [. . .] to enjoy the breed of fullsized men or one fullsized man unconquerable and simple" (iii–iv). A principle of correspondences is apparently involved in this fullness, as indicated by the remark about the "corresponding largeness" in the "spirit of the citizen," without which national "largeness" would be "monstrous," and by the demand for what might "suffice for the ideal of man." The geographic effusion itself is no mere enumeration of place names from the map but a series of "tallies" between poet and land, through which the two become mutually realized, "fullsized."

Another departure from the wretched model that Whitman

33

at first seemed to be imitating is in the long lists and enumerations. In the "prototypes" such lists served no other purpose besides that of rhetorical ornament, and they were composed as rather unimaginative periodic sentences, displaying the standard of sensible grammatical accuracy normally available to a reasonably literate journalist like Whitman himself, as his youthful efforts generally testify. Thus, his obvious disdain for all but the most elementary rules of grammar in these passages cannot be written off as a simple indication of incompetence. On the contrary, these long lists, really the first of the familiar "catalogues" of *Leaves of Grass,* represent an amplification of the manner introduced in the first paragraph: they do not give the impression of enumerations so much as of a search for a precise formulation.

Paradoxically, the sketchy, improvisational quality of each single image or phrase is the most convincing proof of the validity of the total effort. Being consistent with the effects of live speech created earlier, their sketchiness gives the catalogue a quality of spontaneity that no evidence of its actual contrivance can vitiate. In a sequence describing "the common people" of America, "their manners speech dress friendships—the freshness and candor of their physiognomy—the picturesque looseness of their carriage . . . their deathless attachment to freedom—their aversion to anything indecorous or soft or mean" (iii) and the rest, one is persuaded not by the statements but by the voice that makes them.

A different way in which the same tentativeness or obvious insufficiency of any one image contributes to the "fullness" of the utterance can be seen in the following passage, a clause that, typically dangling in a syntactic void, "tallies" the poet's "flights and songs and screams" with a veritable ornithological litany:

The wild pigeon and highhold and orchard-oriole and coot and surf-duck and redshouldered-hawk and fish-hawk and white-ibis and indian-hen and cat-owl and water pheasant and qua-bird and

pied-sheldrake and blackbird and mockingbird and buzzard and
condor and bight-heron and eagle. (iv)

What this catalogue encloses will imply rather than exclude what
it leaves out. That, in fact, will be seen as the very justification of
the catalogues in Whitman's scheme: they do not describe an
image but prescribe a vision.

As if to confirm the upshot of these impressions, that by
pretending to *write* of a Sunday-supplement America he was actually *speaking* of that other, enigmatic apparition that was
glimpsed through his first words, Whitman concludes this first
movement of his essay with the call for a poetry of indirection:
"The expression of the American poet is to be transcendent and
new. It is to be indirect and not direct or descriptive or epic"
(iv). Whatever else he may be driving at here, the all-too-familiar
echo turns Whitman into a Polonius urging his reader that he
should "by indirections find directions out." He need not define
or expound the method itself of indirection, since he has been
demonstrating it all along. Finally, in the sentence that prepares
the shift in emphasis from "America" to "the poet" and leads
into the second major movement of the essay, he practically
spells out what he is doing: "with decision and science" and the
patient labor of "one among the wellbeloved stonecutters," he
is making a new form, "the solid and beautiful forms of the future," possible (iv).

III

So far, the pattern of expression has been based upon the palpably felt but unacknowledged tension between a direct and an indirect argument. While the logical discourse rarely managed to
escape the confines of bombast and platitude on the one hand
and sheer impossibility on the other, the undercurrent of images
and inflections imparts to the statement an ever increasing coherence and authority. It is obviously quite difficult to read the
essay without becoming, on occasion, impatient with it for one

good reason or another, but it is impossible not to listen to it. Faced by such a puzzle, "when the language of words fails," says R. P. Blackmur, "we resort to the language of gesture." [6] The second major movement of the essay is important above all because it indicates both the principle by which the two kinds of language act upon each other and the manner of their fusion into a single meaning.

The movement is the first treatment of the theme of "the poet" in the essay. Although somewhat chaotic in appearance, largely because of a stubborn laxness of diction and a number of emphatic asides that run counter to the main thesis, the rhetorical argument follows a simple and not very original line of reasoning. It presents in their logical order assumptions about three obviously related topics: the qualifications, the material, and the method of the poet capable of "the gigantic and generous treatment worthy of" the America of the preceding movement's patriotic oratory.

His qualifications are based, above all, on the frequently quoted pronouncement that, "of all mankind the great poet is the equable man" (iv). The phrase equivocates, and there is no reason to doubt that it does so by design. Whether the poet is "great" because he is "equable" or, the other way around, a man is "equable" because he is a "great poet" does not seem to have disturbed Whitman at all, although the dilemma is a rather straightforward demonstration of what Howard J. Waskow describes as one of the risks of literary organicism. "This [dilemma]," he writes, "can mean that everyone is a poet, each man a god; but at the same time, it diminishes the significance of the individual artist." [7] Whitman, however,—in this "direct" reading—merely sidesteps the problem in a suspiciously disingenuous way: "the others are as good as he, only he sees it and they do not" (v).

The poet's "equability"—that is, qualification for being "great"—is further explained by the claims that "he is no arguer . . . he is judgement [who] judges not as the judge judges but as the sun falling around a helpless thing," and that "what the eyesight does to the rest he does to the rest" (v). These gifts enable him to perform his essential task, which is "to indicate the path between reality and [folks'] souls" through revealing and thus bringing to life "the poetic quality" latent in every experience of existence (v). This "poetic quality," that is, the quality susceptible to poetry, is the poet's material, and since it cannot be absent from anything, all existence is made available through it to his "treatment." As Whitman himself chooses to put it, "if [the greatest poet] breathes into any thing [. . .] it dilates with the grandeur and life of the universe" (v).

While it does not make things necessarily clearer, the phrase undoubtedly has a much more attractive ring to it than the clumsy elucidation. Its resonance and power are typical of the whole movement, which is possibly the best known and most frequently quoted portion of the essay. It is especially important, therefore, to keep in mind Whitman's injunctions about indirection. The temptation to take him at his "direct" word may become altogether too great to resist, in which case misunderstanding and disappointment are bound to follow. As one may suspect from the summary above, once the haze of prolixity and imprecision is more or less cleared away there is little left of the "direct" argument besides an uninspiring recapitulation of some of the stock ideas of Romantic theories of poetry, echoing any number of potential, if ultimately unlikely, sources from Shelley to Emerson while failing to measure up to any one of them. One must also come to terms with generous samples of that stridency which could often provoke the derision of readers unwilling to heed Whitman's call for indirection.

One can, of course, ill afford the luxury of ignoring that warning: witness the example of D. H. Lawrence, who took Whitman at his word but, perhaps willfully, mistook his gesture. Thus, when Whitman declaimed in some such key as "what is impossible or baseless or vague? after you [. . .] had all things enter with electric swiftness softly and duly without confusion or jostling or jam" (iv), Lawrence could reply that "if that is so, one must be a pipe open at both ends, so everything runs through," and depart believing that he had cut down his "limited Walter" to proper size.[8]

The contradiction Lawrence gleefully exposes is undeniably there: an omnivorous ego, absorbing illusions of what is outside itself, yet unable to ascertain an identity of its own. At one turn, "the others are as good as [the great poet]," and he is thus but another part of the world to be "judged"; at the next turn, he is the judge. "He is a seer," but he is also the seen. In one moment, he is certain of having fully "adjudged" the universe, properly perceived all reality, and he is firmly established in a "real" world, but, in the next moment, the whole process is reversed: there is nothing left, in a subjective, illusory universe, except his ego, which has devoured all that came its way—all is nothing but himself. It is, however, this very stridency, this habit of protesting too much that should make one who has been not only reading Whitman's words but also listening to them suspect behind these breathless dithyrambs a self-doubt corresponding in scope and intensity to the self-confidence they flaunt.

IV

It will not do, then, to dismiss, like Lawrence, as mere absurdity the profoundly paradoxical insight which is the source of Whitman's artistic vitality. The broadest definition of this insight is in Whitman's remark that "there are in things two elements fused though antagonistic." [9] The numerous excellent studies of Whitman's position in intellectual history tend to agree that the mode of comprehension implicit in the above phrase—symptomatic of "the cultural shift in which the philosophic and aesthetic mind moved from a conception of reality as mechanistic to a conception of reality as organic" [10]—is the premise that provides the conceptual pattern of all his thinking.

In one of the most exhaustive treatments of the subject, Howard J. Waskow explains this premise as "a curious compound of poetic intuition and Hegelian logic" [11] and identifies it by labeling its final result a "bipolar unity"—a term borrowed

from Emerson's journals and designating "a new entity that results from the mutual pressure of [contraries]." [12] This special
vision originates, as Waskow goes on to show, in Whitman's capacity to accommodate a "belief in a dualistic mechanistic universe" on the one hand with a "belief in a monistic organic
world" on the other.[13] The "bipolar unity" that ensues is the
principle of coherence in the paired opposites Whitman could
devise with such prodigious facility: body and soul, one and
many, identity and distinction, universal and particular, male
and female, humanity and deity, land and sea, life and death, to
mention the more important among them.[14] Out of the configuration of such complementary opposites with the poet's sensibility a characteristic pattern of "dialectical triads" emerges, what
Alfred H. Marks called "triadic imagery." [15] In the terms of this
pattern, Marks writes,

> Whitman's universe is to be seen at any point in time as a great
> sphere holding in unity two hemispheres. . . . The synthesis of any
> concept in one hemisphere with its opposite number in the other
> hemisphere is a symbolic representation of the central truth of the
> system, or unity in diversity.[16]

Such a system, of course, does suggest extensive borrowings from Hegel, but one need not dwell long on its ancestry
and relations in the history of philosophy. That background has
by now become rather familiar; besides, discussions of the sort
tend to overrate Whitman's powers of pure intellection as well
as the significance of his scattered statements with an explicitly
"philosophic" purpose, in which ambition consistently outstrips
competence. The right perspective in these matters, including
the poet's apparent Hegelianism, seems to have been well indicated by the following remarks of Frederic W. Conner:

> [Whitman's] thinking was largely temperamental. He borrowed
> plentifully from the ideas current in his time, but his borrowings
> were never closely examined and were for the most part mere gar-
> ments to clothe intuitions. . . . His metaphysic, if such it may be

called, was merely the older transcendentalism modified to square with the veneration of material reality inspired in him by his peculiar temperament and experience and by science; but his third hand Hegelianism gave him terms in which to define it . . .[17]

Thus, although discussing "Whitman's use of the logical technique which Hegel popularized," Alfred H. Marks himself adds that the most likely immediate source of the "triadic imagery" was Emerson rather than Hegel, as any number of illuminating passages from works like *Nature*, "Compensation," and "Plato" could testify.[18] The self that Whitman creates to unify the paired opposites, the self Waskow calls "the central Whitman,"[19] is farther removed from the Hegelian synthesis than from the versions of "bipolar unity" in "older transcendentalism," and the prototype of a "triadic image" would be found not so much in Hegel's dialectical formula as in such characteristic figures of Platonism as the comparison of the soul "to a pair of winged horses and charioteer joined in natural union," the trope Wallace Stevens quotes from the *Phaedrus*.[20]

There is, however, more to this "curious triplicate process" than a "logical technique."[21] The intuitive experience itself that could prompt such formulations (and provoke the impatience of readers of a Laurentian persuasion) is given its classic statement in American literature by Emerson in the notorious "transparent-eyeball" passage in *Nature*;[22] his enthusiasm is easily recognizable in Whitman's own raptures about "the curious mystery of the eyesight." That this experience also creates an epistemological predicament was made most memorably clear, long before Whitman's critics, by young Ishmael on the masthead.[23] On the verge of "seeing all and being nothing," Ishmael possibly remembered such ominous warnings as Coleridge's cryptic remark about the dangerous "restlessness" that the "despotism of the eye" can induce [24] and, by not moving "foot or hand an inch," by keeping, in sober Cartesian fashion, Ishmael the seer apart from Ishmael as seen, avoided the fatal plunge through "transparent air" into "vortices" that would have proved properly "Descartian" otherwise.

Ishmael's comprehension of the dangers of the "Platonic" mode of perception as well as his manner of protecting himself against them bear out, probably unwittingly,[25] some observations Goethe made in 1823 about what he called "the concept of metamorphosis." The problems inherent in the transformative, identity-loosening powers of the transcendental insight have rarely been stated with greater lucidity and conciseness:

> The concept of metamorphosis is a highly estimable gift from above, but at the same time a highly dangerous one. It leads to formlessness, destroys knowledge, disintegrates it. It is like centrifugal force and would lose itself in the infinite if a counterweight were not provided. I am referring to the specification force, that tenacious capacity for persistence inherent in whatever has attained existence, a centripetal force that cannot be disturbed in its deepest nature by anything external.[26]

Ishmael's experience is a recognition that this fundamental dynamism is indispensable for the accommodation of transcendental ecstasies, and the same recognition, not a mere gratuitous "generosity of the soul," lies at the core of Whitman's intuition about the "two elements fused though antagonistic" in all things. "Bipolar unity," for Whitman, is a pattern of balance, essentially, in which the two "elements" imply each other *by* being "antagonistic," and must do so or else disintegrate.

Thus, fitting Goethe's remarks (or Ishmael's experience) to the "curious triplicate process" of Whitman's awareness, one can define the "central Whitman" as constituted of the tension between "centrifugal" and "centripetal" forces, that is "self-shunning" and "self-seeking" impulses. His perception and his creation alike are, as Waskow notes,[27] functions of these forces, and in both cases the "triadic" pattern is the functional formula.

Lawrence's disgusted impatience, then, with his "dilating Walter" would have been justified only if "Walter" had left the matter stand where Lawrence himself preferred to claim it did. But, as someone said, "men are tricksy-tricksy, and they shy all sorts of ways";[28] just how "tricksy-tricksy," how inventive in "shying" they can be, this recapitulation of the major conclusions about Whitman's ways of meaning might help to show.

V

In the 1855 Preface, Whitman for the first time acknowledges these assumptions for his own. The formulation "two elements fused though antagonistic" is found among notes that date back, so far as it can be ascertained, to the time of the composition of the first *Leaves*,[29] and perceptions of "bipolar unity" are recorded in the earliest notebooks.[30] But the first complete triadic image that could be publicly ascribed to Whitman (not a name yet, really, only an increasingly characteristic voice that matches the picture of brazen indolence on the inside of his thin volume's first leaf) is in the figure which rounds out this second major movement of his essay.

Winding up his review of the poet's method, the speaker explains that "the greatest poet does not moralize or make applications of morals . . . he knows the soul," and he concludes:

> The soul has that measureless pride which consists in never acknowledging any lessons but its own. But it has sympathy as measureless as its pride and the one balances the other and neither can stretch too far while it stretches in company with the other. The inmost secrets of art sleep with the twain. The greatest poet has lain close betwixt both and they are vital in his style and thoughts. (vi)

Being the first, this figure is also one of the fullest expressions of the "triplicate process": the concept of balance, an essential feature in the pattern, is directly stated, and "pride" and "sympathy" translate with remarkable precision the "centripetal" and "centrifugal" forces of Goethe's argument into affective terms, that is, terms that suit the carefully cultivated effect of a spontaneous, speaking voice throughout Whitman's text.[31] The importance of these lines is crucial to the reading not only of the Preface but of the whole volume itself, since it proves to be the formal as well as the conceptual paradigm of the essay.

"CURIOUS TRIPLICATE PROCESS"—IN THEORY

The figure's relevance is made conspicuous by its position at the end of the second movement, the spot corresponding to the one that contains the call for indirection in the first, and it is twofold. The success of the image's realization forces the reader to reconsider the preceding portions of the essay by applying the principle of triadic coherence to them, and the pattern of meaning thus outlined will orient, in turn, one's approach to comprehending the rest.

The first result of any such reexamination, however, will be the discovery of another important feature of the principle itself: the completeness of bipolar unity is dichotomically conceived and does not have to be, although it often is, symmetrical. The "formula" is announced in the text itself. When Whitman writes,

> From the eyesight proceeds another eyesight and from the hearing proceeds another hearing and from the voice proceeds another voice eternally curious of the harmony of things with man (vi),

the correspondence he announces seems to consist of matching halves, as in Professor Marks's simile of the "two hemispheres," but what follows leaves no doubt that any one part is capable of implying the whole, according to this "law of perfection": "To these respond perfections not only in the committees that were supposed to stand for the rest but in the rest themselves just the same" (vi).

The recognition of the dichotomic nature of Whitman's conception of "bipolar unity" helps to account for two characteristic features of his style: his catalogues and his idiosyncratic use of the word "full" and its variants. In this light, it is no longer startling that words that describe amplitude—"full," "fullness," "tally" and the like—express the concept of perfection.[32] One variant to emerge with especial power in the first edition, if not in the Preface, is the verb "satisfy," meaning, as employed by Whitman, "bring to perfection."[33] The catalogues' curious power to imply what they do not list, to prescribe rather than describe a vision, has been noted earlier: Whitman's remark about the "committees" confirms this judgment and makes clear that the "greatest poet" chose the catalogue-method because of this very power. His metaphor for the catalogues— "committees"—is extremely suggestive, and in many ways it remains the most convincing interpretation and, if it is needed, justification of the device. To appreciate, however, the metaphor's precision, one had to encounter first the hitherto hidden alternative possibility of coherence in the figure of the greatest poet arising between the sympathy and the pride of the soul.

Reexamined in this light, the apparent incongruities and contradictions of the first two movements of the essay arrange themselves into a bipolar unity of style and idea. Behind the awkward ecstasies and oracular incoherence in the direct statement of the "greatest poet's" material and method a consistency of insight is revealed, convincing one of the individuality of the arguer if not of the originality of the argument itself.

Thus, the incongruities in the sensibility of the poet turn out to be the qualities that actually make it up. Through his being the seen by being the seer, the judged by being the judge, "he is judgment" and "the president of regulation." That he is the "equable man" becomes, in this system of "precision and balance" (vi), a more carefully chosen phrase than at first it seemed, and so does the assertion that "he is complete in himself" (v).

A power attendant upon this "fullness" is his singular way with the "poetic quality"—defined earlier in this chapter as "the quality susceptible to poetry"—in all that exists. The definition can be amplified now to read "the quality which allows any one thing to be drawn into a 'bipolar unity' "; thus, for the human consciousness, the poetic quality is an aptitude to recognize the corresponding quality in the objects of its perception. Beauty resides in the experience of recognition, in the discovery of the relationship between "reality and [the] soul" (v). It is a state of being the two bring forth: reality evokes an awareness in the soul of which the soul would be incapable on its own, and the soul grants a presence to reality of which reality alone would be incapable.[34] In "triplicate" terms, it is the event of the configuration of two constituents, fusing them into a new essence yet reconfirming, at the same time, the constituents' individual identities.

The poetic quality of the human consciousness, that is, its capacity for this awareness, is common to all, to poet and listener alike, only the degree of its intensity varies. "Outdoor people" (v), as Whitman calls those who interpose very little between themselves and a nature yet unsubdued by human ambition, need no assistance from the poet: they "perceive the beauty well enough . . probably as well as he" (v). He serves the rest of "folks," "the others [who] are as good as he, only he sees it and they do not": the "poetic faculty," Henry Alonzo Myers noted, is likened here to clear vision.[35]

Whitman feels no need to belabor the question of giving the permanence of form to what this faculty yields; he simply takes it for granted that the poet will "go directly to the creation" (vi). He admits to no clear-cut distinction between the subject of vision and its object, between perception and expression.[36] Commenting upon the "great poet's" method, he pauses only to make the futility of such distinctions clear in this memorable passage:

> The profit of rhyme is that it drops seeds of a sweeter and more luxuriant rhyme, and of uniformity that it conveys itself into its own roots in the ground out of sight. The rhyme and uniformity of perfect poems show the free growth of metrical laws and bud from them as unerringly and loosely as lilacs or roses on a bush, and take shapes of chestnuts and oranges and melons and pears, and shed the perfume impalpable to form. The fluency and ornaments of the finest poems or music or orations or recitations are not independent but dependent. All beauty comes from beautiful blood and a beautiful brain. If the greatnesses are in conjunction in a man or woman it is enough. . . . the fact will prevail through the universe. . . . but the gaggery and guilt of a million years will not prevail. Who troubles himself about his ornaments or fluency is lost. (v)

The "greatest poet's" whole imaginative existence is contained in "indicating the path between reality and the soul." "Reality, poet, poem, and the ideal reader all are one" in such a conception, Waskow observes.[37] In these images of roots and ground and plants and seeds and growth that lead naturally toward the context in which "grass" can become a major symbol, Whitman is "the optimistic symbolist, the extreme organicist," [38]—in just about everything except, possibly, his neglect or ignorance of some key terms in the theorists' jargon, for which he substitutes verbal idiosyncracies of his own.

Whitman's organicism has been frequently treated and at length. Thus, it will suffice here to note one feature of the passage just quoted, since apart from the characteristic diction it alone distinguishes his "system"—if it can be called a system at all—from "orthodox" theory. Even here, at his most "organic," Whitman prefers to speak in dualistic terms, in correspondences and analogies; the resolution of this apparent contradiction is in his intuition of bipolar unity, which his imagination exploits with greater vigor and consistency than the coiner of the phrase, Emerson. For Emerson, "natural facts" pointed unequivocally away from themselves, toward the "spiritual facts" of which they were symbols and which alone constituted the one true reality of the Spirit; for Whitman, the balance between the poles is unqualified; they represent equivalent and mutually creative fields of meaning, and the operative word of his scheme is "conjunction." [39] "The fluency and ornaments [. . .] are not independent but dependent" upon what they evoke, and vice versa. Sensible harmonies do not merely indicate harmonies that transcend the senses; the two kinds together form the ultimate "rhyme," the complete harmony. The sonorities of verse stand in conjunction with that "sweeter and more luxuriant rhyme" they are "dropping the seeds of," "beautiful blood" is "fulfilled" by "beautiful brain," and "reality" (or elsewhere "body") by "soul." The sense Whitman has lent to the word "beauty" suggests very convincingly that, in "beautiful blood and beautiful brain," "beautiful" is a deliberately eccentric reference to the poetic quality, the requisite of the "triplicate process," without which the two "greatnesses"—the "poles" of bipolar unity—could not be drawn into conjunction.

Once this difficulty is out of the way, the all-important phrase about "the path between reality and the soul" can be finally elucidated, too: it does not describe a process of spiritualization, a movement *from* reality to soul, but the connection, the creative tension between the two. It is thus recognized as a "dialectical triad" in which the path represents, in Marks's words, "the third member, . . . the unity which contains contradiction [by mediating] dramatically between the extremes." The "great poet" *indicates* this path in his very self: "the Poet-self which [Whitman] created for himself was designed both to contain the extremes and to unify them." [40] The same principle is at the heart of the passage on time. It is but another way of attempting to express the function which gives the "greatest poet" his being, since "to indicate the path between reality and [the] soul" means also "to compete with the laws that pursue and follow time" (vi). The attempt is another triad, which shows the "poet-self" again as the "third member," the resolution this time of temporal opposites:

> Past and present and future are not disjoined but joined. The greatest poet forms the consistency of what is to be from what has been and is. [. . .] [H]e says to the past, Rise and walk before me that I may realize you. [. . .] [H]e places himself where the future becomes present. (vi)

VI

Thus, the "triplicate process" gives unity to Whitman's thinking even if the philosophical pretensions of his conclusions cannot be taken very seriously. The terms that dominate the first two movements of the essay—reality, soul, time, full, America, beauty, poet—owe the curious power they wield to their being part of what keeps asserting itself all along as a manner of meaning while proving to be a very indifferent system of thought. It would be impossible or, at any rate, futile to define or even paraphrase their significance independently of each other, as of self-contained concepts. After irretrievably divesting them of their conventional meaning, Whitman does not assign a new, intrinsic sense to these terms but displays them, instead, in contexts that reveal the manner in which he wants them to be construed.

It has been noted ruefully and often enough that his concept of "soul," for example, will remain forever elusive because the philosophical tradition that supplied him with whatever premises of systematic thought he had was itself too far into the clouds. One can add that even on these few pages of the essay the word is used in a logically inconsistent way. With its measureless pride on the one hand and sympathy on the other, "soul" would seem to be a way of saying "self," but how can this reading sustain phrases like "the native elegance of soul" (iii) or "the path between reality and [. . .] soul," or, for that matter, Whitman's refrain and the very seed from which his whole poetry sprang: "I am the poet of the body, and I am the poet of the soul"? [41] But while all efforts to pin the word down seem to add up to a self-defeating proposition, it appears quite sufficient to conceive of "soul" in terms of its position in a given configuration of "the triplicate process." Like "all things," "soul" contains the "fused though antagonistic" "two elements" of "pride" and "sympathy," that is, the corresponding, "centripetal" and "centrifugal," impulses of introversion and extroversion; therefore, it consists of a "bipolar unity" in itself. It also evokes its opposite ("reality," "body") to form another "bipolar unity" or "dialectical triad." [42] That the "poetic quality" is "in the soul" and "only the soul is of itself" corroborates what the complementary opposition of "body" or "senses" to "soul" tends to imply: what "body" is to the world perceivable by the senses, "soul" is to the realm of comprehension the senses cannot attain alone. Just as the body is the means by which identity is achieved in the "float" [43] of "reality," the sensible world, the soul is the instrument of identity in the float of the imagination.

Claims of this sort, however, had better stop short of being definitions lest they impede the flexibility of Whitman's quaint dialectic, which is the very essence of the scheme's vitality, although it can often seem mere imprecision.[44]

That flexibility depends largely on the metaphoric uses of the theme introduced in the paragraph announcing that "the known universe has one complete lover and that is the greatest poet" (vi). It is generally held that Whitman's conception and capacities of love, what Allen describes as his "Christlike love for humanity, his St. Francis-like sympathy for all living things, and the psychic turmoil for which he could find expression and release only in his life-book," [45] evolved from his complex and confused sexuality. Love, in his experience, grew from sex into sympathy and from instinct into intention. He incorporated this growth into his work not by "[lifting] love above sex . . .[but by] striving to lift sexuality into love," as Henry Seidel Canby observed.[46] This passage about the "complete lover" is, in order of publication, Whitman's first statement on the subject and hence the one that conditioned, one way or another, both his later formulations and the various accounts his readers were to give of it. It is worth noting, then, that it presents the traditional view from a curiously oblique angle. Such an early statement, according to this view, should speak of Eros in language from which Caritas could eventually spring; instead, Whitman speaks of Caritas in the language of Eros. What this poet aspires for may be as disembodied and "transcendent" as the ponderous abstractions he seems to be fond of mouthing, but his desires are ecstasy-bound and express themselves in images and words of passion. The "eternal passion" through which he is "rapport" with "all expected from heaven or from the highest" is "showers and thrills" and a "burning progress to contact and amorous joy" (vi).

Common experience, which can recognize the sexual element in all love but knows that all sex is not love, may be exasperated by Whitman's oversimplifications, but their metaphoric power is difficult to resist. Of course, the figure seems prac-

tically grotesque at first. It reveals an imagination either spite-
fully contemptuous of the actualities of sex or, in a curious
way, ignorant of them. But these apparent limitations, the very
poverty, of his experience of sex allow Whitman the freedom
first to conceive of all existence through the metaphor of the
procreative attraction and commingling of the sexes and then to
call his metaphor love. The "complementary opposites" that
make up all that exists are, like male and female, complementary
by being "antagonistic," and they do not merely fuse: they
mate. For Whitman, that means that they love. As one critic
phrased it:

> [Whitman] moves from the physical (biological) differentiation be-
> tween male and female to the dichotomy of experience—through
> love—that pervades the whole of the universe. There is a dialectic
> interaction on the basis of love of all phenomena, and from a cos-
> mic point of view the procreative force operates in all things.[47]

This connection between love and the "conjunction" of the
elements of existence is a fundamental assumption throughout
Whitman's work. In the Preface, too, the essential creative device is not merely the mechanical dialectic of bipolar unity but
its infinitely versatile metaphoric conception, the "merge," for
which Whitman's taunts will soon coax his reader.

The paragraph on the greatest poet's "eternal passion" is in
itself hardly an explicit statement of this connection. Its full significance is revealed only by the crucial figure that soon follows
it: that of the poet arising between the sympathy and pride of
the soul. The principle of triadic coherence makes sense out of
this "eternal passion" by releasing its metaphoric power and assigning a function to it within Whitman's scheme. In turn, the
apparatus of meaning whose presentation culminates in the triadic figure would have been incomplete without this metaphor
of what Waskow with somewhat excessive delicacy calls marriage.[48]

Once it has been made clear that the greatest poet's power
to "dilate" "anything that was before thought small" is "burning

progress to contact and amorous joy," the triadic figure's images of stretching, sleeping, and lying down take on unmistakable erotic and procreative connotations.[49] This context reinforces the dialectical principle the figure stands for by endowing it with a degree of immediacy it could not possibly have as a mere formula of logic. When the very process of being is expressed through a preposterous and exhilarating personification as the universal love-making of opposites, all existence is, in a sense, humanized, while human experience is shown not as a world in and of itself but as subordinate to a total system. This purposeful equivocation between human and non-human orders of existence is also the burden of the memorable sentence that concludes the passage on the "complete lover": "The sea is not surer of the shore or the shore of the sea than he is of the fruition of his love and of all perfection and beauty" (vi).

In Emerson's "Plato," which appeared only five years before the first *Leaves*, there is a metaphor that resembles very closely this simile of the shoreline. "Our strength," Emerson writes, "is transitional, alternating; or, shall I say, a thread of two strands. The sea-shore, sea seen from shore, shore seen from sea."[50] Whether it was indeed this passage that suggested Whitman's phrase or it occurred to him during one of his countless walks along the beaches of "Paumanok," the differences between the two offer a summary illustration of the way in which the metaphor of love operates in his vision and style. In Emerson, land and sea are lifeless and motionless objects of perception; they depend on being seen. In Whitman, the personification sets them free to interact directly, to "merge." Emerson's sentence is a hissing tongue-twister. In Whitman's phrase, the sibilants' modulated alliteration and the vowels' symmetrical dip and rise in pitch reflect the gentle rush and retreat of the waves, the ceaselessly undulant rhythm not simply of water splashing ashore but of earth and ocean making "sure" of each other.[51]

Thus, through his metaphor, Whitman can embody his intuition of the process of being. The dialectic of bipolar unity simply formulates this intuition into law. But without the introduc-

51

tion of the metaphor first, the principle announced by the triadic figure would have been only a boring and rather nonsensical abstraction.

VII

Sea and shore are complementary; hence, they are "lovers," and they "merge." The greatest poet is the "one complete lover" in "the known universe" because he alone can be a complementary opposite to all. What distinguishes him is his "clear vision," his ability to see, when others do not, the "poetic quality" in everything. The distinction that "the others are as good as he, only he sees it and they do not" could be dismissed in a "straight" reading as banal or at best disingenuous, but its implications gain central significance in the light of the triadic principle and the metaphor of love. These reveal, as mentioned earlier, that "indicating the path between reality and the soul" is not simply the function but the very being of the "greatest poet." It follows that there can be a "greatest poet" only *when* he possesses his "clear vision"; in other words, his "clear vision," along with his other attributes, is not a permanent characteristic but the mark of a special awareness. The "greatest poet" is anybody ("the others are as good as he") in this rare, only intermittently attainable state of mind. Even a sometime printer-editor from Brooklyn, New York could aspire to attain it.

This observation leads to some important conclusions. First of all, if the "greatest poet" is a state of mind, so is the other dominant theme of the essay, "America." As noted before, the alternation of emphasis between the two themes organizes the essay into five major parts. The foregoing detailed discussion of the triadic principle and its function in Whitman's work should suggest that such an arrangement is not an artificial, totally arbitrary one.

Clearly, the two themes correspond to form a bipolar unity. They represent the complementary impulses which have been variously described in this study as extroversion and introversion or centrifugal and centripetal forces and which one may label respectively, "democratic" and "unitary" after Richard Chase's analysis of what he called "the paradox of identity" in "Song of Myself." [52] As such, they are the two aspects of a concept in dichotomy. It is interesting to note, for example, that in the first, keynote paragraph of the Preface, one can substitute "the greatest poet" for "America" ("The greatest poet does not repel the past . . ." etc.) without upsetting the logic of the argument, since everything the speaker claims for "America" he will also claim for "the greatest poet." The question of why Whitman chose to stress "America" in opening his discourse must be left unanswered for a while yet; however, the structure of the essay can be outlined at last as it is defined by the "triadic" interaction of the two themes.

The first movement states the "democratic" theme, "America," through an unconventional combination of conventional assumptions about it. The second movement does the same thing with the "unitary" theme of the "poet" and, in the process, gradually reveals the principle and mechanics of the coherence one could sense in the essay from the beginning without being able to account for it by traditional means. In the next two movements each theme is viewed in the light of the other: "America" as it is conceivable in the individual and "the great poet" as it is expressed through the collective values of his environment. While throughout these four movements one of the themes is always implied and only eventually evoked by the dominant other, the fifth and final movement explicitly states both. To be more exact, since the movement deals with the direct practical effect of the two themes upon each other, it contains both in a system of "precision and balance," in which "neither can stretch too far."

As complementary aspects of an envisioned state of mind, "America" and "the poet" project an ambition, a goal. The formal realization of the mode of being that is the fulfillment of this ambition is what Whitman calls poetry. Thus, as the outward form of the realized aspiration that is "America," "the United

States themselves are essentially the greatest poem," even if unessentially, as a political and social actuality at any given time, they can be a discouraging reminder of how unrealized that aspiration is. Whitman furnishes proof in the Preface itself that he harbored no illusions about the everyday perversions of the democratic ideal. The same concept of poetry is the "essential" justification of *Leaves of Grass* in general and of the volume's first poem in particular. They are to the ambition that is "the greatest poet" what the United States are, "essentially," to the vision that is "America."

By containing the themes that constitute this double-faceted ambition the Preface does not articulate the ambition itself but embodies the mentality that could conceive of it and that is therefore the indispensable condition for its attainment under either or both of its aspects. The concept of poetry just described makes the Preface, in turn, indispensable for an understanding of the volume. Whitman insists on what was defined earlier as "the listener's intimate experience of the poet's person" because his whole poetry consists of a person's becoming a poet. Through expressing the mentality capable of this transformative or, in a sense, transcendental ambition the Preface evokes in the listener a living, "meta-verbal" sense of the personality that could become the poet. Thus, it creates the context without which the poems could have only incidental significance.

VIII

Since the demonstration of the workings of the triadic apparatus should serve as a key for the thematic reading of the essay, there seems to be no need for a detailed discussion of the successive steps in the argument of the last three movements. When Whitman opens the third movement, for example, with his praise of simplicity as "the sunshine of the light of letters," (vi) he may seem "like . . . Leo Tolstoy [who] glorified everything that he himself was not and never could be"; [53] however, once his fundamental assumption that all being consists of "the mutual pressure of contraries" has been made plain, the method of indirection follows from it as a logical and simple conclusion. As a matter of fact, no stronger objection can be raised against Whitman's system of bipolar unity than that it is far too simple, if not an outright over-simplification. To be sure, lacking the grace of an insight as overpowering as Whitman's, one's comprehension of his passionate cosmos may well be a complicated and rather half-hearted operation. But granted that insight, his ways are simplicity itself.

After simplicity, other crucial qualities of the new poetry follow: "unconstraint," that is, the "silent defiance advancing from new free forms" (vii); equality, which means "generosity and affection and [encouragement of] competitors" (vii); receptivity to "exact science and its practical movements" (vii); and, finally, "sanity" and "perfect candor" to "investigate" the "past and present and future" of "men and women and the earth and all upon it" (viii). Although these virtues are ascribed or available only to the individual, what they present is the idea of a community: the potential for "America" in the "single separate person." The "silent defiance" Whitman speaks of is that "antinomian impulse" Roy Harvey Pearce takes to be the single most distinctive feature in the literature of the New World,[54] and the origin of not only *Leaves of Grass* but the country itself is characterized by the observation: "The cleanest expression is that which finds no sphere worthy of itself and makes one" (vii).

Dominating the whole movement from its center stands the phrase that formulates in "triadic" terms the law of individual existence by which communities like the envisioned "America" can come into being: "The most affluent man is he that confronts all the shows he sees by equivalents out of the stronger wealth of himself" (vii). The diction in this sentence is remarkably precise. "Stronger" is a hint at one of the most pervasive concepts in Whitman's poetry, the ultimate resilience of the self, through which the poet's "final merit" achieves its countless triumphs over the identities it has challenged or has been challenged by. Equally effective is the adjective "affluent." It not only fits the immediate metaphoric context in which it appears, it also anticipates the context of "prudence," which will enclose, in the following (fourth) movement of the essay, the triadic statement that corresponds to the one in the third: "The prudence of the greatest poet answers at last the craving and glut of the soul [. . . and] matches every thought or act by its correlative" (xi).

This "extreme caution or prudence" (ix) is the last of the major topics that make up the fourth movement. "Political liberty," which "takes the adherence of heroes wherever men and women exist" (viii), is the first. "The superiority of genuineness over all fiction and romance" (ix) follows, then "the openness" that "wins the inner and the outer world" (ix). Only then does the speaker finally launch into his lengthy tirade on "caution." This is the outburst that some say was inspired by the celebrated "chart of bumps" the "practical phrenologist" Lorenzo Fowler prepared for Whitman in July 1849.[55]

This movement, as mentioned before, is the inverse of the third. This time, an individual is presented against collective values, "the greatest poet" as the expression of the ambition of a community. The pedestrian prudence of the everyday merely leads to a recognition of "the great fraud" it conceals and, beyond it, to "the thought of the prudence suitable for immortality" (x); similarly, the innumerable abuses that liberty as it is lived must sustain merely point toward the glimpse of perfection in liberty personified as it "sits in calmness and light" (viii). The emphasis is strictly on the individual. "The great poet" is described as a free man among those who abuse freedom and a wise man among the unwisely prudent.

He is also shown as the one capable of stark truth, the one who does not need to have his "histories" diluted into "romances" (ix).[56] He thrives on "genuineness" while others prefer "fiction." Again, a criterion of the community serves to delineate the fully realized, "satisfied," individual, who is, like "most works," "most beautiful without ornament" (ix). Thus, "the absence of tricks" in "the outer world" is contingent upon "openness" in "the inner world," and the description of "those communities where the models of natural forms are public every day" (ix) becomes an indirect representation of "the great poets," who are "justified" by their "perfect personal candor."

As this summary itself indicates, one major characteristic of these two movements is Whitman's practical demonstration of his method of indirection: he consistently illustrates what he means by explaining at length what he does not mean. Through this method emerges another important aspect of his conception of the "mode of truth"—to use Hawthorne's expression—with which he is grappling. This truth lies beneath the surface of appearances. Its essence cannot be "directly" read; one must penetrate to it. By unfolding the logic of the link between the "inner" and the "outer" world—the triplicate process, "bipolar unity,"—Whitman performs the task of making available what Matthiessen, speaking of Hawthorne, called "the 'real': not actuality transformed into an impossible perfection, but actuality disengaged from appearances." [57]

This "actuality" is the "inner world" that Henry Alonzo Myers, departing somewhat from Whitman's use of the term in the Preface, claims "is the very reason and justification for the presentation of a world of experience." [58] Myers has described this "inner world" as a "spiritual democracy governed by two principles, one the unlimited individual, the other the equality of individuals." In these two principles the themes of "the poet" and "America" are easily recognized, and in his argument about "that eternal equality of beings which may be known by seeing each thing in its place and as it really is" there is as good a definition as any of what Whitman calls "the poetic quality" in everything.

"The perfect poet," Myers writes, "will find all beings equal in his eyes, *not in society,* but in the inner world." Therein lies the clarification of the apparently paradoxical concept of equality, "equal terms," in a world of "heroes" and "great masters." Since "equality exists only in a world of unlimited personalities,"

Myers asks, "how can one unlimited personality be either more or less than another?" That is, in fact, the gist of the question that could baffle some readers in "the messages of great poets to each man and woman": "Did you suppose there could be only one Supreme? We affirm there can be unnumbered Supremes, and that one does not countervail another any more than one eyesight countervails another" (vii). What emerges from the resolution of the paradox is "a community of infinite individuals ruled by an eternal and just law of equality." It is the fully realized "picture of [the] inner world," through which, Myers concludes, Whitman strives "to justify the ways of the world to man." [59]

Chapter Three

THE "CURIOUS TRIPLICATE PROCESS"—IN PRACTICE

I

Although the first four movements of the Preface reveal a unified vision that makes conceivable the special awareness toward which Whitman's whole creative effort is directed, this thematic harmony cannot mitigate or even account for the ever louder dissonances in the speaker's style and tone as he reaches the third and, especially, the fourth movement. Just when his argument has begun to make sense, the voice of this "lecturer-orator" becomes increasingly shrill, his sentences and periods insufferably long, and his figures of speech often lame or trite. There were such slips before, too, but, all in all, he more than compensated for them with insights, images, and cadences both original and arresting. A limping sentence like "Other proportions of the reception of pleasure dwindle to nothing to his proportions" (vi) was set off by such self-assured and clear measures as the shoreline image, and even his longest outbursts were tempered by a sense of uncomplicated and simple delight that only rarely allowed his enthusiasm to decline into stridency.

Now, however, he seems to be growing hoarse. His exuberance sours into mere shrillness, and syntactic atrocities like "Of the human form especially it is so great it must never be made ridiculous" (ix) follow one another in such profusion that even the half-forgotten ill effects of the earlier lapses are revived. This changed tone is inevitably part of the essay's total significance and needs to be explained. A good example of the change and a good place to begin the analysis is the harangue on "extreme caution or prudence."

This portion of the essay, it will be recalled, rounds off the fourth movement by contrasting "the prudence of the mere wealth and respectability of the most esteemed life" with "the prudence of the greatest poet," which is "wisdom spaced by ages" and "answers at last the craving and glut of the soul" (x–xi). "Only that person has no great prudence to learn," runs the conclusion,

> who has learnt to prefer real longlived things, and favors body and soul the same, and perceives the indirect assuredly following the direct, and what evil or good he does leaping onward and waiting to meet him again—and who in his spirit in any emergency whatever neither hurries or avoids death. (xi)

In other words, true "prudence" is yet another name for that special awareness which is the central subject of the Preface and of the whole volume itself.

As Gay Wilson Allen, for one, has noted, this discussion of "extreme caution" contains marked echoes of Emerson's essay, "Prudence," and shows also the possible influence of Epicureanism, which probably reached Whitman through Frances Wright's popularization of it.[1] But even if it is less than entirely original, it would be quite effective as part of the main argument if it were not so overdone. From the structural or thematic point of view, the spirited peroration alone, beginning with "Whatever satisfies the soul is truth" (xi), would have fulfilled the speaker's purposes very well. This portion is as pithy and emphatic as any number of earlier passages, with which he knew how to rest content in the first three movements.

Now, however, he cannot leave well enough alone. He car-

ries on interminably, and before he finds his stride again toward
the end, he stumbles through three catalogues, which become
worse as they become longer. The first one is relatively successful with its straightforward, powerful diction in such phrases as
"the independence of a little sum laid aside for burial-money,
and of a few clapboards around and shingles overhead on a lot
of American soil owned" (x). The second list, although less impressive, attracts attention by the odd emphasis in it on sexual
venality. But the third and longest catalogue is a failure, for only
its abstractions and generalizations do not strike the listener as
utterly banal. "All the self-denial that stood steady and aloof on
wrecks and saw others take the seats of the boats" (x) is far too
close to the boy who stood on the burning deck, and the "vast
sweet love and precious suffering of mothers" (x) is not much
further away. The Preface evidently contains not just catalogues
used as "committees supposed to stand for the rest" but also instances of sheer verbiage in which a torrent of sound attempts
to conceal the lack of invention.

Why has this embarrassed excitement crept into Whitman's
voice? Part of an answer may be found in the argument of Edward Hungerford, who demonstrated convincingly that the list
of virtues introducing the tirade is a close parallel of the phrenological evaluation of Whitman's character.[2] The exponents of
this "pseudoscience of head bumps, rudimentary eugenics and
moral perfectibility"[3] claim to be able to read the character of
an individual by an expert analysis of the "topography" of his
skull. Phrenology originated in Austria, reached these shores in
the early 1830's, and almost immediately became very popular.[4]
The decline of the fad, however, was almost as rapid as its rise,
for by the 1850's very few people seem to have taken it very
seriously,[5] although it lingers on even today, relegated to a place
among other shabby esoterica like graphology or spiritualism.

A reviewing assignment in 1846 was probably Whitman's
first contact with phrenology.[6] His interest in it grew, and finally,
in the summer of 1849, he had his "chart of bumps" drawn up in
the "Phrenological Cabinet" of Fowlers and Wells, in New York.

His bumps must have amazed the analyst Lorenzo Fowler himself. As Hungerford writes,

> phrenology found Whitman an astonishingly developed man. There was no element of human nature lacking in him, and his faults, if they were to be regarded as faults, were due rather to the surplus of good, human qualities than to any omissions.[7]

Even in his most "dilating" moments of boundless self-confidence, Whitman could not have flattered himself more than this report did. It is hardly surprising, then, that as Hungerford adds, "Whitman's idea of the perfect poet has become subtly intertwined with his conception of himself, and this *liaison* was conceived in phrenology and expressed in its terms."[8] However, it would be perhaps more precise to speak not of Whitman's concept of himself but of the phrenologist's concept of him. Whitman himself, apparently, knew that, attractive as it may have been, Fowler's chart of bumps was in some important respects off the mark. Hungerford implies as much by his bemused comment that in Whitman's explanation of true prudence,

> we have a superb example of rationalization. Whitman reshapes prudence to satisfy the desires of his own heart. The truly prudent person is he who plunges gloriously into life. The truly prudent poet is, it seems, strangely like Walt Whitman.[9]

Whitman's loud insistence on his curiously incautious version of caution may well have been meant to satisfy the desires of his own heart, but he certainly was not just trying to fit himself to the phrenologist's portrait. With that he was not afraid to tamper: the greatest poet is assigned "large hope," for instance, in which the Brooklyn editor was found somewhat deficient. However, since the absence of "hope" would have been a strange deficiency in an embodiment of noblest aspirations, the picture is amended without hesitation. There is undoubtedly more to this troubled torrent of words than an attempt to live up to the chart of bumps.

"CURIOUS TRIPLICATE PROCESS"—IN PRACTICE

For all his protestations to the contrary, Whitman had not always been above the attractions of the inferior kind of prudence that the speaker in the Preface keeps contemptuously denouncing until his throat becomes sore. "Business, moneymaking," notes Newton Arvin, "was undoubtedly the prime activity of the age, and Whitman the optimist . . . was determined to find this activity a splendid thing." [10] The evidence is both ample and familiar that this admiration did not take him such a strenuous effort as all that, for he knew well the value of a dollar and appreciated it not only when he was building and selling houses but also when he was offering poems for sale.[11] And it bothered him not a little that he was not much good at this "prime activity." Arvin speaks of the "constant, though on the whole . . . quiet clash between what [Whitman] really saw and what he wished to see, . . . between his instinctive loyalties and his superficial complacencies." [12] These "complacencies" of his were not quite as superficial as one might wish that they had been. He, at any rate, took them seriously, especially, it would seem, during the two or three years before the first Leaves. The wry humor in some of the comments he made late in life on this crucial period of his career merely underscores the fact that not to have "made it" on the terms of the philistine world did not leave him undisturbed.[13] He was a failure at thirty-five, among other things as a breadwinner, too. He did not need the affectionate contempt of his family to remind him of it, although he must have had a generous share of that anyway, as his brother George's indulgently condescending old-age reminiscences testify.[14]

This sense of failure had to be part of Whitman's general sense of deception by the "real" world that Jean Catel persuasively argues drove him to writing Leaves of Grass.[15] If in the Preface the speaker cannot stop railing against "the great fraud upon modern civilization," it is because he is still smarting badly from having been taken in by it, although he cannot bring himself to admit freely that he had been one of its dupes.

The shrillness, then, may be due to Whitman's effort to

drown out a sense of failure by rationalizing it to death. It is interesting, however, that his vociferous contempt for his age's "prime activity" was in no way setting him against his age. To be prudent for eternity rather than for transitory things is perhaps the oldest and widest-known bit of wisdom, after all, and to despise material gain while striving for it has been, all in all, the favorite hypocrisy of any mercantile civilization, Whitman's own included. Both by his ill-disguised sense of frustration and even shame over his material improvidence and by his ringing pronouncements about the profit and loss that really matter "in the unshakable order of the universe" (x), he was bowing to the conventions of his world, offering it what it wanted to hear.

Newton Arvin was right, of course, in remarking that "in his own way . . . [Whitman] too was at odds with the public and official morality of his time," [16] but, whatever external manifestations this conflict may have had, rarely if ever did it cease to be an internal struggle as well. A good part of Whitman's sensibility remained always—sometimes for the better, often for the worse—intensely conscious of this "conventional morality," if not necessarily committed to it. The passage on prudence is only the first indication in the Preface, and there are others as well, that this conflict had a very important influence not just on his "philosophy" but, above all, on his manner of expression and on the associative patterns his poetic imagination was to follow.

II

What had been gathered from the prudence tirade helps to clarify some earlier odd moments in the essay, especially the curious treatment of political liberty. Myers' suggestion makes sense that the political version of equality was left to the last third of the essay because of Whitman's preoccupation with the "spiritual democracy." [17] For the sake of "definiteness," the speaker takes first things first. But the overwhelmingly negative emphasis in his reflections on political liberty can be understood only after the listener has finally discerned that when the "lecturer-orator" suddenly begins to talk faster and louder than usual, he is trying to conceal something, not so much from his audience as from himself.

Whitman, as it has often been noted, was capable of politically extreme emotions. Of course, he was the proud champion of "the common people," "the divine average." As Matthiessen summed up one of Arvin's arguments, ". . . Whitman did not 'espouse' the cause of the masses through any self-conscious gesture of identification. The relation was simpler and more natural, for he was quite literally one of them himself." [18] A home atmosphere of Jeffersonian patriotism combined with Quaker, "Hicksite," sympathies was the earliest and hence perhaps the profoundest influence on his mind.[19] This mixture may account for the fact that the mode of his political understanding was essentially religious. As Myers has demonstrated it, Whitman's "spiritual democracy," which he discovered through "the surface world of American democracy," was, for him, *an eternal fact,*" and the "political ideal" of equality was but a manifestation of it. Thus, his commitment to the "good old cause" of "the sovereignty and sacredness of the individual" was a quasi-religious faith, steady, deep, and sincere.[20]

But the list of all the political evil that must befall a nation before its "instinct of liberty" can be "discharged," proves that he could get at least as worked up over "swarmery" as Carlyle himself, whom he was to excoriate viciously once for coining the term to describe what democracy can be.[21] Later, apologizing for the intemperate tone of his refutation of the Scotsman's "ironically derisive" attack on American democracy, he confessed that "[he] had more than once been in the like mood, during which [Carlyle's] essay was evidently cast, and seen persons and things in the same light." [22]

By the time the Preface was written, he must have been familiar with such moods, for his democratic faith had been long and sorely tried. The story of his practical involvement in politics during the forties and of his subsequent disillusionment has often been told.[23] After he had left active political life, Whitman watched from the outside but no doubt with growing disgust and indignation the inglorious machinations through which the forces sympathetic to slavery managed to retain control of the Democratic party and of the government. These were the years of the bitterest controversy over the Fugitive Slave Law, a time,

> when the soul retires in the cool communion of the night and sur-
> veys its experience and has much ecstasy over the word and deed
> that put back a helpless innocent person into the gripe of the
> gripers or into any cruel inferiority. (viii)

Such times, the speaker of the Preface says, arrive along the way toward the extinction of liberty. Yet, only a few years before, as the editor of the *Brooklyn Eagle,* Whitman gave his support, anguished and grudging though it was, to the repulsive law. He gave it for the sake of preserving the union at all cost.[24] In the Preface, there is no longer room for such accommodating sentiments.

Whitman's shifting stand on the Fugitive Slave Law is only one example of "his confusions, his generosities and blurred enthusiasms"[25] that mark the evolution of his political views. The lop-sided treatment of political liberty in the Preface is an expression of the tension that their erratic evolution represents.[26] These views have not only little relevance but also little existence apart from the interaction of elemental drives that was Whitman's whole being.

In the general scheme of the essay, the passage on liberty is meant to show that the "great master" is the epitome of his community's ambition; however, the speaker winds up almost defeating his own purpose by insisting too hard and too long. What was intended to be an affirmation of faith turns out to be a nervous protestation of innocence. The needlessly extended enumeration of the forces corrupting liberty is scarcely balanced by the platitudinous reassurance that "liberty is poorly served by men whose good intent is quelled from one failure or two failures or any number of failures" (viii).

"CURIOUS TRIPLICATE PROCESS"—IN PRACTICE

At first, the imbalance and the dissonant notes of outrage may not seem in any sense significant. But whoever has heard the anxiety beneath the shrillness in the oration on prudence will also remember this earlier passage and recognize in both the same worried concern to be on the side of the angels. In this case, too, such concern is due, to a certain extent, to Whitman's ambivalent attitudes toward the conventional assumptions of his time. Flaunted and abused as it was, the democratic ideal was nevertheless the "official morality," the political orthodoxy of the land. Whitman could not give vent to his "Carlylean" mood without announcing first, for all to hear, his unshakable loyalty to the cause.

But, obviously, the speaker is troubled by a great deal more than convention as he holds forth on liberty. Since Whitman adhered to the democratic ideal with the fervor of a religious faith, he confronted the deviations from the ideal with the wrought-up emotions of the true believer confronting sin and heresy. And he had to encounter them within himself, first of all: his speaker's angry impatience with the corruptions of democracy is not the only "Carlylean" feature in his mood. The preceding portion, in which he finished the presentation of "America" as it is inherent in the individual, concluded with heated pronouncements about the "great master" (viii). Now he is still full of excitement about the "heroes" and "great masters," and there is something quite "undemocratically" isolated and self-assertive even about the beautiful image in which liberty is personified as yet another avatar of the supreme ambition.[27]

Although he does not seem to have admitted it directly, Whitman, apparently, was quite aware of his own tendency to let the "centripetal" forces get the better of him, to allow the "infinite individual" to be replaced by the egomaniac. There are indications in the Preface as well as in the poetry that he knew and dreaded his egocentric proclivities. He was afraid of them not just because they threatened to degrade his cherished insight from "knowledge that [passes] all the art and argument of

67

the earth" (xi) into primitive solipsism but also because they drove him to transgress against his egalitarian faith. If in the Preface his "right explanation about prudence" (x) is a way of shouting down a sense of shame, his perfervid insistence on his democratic loyalty is a way of drowning out a sense of guilt.

Fully realized, with "everything in its place," Whitman's vision is a perfect system of "precision and balance." He is justified in speaking of it as "individual or aggregate democracy," [28] his adjectives marking off two equivalent and mutually dependent versions of the same concept. But the fulfillment of the vision is only implicit in the continuous effort to achieve it; meanwhile, if one of the hands preponderates in the balance, it must be compensated for. In the Preface, whenever a statement or an argument implies or is about to admit isolation, the speaker hastens back into the fold, usually by reasserting his democratic faith, occasionally by falling in with "public or official morality." As indicated above, the process originates in certain forms of guilt; hence, it is all but involuntary, almost compulsive. To put it another way: Whitman does not so much strive to restore the balance as the balance tends to restore itself.

The paragraph on political liberty illustrates one of the ways in which this pattern of association may operate. Another way is seen in the scrupulous care with which the speaker keeps reminding his audience that "the others are as good as [the great poet]" (v), "men and women perceive the beauty well enough, probably as well as he" (v), and "the poet sees for a certainty how one not a great artist may be just as sacred and perfect as the greatest artist" (v). These and similar reminders invariably follow assertions of exuberant individualism. After announcing that "in the talk on the soul and eternity and God off of his equal plane [the great poet] is silent" (v), the speaker feels compelled to digress on "faith," which is "the antiseptic of the soul" and "pervades the common people" (v). Logically a *non sequitur* pure and simple, the digression makes plain enough sense in the light of the associative pattern just discussed. The same principle of compensation accounts for the unexpected sermon that follows the arrogant phrase about "beautiful blood and a beautiful brain" (v). Although "the greatest poet does not moralize or make applications of morals" (vi), the speaker of the Preface is forced to spell out "what you shall do" (v–vi), for he has just blurted out the conceitedly conditional claim that "if the greatnesses are in conjunction in a man or a woman it is enough" (v). The advice he finally gives echoes the noblest Christian pieties, which his world admired the more because it refused to follow them: he is on the side of "official"—if not necessarily "public"—morality again.

The same forces appear to be at work in the transitions from movement to movement. Between the first and second and between the third and fourth, that is, when the thematic emphasis shifts from "America" to "the poet," the change is gradual, spontaneous, virtually unconscious. Again and again the speaker starts with the "democratic" theme and moves on smoothly, imperceptibly, to the "unitary," pursuing the latter to the point where its link with its complementary opposite is all but broken. Then the speaker suddenly catches himself, pulls himself up short. The transition from the second to the third and from the fourth to the fifth movement is an abrupt pause, then a sharp change of subject. After the triadic figure of poet, pride, and sympathy, the voice changes, and the speaker begins to talk of simplicity. Later, he runs out of breath announcing the law of supreme prudence, must stop to collect his wits about him, and continues in a totally different vein, humbly submitting his "great poet" to the judgment of "the immediate age" (xi).

Whitman's persistent maneuvers to maintain a "democratic" balance and thus keep clean his conscience, and perhaps the image he aims to project, resemble his meticulous habit, noted by Asselineau and frequently seen in the Preface, of adding "or woman" or "and woman" whenever he says "man." [29] Both obsessions point up the tension that the speaker's self-conscious optimism cannot long conceal. Whitman's whole being is caught up between self-assertive, individualistic impulses that he can scarcely control and ethical and cultural commitments that he is unwilling and at any rate psychologically unable to abandon.

III

A curious and from the explicator's point of view very significant manifestation of this tension emerges from Whitman's treatment of sexuality. The obvious importance of sex has from the first been among the best-known and most widely discussed aspects of Whitman's work. Against the unlikely chance that his lines would not speak plainly enough, he himself drew attention to it on a number of occasions, risking and then suffering the notoriety that was to follow inevitably. One might recall his frequently cited remark reported by Traubel: "If I had cut sex out I might just as well have cut everything out—the full scheme would no longer exist—it would have been violated in its most sensitive spot." [30] By establishing the "complete lover's" "eternal passion" as the key metaphor of the whole volume, the Preface, too, bears out his claim. And yet, the speaker shows nothing but revulsion and contempt for auto-eroticism, although the evidence available suggests that it made for most, if not all, of Whitman's sexual experience.[31] Thus, a number of crucial passages in the first volume and especially in its first poem are, as Richard Chase, among others, has noted, "of course frankly auto-erotic." [32] Whitman eventually deleted from later editions the lines in which the diction is possibly the most explicitly revealing, but he left the rest to stand substantially as he wrote them. He quite simply could not afford to leave them out, for without them "the full scheme would no longer exist"; he may have also felt that in these cases his words managed to preserve the sheer imaginative force derived from sexuality while they kept concealed what may have seemed offensively aberrant in its specific manifestation.

What is important about such concealment, however, is that it would not be just Whitman's concession to a foolish prudery he himself could only despise. A great deal of it is an acknowledgment of scruples of his own. The same pattern of association that makes him assert his democratic orthodoxy to compensate for "undemocratic" impulses also makes him profess his times' conventional strictures and fears concerning masturbation. Often he does so even in the poems in which the "frankly auto-erotic" inspiration is most evident. For example, in the poem that was to become "The Sleepers," as the protagonist enters a vision which can be understood in terms of an auto-erotic fantasy, a conspicuous feature in the opening *montage* is the "faces of onanists," and they are just as "sick-gray" ("The Sleepers," 8) as any contributor to "the great literature of masturbation-phobia" [33] would describe them.

Straightforward denials of this unsolicited sort invite suspicion by their very presence. Not surprisingly, they got Whitman into more trouble than the passages in which the meaning could be scarcely mistaken but at least no such blunt word as "onanist" embarrassed the delicate reader. Thus, in 1868, the lines William Rossetti asked for and got Whitman's permission to excise from the Preface were the ones containing the speaker's gloomy warnings that the indulgence of passions "[never] can be stamped on the programme but it is duly realized and returned, and that returned in further performances" (x).[34] The difficulty lay in the list of the examples of excessive passion, and the fact that Whitman wrote it to reinforce his horrified disapproval made not the slightest difference. A stubbornly recurring item in this list is "the privacy of the onanist," repeated first as "any depravity of young men" then a few lines further on as "any of the wiles practiced by people upon themselves" (x). This train of thought will also be a faint echo among some other, stronger reverberations in these powerful notes of intentionally biblical resonance that conclude the poem as yet untitled "I Sing the Body Electric":

> Have you seen the fool that corrupted his own live body?
>   or the fool that corrupted her own live body?
> For they do not conceal themselves, and cannot conceal
>   themselves.

"CURIOUS TRIPLICATE PROCESS"—IN PRACTICE

Who degrades or defiles the living human body is cursed,
Who degrades or defiles the body of the dead is not more
    cursed.

               ("I Sing the Body Electric," 116–19)

Whitman protests his sexual probity in yet another way. This
time his excessive precautions suggest a genuinely "guilty" conscience rather than a merely prudent compliance with a prudish
age, for only he could have known in this case that his words
might be construed as an admission that he was a masturbator.
In his list of phrenological virtues introducing the discussion of
prudence Whitman carefully translates "amativeness" as
"fondness for women" (ix). One should, of course, be grateful
for this favor, for "amativeness" is unquestionably a very ugly
word. It is not more of a verbal barbarism, however, than "alimentiveness," nor is it in greater need of an explanatory translation than, in the context of the sentence, "comparison" or "causality." Whitman himself felt no compunction about using it
elsewhere. But in these lines, when he knew even if nobody else
did that the qualities he was enumerating had been pronounced
to be his own, he apparently decided to eliminate from the
phrenological concept some implications that the technical term
would have necessarily retained.

"Amativeness," Hungerford writes, "meant the instinct of
physical love," and, when coupled with "adhesiveness," it constituted the affection Whitman was to celebrate as "love." [35] But
this instinct, the phrenologists themselves argued, manifested itself more often than not through its abuses and excesses, and by
far the most widespread and pernicious among these, they
claimed, was "perversion," that is, masturbation.[36] One of the
phrenologists promoting this brand of "scientifically warranted"
sexual hygiene was Orson Squire Fowler, Lorenzo's brother and
one of the *de facto* publishers of the first *Leaves.* Having believed him on several other subjects concerning himself, Whitman is quite likely to have believed him on this one, too, especially because the conventional attitudes of his culture and, as
noted earlier, his own reluctance—fear, even—to oppose them

squarely predisposed him to do so anyway. There are a number of close parallels and echoes in wording between direct references to auto-eroticism in the Preface and Fowler's "definitive treatment" of it, a shoddily written, dreary little pamphlet published in 1844 under the title *Amativeness or Evils and Remedies of Excessive and Perverted Sexuality*. Their very presence suggests that not only was Whitman, indeed, familiar with Fowler's statement of what at the time was, after all, the commonplace view of the subject, but that he also accepted it as at least socially valid. It was the orthodoxy, like democracy or otherworldly "prudence," against which he dared not openly rebel. The purpose, therefore, of Whitman's carefully restrictive elucidation of "amativeness" appears to be to insure that those implications of the concept that he found embarrassing will not occur to his listener.

Whitman's preoccupation with auto-eroticism is in itself neither particularly surprising nor very interesting. That he accepted the phrenologists' attitude toward it is, however, very significant, for by doing so he was condemning and disowning publicly and morally what the metaphoric structure of his poetry acknowledges and a number of explicit passages all but proclaim to be among his imagination's main sources of power. In Whitman's whole work there are few concerns as pervasive as this "secret" of his sexuality; consequently, there is no example more telling of the constant struggle of contradictory drives within his awareness than his overanxious efforts to repudiate "for the record" the pattern of his own sexuality, even though it was also, in fact, the pattern that gave form to his inspiration.

IV

Thus, whatever the context—sexual, political, "existential"—the basic formula of Whitman's processes of consciousness consists of elemental impulses of self-assertion invariably followed by self-denying reactions of compulsive force. Neither drive can ever become totally dominant; therefore, the process itself is self-sustaining and self-renewing. Whitman's auto-eroticism is as indispensable a feature in his work as his persistent efforts to hide and deny it. The same holds true of his impulsive egocentrism and the profound and often desperately insistent democratism through which he kept it under control. When he spoke of the fused though antagonistic two elements in all things, his words reflected not so much second-hand Hegel as first-hand experience. In these terms he could at last comprehend himself, and when he began to seek out ways by which he could turn this insight into the central instrument of his expression, his transformation from a third-rate hack into great poet also began. Thus, the principle of balance which informs the Preface through the "curious triplicate process" and establishes its "bipolar unity" is really a conceptual extension of the dynamics of the stress between the characteristic, ambivalent impulses that constituted Whitman's—Walter Whitman's—awareness.

Once this fundamental relationship is recognized, Whitman's opening strategem can also be plausibly explained. He begins by stressing the "democratic," "American" aspect of the ambivalent first image and by treating the theme of "America" before the "unitary" theme of "the poet." This gambit is closely related to "the simple and astonishing fact" John Kinnaird was the first to recognize "duly": there is "a disparity between the Preface and the earliest poetry," between the essay, with what Kinnaird sees as its essentially political and didactic orientation, and the poetry, in which "we are never in a consciously American world, but always within the purely magical universe of Whitman's 'self' and its strange visitations." [37]

Indeed, "the shift in focus and intention is clearly there," even if the conclusions Kinnaird draws from it about the Preface are difficult to accept. To use the terms of the present argument, the "democratic" or extroverted, "centrifugal" impulse is preponderant in the Preface, although it cannot, of course, efface its complementary opposite at any point. In the poetry that follows and especially in the first poem, the emphasis is shifted to the "unitary" or "centripetal" impulse of introversion. In this

74

change, as Kinnaird notes, "the duality of poetic motive" and through it "the dialectic of Whitman's career" are revealed.

However, to call the dialectical element represented by the Preface "the public phase of [Whitman's] new identity" seems imprecise and misleading. The contrast between the "centrifugal" Preface and the "centripetal" first poem at any rate should not obscure the fact that each of its constituting halves is made up, in turn, of the tension between the same centrifugal and centripetal forces. The "democratic" impulse is in no sense "public," just as the "unitary" impulse is in no sense "private." The function of each is essential and cannot be divorced from that of its counterpart. The world of the Preface is neither more nor less one of "nationalism and ideology" than that of the poems which follow it, and to hear "the familiar prophetic utterance" of the "would-be national bard" in it is almost like reading *Walden* as a "nature-book" or a blueprint for frugal living.[38]

In themselves, several of the essay's ideas can be understood as political or ideological, and many of these, of course, were later incorporated by Whitman into poems like "By Blue Ontario's Shore." But the fact that Whitman never showed the slightest intention to make these poems do for the later volumes what the Preface did for the first is in itself an eloquent indication that the ideological portions are not what is essential in the essay. Whitman himself had, apparently, some qualms that the Preface might be mistaken for a predominantly political statement. His own paperbound copy of the first edition contains only one marginal notation, and it is the single word "out?" pencilled in Whitman's hand on page viii and indicating with a vertical line running the length of the page the whole paragraph on political liberty.[39] Whitman rejected, of course, the whole Preface from the second (1856) edition because the strategy it had been a part of no longer seemed to fit his design. Thus, the notation on the margin must have been made very shortly after the publication of the first edition, when Whitman's plans for the next one aimed still only at an enlargement of the first volume without giving up its fundamental scheme. The political emphasis in the passage on liberty may well have seemed excessive for the purposes of that scheme.

The "democratic" tonality of the Preface serves, then, as a kind of counterpoint to the self-celebrating music of the poems and as such assures the unity of the whole volume through "fused though antagonistic" elements, that is, through the pattern by which alone could Whitman conceive of integral experience. To achieve this effect, the poet had to give some prominence to the "democratic" theme without upsetting the fundamental balance of the essay itself. It is for this reason that he begins his discourse with a movement on "America." And since the Preface was written after the celebrated first poem,[40] the "democratic" character of the opening personification effectively contrasts the "unitary" image with which the poem begins. "America" and "the great poet," as explained earlier, are complementary ways of speaking of the same concept. The substitution of the one for the other would not have affected the logic of the statement, although it would have radically altered the whole essay's drift. The "I" with which the first poem begins means, in effect, "the great poet" of the essay; consequently, it follows from the argument of this chapter that the essay had to begin with "America."

Thus, the language of Whitman's gestures of anxiety and nervous excitement reinforces and completes the statement that the often ineffectual rhetoric of his words all but failed to make. The essay's thematic structure, outlined in terms of the triplicate process, is based on a natural, spontaneous rhythm of association. This connection supports the assertion made earlier that the Preface achieves significance through elaborating its two main themes, although it is not primarily an elucidation of them: to communicate the mentality that reveals itself in the unfolding of this drama of meaning was Whitman's principal intention with his essay. In that mentality the reader encounters the poet's person, that is, the person capable of both conceiving and fulfilling the ambition of becoming "the poet."

Chapter Four

CONCLUDING REMARKS ON THE PREFACE

I

In the course of making his essay accomplish its central task, Whitman also got a number of other things done, which may not have been quite as essential in themselves but were nevertheless important enough. No discussion of the Preface could be complete without a reasonable account of them.

First of all, Whitman has taught his audience the logical idiom of the triplicate process, and he has introduced the dominant metaphoric scheme of the "merge." These two "lessons" are second in importance only to what has been identified as the central function of the essay. He has also created, "conjured up," an audience for himself by the same deceptively simple strategy as in his later devices of introduction. After ranging far and wide in an apparent search for direction, his address has inevitably found "you," the one person whom the speaker pretends to want to reach and whom he makes each member of even the largest audience feel himself to be.

Since syntactically most of the essay is rigorously impersonal, the exceptions are conspicuously effective. The first grammatical acknowledgment that the speaker is not alone—except for the common-sense assumption that he could not be talking to himself—is in the exclamation, "Now he has passed that way see after him!" (v); then, somewhat later, the sanctimonious words of good counsel are cast in the form of a direct address: "This is what you shall do" (v–vi). The context offers no clues so far whether the pronoun is in the singular or the plural, but the next instances are more explicit: "the greatest poet brings the spirit of any and all events and passions and scenes and persons [. . .] to bear on your individual character as you hear or read" (vi) and "If you have looked on him who has achieved [the flawless triumph of art] you have looked on one of the masters of the artists of all nations and times" (vii). "You" is obviously "generalized" here as part of an informal impersonal construction; thus, it is also in the singular. The "greatest poet's" command is heard a few lines further on: "You shall stand by my side and look in the mirror with me" (vii), and the listener is finally "singled" out. A number of casual remarks confirm this peremptory "definition" of an audience: "When I and you walk abroad [. . .]" (viii), for example, and "[all] that is henceforth to be well thought or done by you whoever you are, or by any one—" (x), or, "did you guess any of them lived only its moment?" (x–xi). The rather excessive use of the impersonal construction becomes thus a conspicuously personal form of address and establishes an audience for Whitman with a degree of precision he apparently finds sufficient for his purposes.

In the concluding movement, the speaker retreats somewhat from this delicately built involvement with an audience, confident perhaps that it is at any rate no longer dissoluble, and offers instead an objective account of the relationship the present one is designed to lead to:

> The touch of [the greatest poet] tells in action. Whom he takes he takes with firm sure grasp into live regions previously unattained . . . . thenceforward is no rest . . . . they see the space and ineffable sheen that turn the old spots and lights into dead vacuums. The companion of him beholds the birth and progress of stars and learns one of the meanings. Now there shall be a man cohered out

of tumult and chaos . . . , the elder encourages the younger and shows him how . . . they two shall launch off fearlessly together till the new world fits an orbit for itself. (xi)

The singular "companion" verifies the conclusion that "you" projects a single interlocutor, and the transition from the one man "cohered out of tumult and chaos" to the "two together" is perhaps the best demonstration of the nature of Whitman's audience and of the way he creates it. It is also characteristic of this dual relationship that it consists of an elder and a younger man. Schyberg saw a "Socratic theme" in this arrangement, but Allen and Matthiessen seem to be historically more precise in calling it an influence of Frances Wright's version of Epicureanism.[1] One could also add that, whoever the dialogue's participants may be, they bring to mind a characteristically romantic variant of the rhetorical device of the direct address. Baudelaire's famous "Hypocrite lecteur" would be the commonplace example, but closer both to home and to the "indirection" of Whitman's method is Ishmael's subtle use of "you," through which, as Berthoff noted, he transforms his chance listener into an accomplice and an active sharer of his experience.[2]

Whitman handles the first person singular in an equally purposeful manner. Of course, the "great poet's" qualities are practically identical with the ones Whitman liked to believe that he himself possessed. There is, however, more than just a simpleminded coyness in his insistence not to reveal in his essay his name or the person Emerson could write a letter to. The "I" steals into the discourse, if anything, even more surreptitiously than the "you." Only once, in the carelessly dropped phrase "when I and you walk abroad" (viii), does the speaker directly refer to himself. On all other occasions, he assigns statements made in the first person singular to carefully identified other voices: "the great poet" (e.g., vii), of course, or a "live interrogation in every freeman's and freewoman's heart" (xii), or simply "folks" (e.g., ix). The reason for this "stratagem" is in his own concept of poetry. He cannot base his outline of "the great poet" on Walter Whitman as long as the principle of equality, of the "innumerable supremes" has not been established. Indeed, while his personal preoccupations may occur earlier, none of "Walter's" personal qualities is explicitly attributed to the "great poet" before his concept of what Myers called "spiritual democracy" [3] is introduced.

II

Another important achievement of the Preface is that it prepares the ears of its audience to receive the language of the poetry that follows. It has been often claimed that Whitman rarely writes with any formal competence, and when he does, he does so in spite of himself. One must remember, however, his earlier writing: in his journalistic work or in *Franklin Evans* his syntactic, grammatical, or lexical competence is beyond serious reproach, even if it is only the dreary, uninspired competence of the hack. Thus, if the manner of the Preface is different, it is intentionally such. Of course, the difference has not been ignored.

For example, commenting on the essay, Alain Bosquet draws attention to "the poor style, the inappropriate terminology, yet at the same time, the deliberate mystification that, one feels, Whitman would like not to give away cheaply." Later, Bosquet adds the warning that in the essay's successes "one must not see the calm calculations of a man who knows where he is going." [4] Although Matthiessen's comment that "Whitman reveals the peculiarly American combination of a childish freshness with a mechanical and desiccated repetition of book terms" [5] refers to Whitman's speech, it would also apply to the Preface, since the essay is, obviously, meant to be heard rather than read.

This last assumption is, of course, the view of those who, like Schyberg, speak of the Preface as not yet poetry but no longer prose. Although it should not seem quite as terrible as all that, this "in-between" position has nevertheless served as grounds for so many all-too-easy condemnations of the writing in the essay that one can perhaps simply acknowledge their general validity. This move should clear the way to the alternative line of reasoning and a more charitable view.

Indeed, the essay fits neither category, but this deficiency is, in a very important sense, one of its chief virtues. It may yet fit into a third category, one proposed by Northrop Frye. "There are," he writes,

> three primary rhythms of verbal expression. First, there is the rhythm of prose, of which the unit is the sentence. Second, there is an associative rhythm, found in ordinary speech and phrase of irregular length and primitive syntax. Third, there is the rhythm of [verse,] a regularly repeated pattern of accent or meter, often accompanied by other recurring features, like rhyme or alliteration.[6]

Prose and poetry, runs Frye's argument, are the two ways in which ordinary speech may be "conventionalized." Ordinary speech itself "is concerned mainly with self-expression," and Frye's description of it may produce a mild shock of recognition in readers-listeners of the Preface:

> One can see in ordinary speech . . . a unit of rhythm peculiar to it, a short phrase that contains the central word or idea aimed at, but is largely innocent of syntax. It is much more repetitive than prose, as it is in the process of working out an idea, and the repetitions are largely rhythmic filler, like nonsense words of popular poetry, which derive from them. In pursuit of its main theme it follows the paths of private association, which gives it a somewhat meandering course.[7]

One of Frye's claims does not seem to apply to Whitman's essay: "Whether from immaturity, preoccupation, or the absence of a hearer, [ordinary speech] is imperfectly aware of an audience." One might, however, indulge in some hair-splitting and question whether the absence of a hearer amounts to the same thing as the absence of an audience. While an audience does, indeed, make speech rhetorical, as Frye claims, the absence of a hearer usually makes speech unnecessary, even in the sense of "putting into words what is loosely called the stream of consciousness." [8] Whitman had neither audience nor hearer, but while he did not care to have a formal audience he definitely wanted a hearer. His audience-making strategies support, as a matter of fact, the observations the critic could make about the "rhythm of verbal expression" he chose as best suited to his intentions. When he imagined, as he had to, an audience for himself, he preferred to conjure up a single hearer rather than a crowd and addressed even his imaginary crowds as if they had been made up of "men and women" listening, each of them, individually, unaware of the rest. He deliberately avoided the burden of being aware of an audience because if his speech had become rhetorical, if it had become "prose," it could not have fulfilled its essential function.

Frye's central claim about ordinary speech also explains Whitman's refusal to write "prose." Ordinary speech is the state of language *before* it becomes either poetry or prose. As Whitman might have put it, it is language with its "innocence and nakedness resumed" (vii). To make as well as to receive the new poetry, one had to start from scratch, and Whitman's bold ways with language in the Preface not only make his poetry plausible but also force his listener back to "the origin of all poems" (25).

Did Whitman know that he was doing all this? Bosquet, evidently, did not think so. Critics of the various manners of imprecision in Whitman's work sometimes imply that a man capable of such errors had to be incapable of sustained thought, calculated effect, and the subtlety by which art conceals its artfulness. In a sense, the answer to the question should be implicit in all the foregoing arguments, but Whitman's practice itself provides several instances of deliberate artfulness that should set such doubts to rest. One example should suffice here.

Throughout the essay Whitman freely appeals to his listener's religious and biblical associations. The phrases that are at all "artful" in his "ordinary speech" are evidently indebted to the King James Version and to the conventions of the pulpit oratory of his day. He speaks of God, faith, soul, "heaven or the highest" (vi) with uninhibited and careless ease. As it turns out, he is well aware of the significance of the frame of reference he is thus erecting, for he exploits it as a foil against which he can play off some of his most important and most intensely felt convictions. Without the biblical intonation in such phrases as, for example, "men and women and the earth and all upon it" (viii) or "his thoughts are the hymns of the praise of things" (v), the speaker's words would not sound half as daring or pointedly blasphemous as they do now when he announces that "in the talk on the soul and eternity and God off of his equal plane [the great poet] is silent" (v) or that "whatever would put God in a poem or system of philosophy as contending against some being or influence is [. . .] of no account" (viii).

This tone provides with special power the remarkable passage which is introduced by a paragraph on science and begins with a paradoxical alignment of faith and knowledge:

> Great is the faith of the flush of knowledge and of the investigation of the depths of qualities and things. Cleaving and circling here swells the soul of the poet yet it* president of itself always. The depths are fathomless and therefore calm. The innocence and nakedness are resumed . . . they are neither modest nor immodest. The whole theory of the special and supernatural and all that was twined with it or educed out of it departs as a dream. (vii)

The biblical echoes with which the diction of the essay has been resounding from the first prove crucially important here, for they practically force the listener to recognize in these lines a bold allusion that might easily have eluded him otherwise. Now it is evident that the passage parallels the first verses of Genesis: the speaker proclaims the "greatest poet's" absolute creative autonomy by likening him to the biblical Creator. As "darkness was upon the face of the deep," so are "the depths and qualities and things" unknown and to be "investigated"; as "the Spirit of God moved upon the face of the waters," so "swells the soul of

* An obvious misprint for "is" in the first edition.

the poet" over these "depths" which are, like water, "fathomless and therefore calm"; as God "divided the light from darkness" and "divided the waters" and "made the firmament," so does the poet create by "cleaving and circling." In the Eden of his new creation "the innocence and nakedness are resumed." Of course, in the light of this self-sufficient new day, "the whole theory of the special and supernatural [. . .] departs as a dream." [9]

In his admirable discussion of "the chanter of Adamic songs" R. W. B. Lewis has also spoken of the poet's efforts of "lowering and secularizing the familiar spiritual phrases . . . with the . . . intention of salvaging the human from the religious vocabulary." [10] Although Lewis does not refer to the Preface specificially, the passage just discussed is the first major example of these efforts. It also illustrates Whitman's most self-confident understanding of what he was doing. Through the speaker's words he is not merely the new Adam, he is also his maker, the creator of his own poet-self. The world of that new—or renewed—consciousness which he projects through the twin figures of "America" and "the poet" is a "salvation" each must attain on his own: "there will soon be no more priests," for "every man shall be his own priest." (xi) [11]

Announcing this "divinity" of himself, Whitman gives proof that not only does he know where he is going, he also knows how to arrive there. The diction of the passage is especially effective. The "flush" of knowledge means, of course, its fullness, its "satisfaction," but the physiological connotations of excitement in "flush" also reinforce the suggestiveness of "cleave." As the biblical parallel indicates, the latter's primary significance is that of halving, dividing, splitting in two; however, the same biblical context suggests that it can also mean knowing in the flesh, making love—this is the sense of the word in Genesis in the verse just preceding the one in which Adam and Eve assume their innocence and nakedness.[12] Whitman thus finds a way of keeping his phrasing consistent both with the biblical model and with the metaphor which is his imagination's central instrument.

Through this connection, he will be able to express the same idea later by the image of "putting [himself] here and now to the ambushed womb of the shadows" (1049). A simpler but equally effective word-choice is "swelling," which can be construed both transitively and intransitively, and which can thus mean both "dilating" and "being dilated": the relevance is obvious.

III

Whitman, then, not only thinks that what he does is entirely new and unique but often proves it by the sovereign skill of his performance. One important implication of this fact concerns the fairly popular topic of the various influences on his work. As it is well known, these range from Epictetus to Shelley, from Plato to Herder, from Egyptology to Italian opera, from Lucretius to the Count Volney, and so forth.[13] It would not take very long to show that, in one sense or another, the Preface bears the marks of all these influences. Then there is Emerson. A not very careful count would turn up some twenty-odd rather close verbal parallels between the Preface and Emerson's "The Poet" alone, and the number would be probably just as high in a comparison with some other essays, like "Plato" or "Prudence."

On the other hand, it is also well known that these ideas, insofar as they are borrowed, "are those of a working journalist, no more," as Seymour Betsky observed.[14] Therein lies, it seems, the explanation of their remarkably wide range as well as of their often remarkable lack of depth. Whitman turns to an unusually large number of alien sources, but the material he borrows becomes transformed in his hands as, for example, the biblical verses did on which the lines just discussed were based. Set against what is original in his achievement, even Whitman's debt to Emerson is rather insignificant. Of course, his indebtedness to Transcendentalism, as shown earlier, is considerably more extensive and more complex, and he may have incurred it through Emerson. But what makes, for example, the Preface live is precisely that aspect of it which separates it from, say, "The Poet."

If Whitman's essay were the exposition of poetic theory for which it has often been mistaken, it would be a rather feeble imitation of Emerson. But, of course, it is not the exposition of a poetic theory, and what its success owes directly to Emerson is, in fact, incidental.

IV

As the speaker approaches the conclusion of his discourse, he becomes noticeably more objective than in the first four movements. He presents the two dominant themes from an equal distance, as it were. His peroration is not so much a summary of previous arguments as the articulation of a position reached by "America" and "the poet" in their mutually illuminating interaction. The proceedings take on a quasi-dramatic aspect as the speaker brings to a head his insistence on the present tense by announcing that "the direct trial of him who would be the greatest poet is today" (xi). This phrase alone should suggest that the Preface is not really a preface at all in the conventional sense of the word but rather a prologue: the poetry "has not happened yet." A kind of drama is thus announced, and the essay, in effect, concludes by calling for the action to begin.

The naive aside on the English language, that it is "brawny enough and limber and full enough" (xi), is entirely unimportant and entirely moving at the same time. Whitman, of course, knew no other tongue, so that as a value judgment his words cannot be taken seriously, but what he has accomplished through the language in the Preface alone gives substance to his claim that English "is the medium that shall well nigh express the inexpressible" (xii).

The burden, however, of the speaker's concluding words is that "today" both "America" and "the poet" will be tried. In his later recension of the essay, Whitman—by that time eager to be "the bard of these States" and the "good gray poet"—wound up with the resounding declaration that "an individual is as superb as a nation when he has the qualities which make a great nation" (xii).[15] In the first edition, however, the apparently overbearing sense of "national" virtues is restrained by the comment that restores the balance between what is "democratic" and what is "unitary": "If the one is true the other is true" (xii). And in the last sentence, "poet" and "country" are still in balance, not in contention but in mutual dependence, in a final, dramatically poised expression of the awareness which is thus still an aspiration and which through "the trial of the poet" may realize itself. That drama of self-realization is the first poem in *Leaves of Grass*.

Part Two

THE FIRST POEM

Chapter Five

WHITMAN'S LANGUAGE–LESSON AND ITS LIMITATIONS

I

The poet of *Leaves of Grass* is born in the lyrical, improvised meditations that make up the first, long poem in the volume. "What I assume you shall assume": one of these categorically imposed assumptions is implied by the conclusion of the Preface that "he who would be the greatest poet" is yet to be tried, that he is not yet a poet. When the poem opens, the speaker of the Preface has found himself in Walter Whitman, but he has yet to find the "great poet" in himself. By the time the second poem is begun, the special awareness that the Preface had merely projected as possible has been realized, it has acquired a personal identity.

In the apparently shapeless flow of words that spreads out over the first threescore pages of the book, much may elude the reader, but the presence he encounters in them is irresistible. He may not always know what the poet is saying, but he knows who the poet is: in the first poem he has met him. That the poet's name did not appear on the title page was interesting; now, when it is revealed, almost in passing, it is little more than incidental information. By that time, much more is known about him, he *is* much more, than just a name. In the rest of the first edition and, in fact, throughout Whitman's whole career, achievement is measured against the poet realized in these first lines. The first poem plays the same role in the world created by Whitman's imagination as the "great poet" does, according to the Preface, in the given world: it is its "equable man," and "not in [it] but off from [it] things are grotesque or eccentric or fail of their sanity" (iv).

In none of the subsequent editions is this poem so obviously dependent on the larger statement to which it furnishes a part as in the first *Leaves*. "I celebrate myself" is no more the first line of *Leaves of Grass* than "Call me Ishmael" is the first line of *Moby Dick*.[1] The first indications of this unity are visual. Just as Melville's phrase gathers much of its force through the curious compendium of preliminaries that precedes it, the impact of Whitman's words is significantly determined by when and in what shape they appear in the volume. Read within the volume as a whole, the poem itself is given its first momentum by the pause sensible to ear and eye alike that separates it from the Preface. Complete enough to mark off from each other the two kinds of statement, this pause is at the same time short enough to preserve a degree of continuity between them. It makes the words which follow sound different and new while it assures that the voice which utters them will remain familiar though changed.

The quaint title is repeated next, connecting speech with poem and linking both to the taunting, irreverently "undisguised and naked" portrait which faces the title-page. Its five subsequent reappearances in the same thick, outsized typeface as at the beginning of the first poem become the stresses of a visual rhythm that paces the whole volume while isolating the major portions of its poetic statement. This rhythm is the first of the two distinct though clearly related visual patterns in which Whitman employs the title. The other one is furnished by the subtly unusual headlining. The words "Leaves of Grass" head every page of poetry (but not those of the Preface), and both spacing and type make them more emphatic than customary headlines would be: "sprouting alike" as a "uniform hieroglyphic," they create a kind of subliminally steadying and unifying effect, a drone bass to the variations on the rest of each page.

Such effects are doubtless intentional. The first edition was designed by Whitman; he even set the type for some of its pages.[2] Nor is the former editor's and printer's expert appreciation of the possibilities of lay-out particularly surprising. As Loren K. Davidson suggests, Whitman "perhaps even composed with an imaginary compositor's stick in his hand."[3] That he did so to a central, firmly conceived purpose, can perhaps best be seen in the typography of the lines. Apparently unrestricted by any formal convention and flaunting a deliberately naive gesture of defying—though not "repelling"—the "past," these must have been in 1855 the most startling visual feature of the volume. As they course across the pages in uneven numbers and at uneven lengths, without rhyme or apparent reason, they surely confused the contemporary reader, for they could not very well look like poetry to him, yet they did not look like the Preface either, which he could assume was prose.

The blatant eccentricity of writing—and then printing—such unordered lines of poetry may even have obscured the eccentricities in punctuating them. Yet Whitman's apparently harmless quirk of indicating apposition among words or phrases within a line by four dots (e.g.: "People I meet . . . . the effect upon me of my early life . . . . of the ward and city I live in . . . . of the nation," [59]) while reserving commas to mark series of progression—consequently they also appear at the end of almost every line—is the first clue that his verses' show of lawlessness has more to it than the idle intent of gratuitously shocking the reader.[4] This same sign (on occasion economically cut in half) already appeared in generous profusion and with more or less the same pedantic function on the pages of the Preface. When it turns up in the poetry, it becomes a visual link between the essay and the poem, a visible reminder that the differences between the two are signs not of disparity but of a fundamental unity. Essay and poem are each better defined by the other than by traditional categories: whether prose or poetry or neither or both, they complement each other (and the rest of the volume) as parts of a single statement.

Thus, the various elements in Whitman's design of the book's physical appearance are no mere decoration. They are part of the poet's main plan; they form what Harvey Gross calls a "visual prosody," a scheme that alerts the mind to the possibilities of poetic and verbal coherence in the work and that thus contributes to it. If the function of all prosody, as Gross says, is to show "human process as it moves in time," [5] it will show poetic process as well. In the first *Leaves of Grass,* the introductory essay, the first poem, and the rest of the poems are arranged visually, too, in a prosodic sequence which establishes each part as the indispensable condition for the parts that follow.

These claims are not meant to cast doubt on the autonomy of the individual pieces in the volume, that is, of poems which have earned attention and acclaim on their own, as "Song of Myself" or "The Sleepers." The very fact that they could command such lasting interest proves that they have power to spare, but some of this power is undeniably lost, along with a degree of sheer intelligibility, when they are removed from their original setting. In reading, for example, the famous first line, "I celebrate myself," directly after the Preface, one is likely to be struck first of all by the speaker's suddenly acquired calm authority and self-confidence. Yet this sudden, conspicuous shift in emphasis and tone is rarely if ever taken into account by the various commentaries, for they usually deal with the poem by itself. There is a great deal to be said, of course, about this line, since understanding it means understanding almost all that there is to the poem. But all further consideration of it is bound to be incomplete without this first reaction, so obviously contrived by the poet.

Whitman begins his poem with a passage that is, in the manner familiar from the Preface, also a lesson in idiom, a sort of survey of the ways and devices of meaning the poem employs.

Made up of the first seventy-odd lines, this passage traverses the whole affective range of the poet's imagination and at the same time introduces the metaphoric pattern and the modalities of discourse through which its forces will find their formal expression. The first line's unashamed self-assertion after the studied impersonality of the Preface activates this crucial function of the passage. The contrast startles the reader to its own possibility, indicating that the intensity of the speaker's awareness of distinctions between himself and the world around him may vary significantly. The special attention invited thus by this contrast to the rhetorical shifts in the direction of address makes one ask questions about the methods of meaning in the poem even before one could get around to inquiring about the substance of it. Accordingly, the effort to interpret the poem must begin with a description and analysis of the ways in which it says what it says. That done, one may go on to see by what principle these methods function, and only after this question has been dealt with can the final, most important one be asked with any reasonable hope of finding some answers: for what purpose is this complex apparatus put to work? what is the poem all about?

II

The speaker's voice is filled with quiet self-assurance as he abandons his apparent and at times annoying coyness maintained throughout the Preface and, announcing his intentions, announces himself in the very first line of the poem. The self-assurance does not leave him in the next two lines, when with the same matter-of-fact simplicity he points a finger at the reader:

> And what I assume you shall assume,
> For every atom belonging to me as good belongs to you.
> (2–3)

The address is direct, explicit, and precise. The "I" does not plead or allow, he commands and states; the reader feels spoken to.

WHITMAN'S LANGUAGE-LESSON

> This hour I tell things in confidence,
> I might not tell everybody but I will tell you . . . .
>
> (386–87)

This passage comes later, but the illusion of intimate, personal contact—held indispensable by Whitman for the realization of his poems—is already complete at the beginning, perhaps more complete than it will ever be further on. Just now, the illusion is so powerful that its effects linger on even after its sources have disappeared. The reader is all too prepared to hear the next lines as if they were addressed to him, although there is nothing in them that would warrant his doing so: [6]

> I loafe and invite my soul,
> I lean and loafe at my ease . . . . observing a spear
> of summer grass.
>
> (4–5)

These words are not necessarily directed at anybody. They sound as if the speaker's mind were beginning to wander away from his listener, who is allowed to stay around but might as well leave. The next group of lines confirms this impression, for in these the listener is no longer needed, and the poet appears to be talking only to himself:

> Houses and rooms are full of perfumes . . . . the
> shelves are crowded with perfumes,
> I breathe the fragrance myself, and know it and
> like it,
> The distillation would intoxicate me also, but I shall
> not let it.
>
> (6–8)

His self-absorption increases as, by now entirely oblivious to any presence other than his own, he articulates his urge to "go to the bank by the wood and become undisguised and naked" (11). Finally, in the next cluster (13–21), syntax itself disappears along with the last vestiges of dialogue or rhetorical intent, and speech

96

becomes merely the primitive, dimly conscious record of random sensations.

These splendid lines contain the turning point of a curve that the poet's perceptions and utterance describe. From the completely extroverted gesture of deliberate communication in "What I assume you shall assume" his concern has turned gradually inward within the self, until in this passage it reaches the point beyond which communication is not only unwilled but impossible. Imagination, which at the outset is the vehicle of both his perception and his will (the experience at "the bank by the wood" is, after all, imaginary or "imagination-induced") is superseded by sheer sensation. Sensations whose source is outside the self ("Echoes [. . .] buzzed whispers [. . .] The sniff of green leaves and dry leaves," etc.—14, 16) are intermingled—confused—with sensations originating within: "The smoke of my own breath" or "the beating of my heart" (13, 15), for example. And as it drowns out imagination and even consciousness itself, sensation also overwhelms the utterance. The lines become longer and more crowded, their rhythm more hurried. The passage is dominated by a triple beat, but from the relative calm of "The smoke of my own breath" and its reduplication in "Echoes, ripples and buzzed whispers . . . . loveroot, silkthread, crotch and vine" (14) it is broken down into the rushed, unruly notes of "The sniff of green leaves and dry leaves, and of the shore and dark-colored sea-rocks, and of hay in the barn" (16).[7] In the next line, the inward impulse attains its optimum:

> The sound of the belched words of my voice . . . .
> words loosed to the eddies of the wind,
>
> (17)

The three-beat pattern is abandoned altogether. Within the cluster, the rhythm of the line is totally irregular and thus reinforces what its sense contends: language has regressed to the point of sheer spontaneity. To paraphrase a remark by Santayana, it still

"constitutes an act, although it cannot yet 'register an observation.' " [8]

The movement inward is complete. The self asserted in the
yielding of reason to the jubilant, excited explosion of the
senses is an instinctive, independent, all but impenetrable world
unto itself. In this version, the self can talk only to itself. Thus, it
is the antithesis and complement of the version presented by
the first lines, in which the self could know itself only by knowing others, by talking to "you."

Once the discourse has thus moved from one extreme to
the other, from complete extroversion to complete introversion,
from the world outside the self to the core of the world within it,
the direction of both perceptual and rhetorical energy is reversed and becomes "centrifugal." The imagination gradually
regains control from the senses. After the interruption by the
emphatic, drawn out, divided stresses of the crucial line, the
triple beat is resumed now that the critical moment is past:

> A few light kisses . . . . a few embraces . . . . a
> reaching around of arms.
>
> (18)

The voice then is sufficiently becalmed and mindful of an audience to shape what after the disorder of the preceding lines
seems a remarkably controlled image:

> The play of shine and shade on the trees as the
> supple boughs wag,
>
> (19)

Sensations alone are no longer enough to make this observation; they must be composed, articulated.

Next, a conspicuously "imaginative" figure is introduced as
the discourse is led into "the rush of the streets" from the well
circumscribed, specific, single setting of "the bank by the wood"
where the earlier action occurred. This shift disrupts the unity of
place and thus effectively denies the factual authenticity of the

event while leaving its "reality" intact. The experience, the poet seems to say, is "real," although it never "really happened." Thus, his speech, which in conveying his involuntary grunts and moans attained for a moment the lowest common denominator (and most primitive "convention") of communication, now begins to take some account of the listener again; it becomes more "public" and also more artful. When he goes on to break the unity of time he does so with a couple of trite and self-conscious figures of speech: "the full-noon trill . . . . the song of me rising from bed and meeting the sun" (21). These phrases are as patently "literary" as "the smoke of my own breath" or "the passing of blood and air through my lungs" was clinical.

It just so happens that through what is at least a happy coincidence, if not the work of Whitman's "imaginary compositor's stick," the page must be turned at this point. The lines that follow resume the conversational, civil tone with which the poem began and find again their listener, too. He regains the poet's undivided attention in the form of some good-natured scorn, plenty of good advice, and a few peremptory commands:

> Have you practiced so long to read?
> Have you felt so proud to get at the meaning of poems?
>
> Stop this day and night with me and you shall possess
>   the origin of all poems, [. . .]
> You shall not look through my eyes either, nor take
>   things from me,
> You shall listen to all sides and filter them from
>   yourself.
>
> (23–25, 28–29)

For all their solicitude for their listener, these lines cannot quite conceal a Horatian gesture of banishing the uninitiated from earshot by making involvement with themselves seem entirely new and thus difficult and forbidding. But what poem does not, in the end, have to be "filtered from oneself?" [9] Besides, Whitman frustrates on the spot the well-intentioned effort not to "take things from him," for, as Waskow has remarked, "despite

99

his denial, [he] tries to make the reader look through his eyes." [10]

III

More important than this last injunction is the polarity which these first lines present. Their two versions of the self recall the distinction which emerged in the Preface between the "democratic" and the "unitary" aspects of the personality. The "I" begins "democratically," becomes "unitary" in the triumph of its senses, then recovers its "democratic" aspect. Observing more or less the same process in the passage, E. H. Miller has heard in the "unitary" voice of the "hard-breathing" lines the realization of an "orgiastic self" after it has been freed of "the closed order and artificialities represented by the man-made house and the synthetic 'perfumes.' " It is, however, less easy to agree with Miller when he goes on to describe this "closed order and artificialities" as "cultural and social repressions or the false self." [11] Granted that it is in firm control over its relations with the external world and that it employs conventions and, witness some of the metaphors, less than pleasing artifice, there is, nevertheless, nothing false about the self of the "democratic" lines. That it is not as attractive as the spontaneous, "unitary" "I" is undeniable, but it still remains a fact of the poem, a fact to be reckoned with, not dismissed.

A. L. Cooke's elucidation of the same passage is more cautious:

> The words "perfumes" and "fragrance" are to be interpreted . . . as symbols for the delightful and intoxicating knowledge emanating from books—knowledge crystallized by books into creeds or schools, in a word, *distilled* knowledge; and "the atmosphere" is to be interpreted as a symbol for Nature—the source of *undistilled* knowledge, first-hand knowledge, the primary source (or "origin") of all poems.[12]

Between the two ways of knowledge, the poet chooses that of the atmosphere—only for the time being, of course, since the two sustain each other after all. His poem itself reveals that he cannot keep away very long from "distilled knowledge." [13] And equally dependent on each other, at least in Whitman's work, are the two ways of speaking which, as Professor Cooke notes, are implied by and correspond to these two ways of knowing. She distinguishes between the "literal statement" in the lines directed to "you" and the "figurative statement" in the lines of the "unitary" voice.[14] The same distinction, variously made, has been a recurring item in discussions of Whitman's poetry from the first. As early as 1872 Swinburne remarked that in Whitman "there are two distinct men of most inharmonious kinds; a poet and a formalist," [15] and as recently as 1966 Howard Waskow, noting "two modes of talk" in the poem's first lines, found much the same thing as Swinburne: "imagism" and "didacticism," which he saw as "the two poles in Whitman's 'bipolar unity.' " [16] Obviously, didacticism here corresponds to the "democratic" voice, to Swinburne's "formalist" or Miller's "false self," who makes Cooke's "literal statement," and imagism corresponds to the "unitary" voice, the poet, the orgiastic self, who makes a figurative statement.

The sort of polarity that these first lines display pervades the whole poem and, indeed, Whitman's whole poetry. The passages Dana quotes in the very first review of *Leaves of Grass* already seem to have been selected in order to illustrate a contrast between two voices.[17]

One voice is heard in the familiar description of the aftermath of the "old-fashioned frigate-fight" ("Stretched and still lay the midnight," etc.—918–32). Although the context could not be more personal (he is recounting an imagined memory or, more accurately, a memory that his imagination has expropriated) [18] the poet merely describes what he sees and does not allow into the passage a single image or word that would reveal what he feels.[19] (Perhaps "impassive guns" [928] is an exception—but what an impassive exception it is!) He is implementing here his boast: "I take part. . . . I see and hear the whole" (856). The line echoes Emerson as "transparent eyeball": "I am nothing; I see all." [20] Indeed, having reached the high point in his narrative

("Toward twelve at night, there in the beams of the moon they surrender to us" [917]), the "I" is soon absorbed by his vision; he almost disappears in it. The texture of his vision, its intensity and precision, cannot, of course, be divorced from his personality, but its structure is independent of it. The individual self has become merely the means through which a world external to it is reflected.

After this strict self-restraint a contrary mode of expression dramatically reasserts itself as, in the cluster's last line, the speaker suddenly chokes up, overcome and at a loss for words, then finally finds the one that, elusive as it is, sums up masterfully a whole complex of emotions: "These so. . . . these irretrievable" (932). The vision, just now an objective, independent world, is reabsorbed into the life of the individual sensibility.

That life is the sole subject of the other voice, which Dana apparently heard in another vision of night, sea, and shore, in the poet's call "to the earth and sea half-held by night" (434–61). The major figures evoke in the poet the same imaginative associations as in the sea-battle. The "stretched and still midnight," the "darkness" that bore the "two great hulls motionless" on its "breast" is here, too, "nourishing," "still nodding," and "barebosomed"; the earth, whose "smells of sedgy grass and fields" were mingled to the "delicate sniffs of seabreeze" and the "strong scent" of the "litter of powder parcels" "in the beams of the moon" is here, too, "voluptuous coolbreathed" and "rich apple-blossomed" in "the vitreous pour of the full moon just tinged with blue"; and the victory was won upon the same "sea of the brine of life" which was for the "formless stacks of bodies and bodies by themselves" still a "sea of unshovelled and always-ready graves." Yet, in spite of the similarities, this passage is radically different from the frigate-fight episode. This time the lines are the poet's impassioned invocation to these primordial forces, not his detached description of them. This time, they are subservient to his imagination. They are the raw material out of which it can give communicable shape to his emotions, to his state of mind.

Although the passage has hardly any argument to speak of, its sense is plain. In a series of symbolic sexual encounters the poet exultantly rehearses his germinative insight that "a kelson of the creation is love," or, as the unwieldy paraphrase has it, "there is a dialectic interaction on the basis of love of all phenomena."[21] The world reflected by these feverish, exuberant lines is private; it exists only so far as it expresses the speaker's momentary sense of self. The "transparent eyeball" attitude is reversed; the poet is all; he sees nothing besides himself in everything he looks at.

Such familiar categories as didactic and imagistic or the simplistic subjective and objective (than which, says Ruskin, "no words can be more exquisitely, and in all points, useless")[22] are not suited to deal with this contrast of styles. Perhaps Schiller's celebrated distinction between "naive" and "sentimental" modes would be the least inadequate.[23] But the most pertinent terms have been furnished by Whitman himself. What Dana's passages have in common with the two voices in the opening lines is the tension between the poet's exclusive concern with himself, on the one hand, and with what is not himself, on the other—the same tension that sustained the dialectic of the argument of the Preface. The "bipolar unity" of "measureless pride" and "sympathy as measureless as pride" that arose from the essay's language of gestures emerges now from the poem's language of words, too. The "curious triplicate process" is a compositional as well as a conceptual device.

This process, as described in an earlier chapter, operates through the metaphor of "the merge," the preposterous and delightful conceit of all existence as "the universal love-making of opposites." Because it is "satisfaction" by a complementary opposite, the "fulfilled," "full-sized" existence through the merge is also the attainment of the rare and intermittent kind of knowledge that Coleridge described as "the coincidence of an object with a subject."[24] This idiosyncratic variant of the biblical "knowing in the flesh" is thus, to recall an earlier argument, the poet's means of self-realization. It is his key to "the path between reality and the soul," the experience in which appearances can fall away, and the soul (the "poetic quality" within the man) and reality (the "poetic quality" beyond the "shows" of his world) become free to illuminate each other. In the discovery of the relationship between the soul and reality resides beauty; its realization is life itself, the very being of "the great poet."

In the Preface the metaphor of the merge is introduced in a carefully indirect manner, through implication and allusion, although it is firmly established as the whole book's central device of meaning. The poem, however, soon elaborates it in erotic imagery of great power, delicacy, and wit. It is brought into the open without delay: the context of the first lines' movement from "sympathy" to "pride" and back again is an explicitly sexual event, a sequence of tumescence, orgasm, and detumescence, in which the speaker, "mad for [the atmosphere] to be in contact with [him]" consummates his "love." The paradox of "fused though antagonistic elements" is accomplished when the surging excitement of passionate self-seeking and self-assertion culminates in the self's becalmed submission to a smoothly expanding vision irradiated by the afterglow of the senses. The quietly jubilant, unassuming lines, in which the momentarily "self-blinded" "I" rediscovers his world, anticipate the mood of serene wisdom in the celebrated and analogous passage in which he evokes the memory of attaining "the peace and joy and knowledge that pass all the art and argument of the earth" (82).

In this state, to be and to know add up to the same thing, which is contained under both aspects in the metaphor. The "merge" is, above all, the process whereby, to use a familiar phrase, "the Actual and the Imaginary may meet"; [25] it produces the actual knowledge of an imaginary existence. Thus, the same logic that, by dint also of a long tradition, allows for sex as the metonymy of being begins also to make sense out of the protagonist's curious love affair with thin air, that is, of the autoerotic emphasis in the experience described by the poem's first lines.

This emphasis needs little further demonstration. Images of

isolation predominate in the passage. Hints at the presence of a sexual partner ("A few light kisses," "a reaching around of arms") are tentative, impersonal, and trite. By contrast, the male genitals are identified in a forceful and original flourish of metaphors in the midst of the non-figurative account of the confused excitement of the senses: "Loveroot, silkthread, crotch and vine" (14).[26] There is nobody present except the "I," and he neither talks nor listens to anybody or anything besides his throbbing blood and hurried breath. Thus, he is free to imagine that he has "merged" with the atmosphere, as in the factuality of coitus, of course, he could not be. The "merge" is achieved in the actual ecstasy of an imaginary embrace, necessarily; only in this manner are left uninhibited the energies of imagination which are essential if the "triplicate process" is to be satisfied.

The merge accomplished in this first episode is thus threefold. The poet's sexual climax is also the metaphor of his attainment of an ecstatic vision which fuses apparent discordances into universal harmony. In the language of the passage an extroverted, "centrifugal" impulse is reconciled by an opposing introverted, "centripetal" impulse into a bipolar unity of rhetoric. Finally, the poet's "belched words" burst from him like seed in his metaphorical sexual climax; they are "the stuff" Whitman is "jetting for far more arrogant republics" (1002), merging himself with all those who hear him into that "greatest poem" which is the United States of his vision. However construed, the merge culminates in "the sound of the belched words of [his] voice"; they are, in fact, the merge given form and made thereby perceptible. Through this formulation Whitman identifies at the outset the essential quality of his utterance, and he will reaffirm it just before the conclusion: "I sound my barbaric yawp over the roofs of the world" (1323). The actual words of the poem are—to borrow Whitman's own term from "Out of the Cradle Endlessly Rocking"—merely a "translation" of this "barbaric yawp," of these "words loosed to the eddies of the wind" in what is not so much an imaginary orgasm as an orgasm of the imagination.

The poem has thus begun with a working example of Whitman's idiom, logical as well as metaphorical, with an illustration of the "curious triplicate process" as expressed in the "merging" of "antagonistic" elements in a metaphoric sexual union. An important part of this "language-lesson" is the paradox that only when the poet forgets the presence of an audience can the reader begin to make sense out of what is being said. The imaginary episode "by the bank," recounted in complete indifference to the listener, is the first segment of the poem which is intelligible on its own terms. The "centrifugal" lines which surround it are, on the contrary, cryptical. The poet's "advice" about the "origin of all poems" is mystifying rather than helpful, and the first five lines, powerful as they are, seem intentionally enigmatic at this point. They function rather like an absorbing riddle, impossible both to fathom and to abandon. Although they are addressed directly to the reader, they tell him nothing; he cannot possibly know yet what is going on in them and, quite simply, what they mean. Indeed, his involvement with the poem, especially in an intellectual sense, can be described as an effort to understand these five lines by listening carefully to the rest, by hearing the poet out. When he turns spontaneously to the words aimed only indirectly at him, the reader accepts, as it were, the lesson the paradox teaches: the poet uses "indirection" not because of his whim but because "direction" simply will not work.

IV

Only now does Whitman announce as an axiom his fundamental insight about the "fused though antagonistic" two elements in "all things," after he has effectively evolved from it a logical and structural idiom in the Preface and a poetic idom in the idyll with the atmosphere. Here, too, the shifts in tone and in the direction of the address are worth noting. First the speaker must detach himself from his listener in two of those characteristic lines of transition in which what he hears himself saying seems to absorb him so completely that he loses all awareness of an audience:

> I have heard what the talkers were talking. . . . the
> talk of the beginning and the end,
> But I do not talk of the beginning or the end.
>
> (30–31)

Then the voice changes again, for it is addressed to no one, not even to the speaker himself. It becomes oracular as he declares the law of his vision first in dimensions of time and then of space:

> There was never any more inception than there is now,
> Nor any youth or age than there is now;
> And will never be any more perfection than there is now,
> Nor any more heaven or hell than there is now.
>
> Urge and urge and urge,
> Always the procreant urge of the world.
>
> Out of the dimness opposite equals advance. . . . Always
> substance and increase,
> Always a knit of identity. . . . always distinction
> . . . . always a breed of life.
>
> (32–39)

From the second (1856) edition onward these lines appear with "always sex" added after "always substance and increase." Although Whitman retained the emended line to the end, it seems to have lost as much in power as it has gained in explicitness. Beyond that, "to elaborate is no avail" at this point, whether or not "learned and unlearned" do indeed "feel that it is so," as Whitman claims (40). Both as a logical and as a metaphorical system, Whitman's "curious triplicate process" has already been quite elaborately analyzed in this study; besides, whatever its intrinsic validity, the system is indeed the perceptual, structural, and metaphorical axiom of Whitman's poetry.

After the oracular declaration the poet recovers his "personal" voice and goes on not to elaborate on what he has said but to enlarge his account of what obsesses him, trying out one new way after another of phrasing the same thing and finding each of them imperfect enough to impel him to another attempt. This voice can be properly called "prophetic," since it does struggle with a conviction so overwhelming that it amounts to a vision. It modulates from the public and instructive through the meditative, which does not exclude an audience nor does it require one any longer, to the private, in which the motions of the mind are articulated without any intent of communication.

To prophetic frustration the poet responds at last in a prophetic fashion, with a rhetorical question which projects a dramatic vision that is a symbol of his own:

> I am satisfied. . . . I see, dance, laugh, sing;
> As God comes a loving bedfellow and sleeps at my
>   side all night and close on the peep of the day,
> And leaves for me baskets covered with white towels
>   bulging the house with their plenty,
> Shall I postpone my acceptation and realization and
>   scream at my eyes,
> That they turn from gazing after and down the road,
> And forthwith cipher and show me to a cent,
> Exactly the contents of one, and exactly the contents
>   of two, and which is ahead?
>
>   (51–57)

With its sudden sensuous power after the groping abstractions before it, this passage is the center radiating vitality into the surrounding lines. What the poet is realizing here as perception he will try to articulate a few lines further on: the "trippers and askers"—the Preface calls them "the shows of the world"—"are not the Me myself" (58–65). Without the poetic success of this visionary scene, however, the direct argument which now follows it could only sound as hollow or obscure as the tentative, dimly perceived phrases which precede it.

The earlier lessons in idiom are beginning to pay off here. In

108

the *plein air* episode of the opening lines both the scene itself and the language which described it were close enough to common experience to allow their interpretation solely through an insistent enough analysis of the words in their conventional sense. In this passage, however, image and diction alike are highly idiosyncratic and, isolated from the rest of the volume, obscure and confusing. And still, one finds little in it that is not already familiar. The special sense in which Whitman uses "satisfied" has been well enough established in the Preface, and what he had to say about the imprudent kind of prudence gives his rhetorical question a particular ironic vehemence when it is asked in monetary and economic terms.[27] The proper context for interpreting the erotic setting has been amply prepared by the earlier passages using the sexual metaphor. As the speaker rephrases the abstraction as experience, the physical love of the poet and his loving bedfellow now both confirms the insight about the opposite equals and reestablishes what seems to be the proper relationship between the two orders of perception.

Some problems are left, however, still unresolved. "On the peep of the day" the loving bedfellow departs, and one could leave it at that if it were not for those baskets he has left behind. The touch of imprecision in "Exactly the contents of one, and exactly the contents of two" is not strong enough for a quibble with the assumption that there are two such baskets. Their "plenty" and the fact that they are covered with white towels have been read by some as an allusion to communion baskets and the whole passage as "a psychological sequel" to, and therefore a kind of preparation for, the mystical union of the soul with the body in the famous lines of Section 5 of the later revisions (73–89). The lovers, runs one elaboration of this view, are "personae" of Body and Soul, and the whole sequence is a statement of

> the theme of the mystic affection of soul for body, of soul for soul, as a value that can only be accepted and realized, not measured or defined. As a bountiful gift of special value it is symbolized by the white-toweled baskets.[28]

Not incompatible with this reading although assuredly different is E. H. Miller's view that the image of the "baskets covered with white towels bulging the house with their plenty" is clarified as a "genital association" in the description of the twenty-eight bathers by the twenty-ninth in one of the poem's best-known passages: "The young men float on their backs, their white bellies swell to the sun" (209). In these lines, writes Miller, "the 'I' projects his hungry amorous feelings upon the environment, the landscape, and even God Himself." He also notes that "since 'baskets . . . bulging' suggest impregnation, the image takes on a bisexual character not unusual in Whitman's writing, here specifically preparing for Section 5 [that is, for 73–89]." [29]

One problem, however, still remains: if the two baskets are indeed a plausible if somewhat bizarre metaphor for the lovers' exposed bodies, how can there be still two of them after the "loving bedfellow" has left at dawn? The question is not as pedantic as it sounds, for it leads to the integration of Miller's extremely illuminating suggestions into the interpretation of Whitman's total design. Neither is it impossible to answer once one assumes that the "loving bedfellow" was not a sexual partner as well. The figure then emerges as one of Whitman's characteristic triads, similar to the ones found in the Preface. The bedfellow is the "breed of life" that the lovers identified through the basket metaphor produce. He appears between them just as, in the important phrases in the Preface, the "greatest poet" lay "close betwixt" the soul's "sympathy" and "pride" (vi) or indicated "the path between reality and the soul" (v). He comes "as God": the speaker draws the God of the Scriptures onto his "great poet's" "equal plane," just as the Preface promised (v).

In "God the loving bedfellow" one can thus recognize the "great poet" as he has been projected by the Preface: the rare, intermittently attainable awareness in which the speaker's personality is fulfilled, "satisfied." The entire vision is the speaker's testimony to this potential in himself as well as his awestruck contemplation of it. "Gazing after and down the road," the immanent, untranscended, "un-satisfied" self contemplates its transcendental, "satisfied" version.

After it has been asserted in a symbolic vision, this curious, highly idiosyncratic sense of self is explained in a series of dramatic-ironic vignettes which illustrate some of the many possibilities of being that the "Me myself" is not. Once these "trippers and askers" are evaded,[30] the speaker concludes the first major portion of his poem with a description of "what I am" as a human figure. Standing "apart from the pulling and hauling," this figure is remarkably similar to the one seen in the memorable, open-collared, jaunty portrait of the frontispiece:

> Looks down, is erect, bends an arm on an impalpable
>   certain rest,
> Looks with its sidecurved head curious what will come
>   next.
>
> (68–69)

And the description is given in the third person, as yet another proof, if further proof was needed, that the "Me myself" is not to be confused with the speaker whose voice is heard in the Preface or in these lines.

Only at this point is, therefore, the theme which was first announced in the poem's first line fully stated. "Myself," which is "what I am," looks like the bearded figure gracing the frontispiece, and the voice of the speaker belongs to neither in any clear-cut fashion. To explore and clarify, in Whitman's own words, the "purport of all these apparitions of the real,"[31] to find the relationship between this voice and the elusive yet insistent presence which has haunted it from the book's first page is the poem's theme—and the reader's chief concern. For the latter, this means that the question with which he began—"Who is the man in the picture?"—has been narrowed down to "Who is the 'I,' the 'Me myself'?"

The answer, presumably, waits to be found in the rest of the poem. The exposition offers one more clue, the most important, for its discovery. It has given a rather extensive practical example of Whitman's characteristic techniques of meaning, along with "the procreant urge of the world" as their theoretical formula. The analysis of the peculiar contrast between this theory and practice will complete the description of the distinctive ways in which the poem says what it says and clear the way to our study's next major question, concerning the principles by which these methods of meaning function.

V

Despite the very reasonable suspicion that Whitman's dialectical formula in its mechanical, "pure" application could lead only to unrelieved dreariness and boredom, the possibility of using it as a key to the poem's structure can seem rather inviting. After all, the resonant announcement of it is still ringing in the listener's ear, and his mind is still wrestling with pointedly symmetrical elucidations:

> Lack one lacks both . . . . and the unseen is
> proved by the seen,
> Till that becomes unseen and receives proof in
> its turn.
>
> (45–46)

If he then expects a poetic structure analogous to a conception of the self as constituted by the dialectical interaction of what it is "within" and what it is "outside," he is not alone to blame. Indeed, he may get better results than one can hope for from triadic formulas and the like.

An example of such results is Richard Chase's inventive and by now familiar way of "feeling the shifting modes of sensibility in the poem" as a dramatic, more specifically comic, articulation of the "paradox of identity" at its center. This paradox—Whitman's "My myself" or perhaps "I and this mystery"—is based on the fact that "both politically and by nature man has 'identity,' in two senses of the word: on the one hand, he is integral in himself, unique, and separate; on the other hand, he is equal to, or even the same as, everyone else." The "comic drama of the self" unfolds through the self's "escaping a series of identities which threaten to destroy its lively and various spontaneity."

That the two aspects of the self are "dialectical opposites" is as clear to Whitman as it is to Chase—the poet would call them "opposite equals,"—and the scheme at least implied in Chase's view is not significantly different from Whitman's "triplicate" logic: "the 'self' who is the protagonist of Whitman's poem," Chase writes, "illustrates the fluid, unformed personality exulting alternately in its provisional attempts to define itself and in its sense that it has no definition." [32]

The remarkable image at the poem's beginning may be read, then, as a symbolic expression of the metaphor of this paradoxical self:

> I loafe and invite my soul,
> I lean and loafe at my ease . . . . observing a spear
> of summer grass.
>
> (4–5)

"Soul" would refer to the "unitary," "single, separate" self, and "grass" to its dialectical opposite, the "democratic" self. These "opposite equals" make up, "advancing," the "I," the "breed of life." One might assume then that the structure of the poem is founded on the alternation of passages dominated by one of these two major symbols.

Some such scheme would perhaps make a kind of sense, but of course it simply does not work; at least, it does not operate in this mechanically symmetrical fashion. If it did, the poem would degenerate, Chase justly observes, into "a universe that is both mechanical and vaguely abstract" and, consequently, quite dead.[33] The major symbols obviously do not conform to the mechanical pattern. The "grass" symbol, for one, actually disappears from sight through most of the poem.[34] Present only through implication, it cannot sustain the share of the structural burden that this less than imaginative, rigid pattern would assign to it.

This oversimplification of the structure, however, is challenged by the introductory lines even before the actual configuration of the symbols renders it spurious. Following the letter of Whitman's law of "triplicate" logic as categorically as he has announced it, one should expect "opposite equals" "advancing" in the poem's style as well as in its images and ideas. Rhetorical extremes, as seen earlier, do in fact establish a polarity which is also, in the broadest sense, structural; they do not, however, organize the poem. After the first, paradigmatic episode, the occasions of the poet's turning outward or "other"-ward, to "you," bear no symmetrical relationship to his turning inward or "self"-ward. These extremes, as a matter of fact, do not dominate even the exposition and are rarely attained in the poem. They function rather the way the "grass" symbol does, according to Matthiessen: they provide "a substantial background of reference" as dialectical poles, without serving as practical instruments of order.[35] Instead, the voice most steadily heard in the opening section is the curious, meditative one, in which the poet enumerates his trippers and askers or spells out the difference between the atmosphere and houses and rooms. As noted earlier, in these lines Whitman seems to be talking mostly to himself.

This meditative, ruminating, though not necessarily calm voice, which gradually asserts itself after the resonant merge of tonal contrasts in the opening lines, prevails through most of the poem. Of the 1,336 lines of the poem, only about a hundred represent what T. S. Eliot called the "second" voice of poetry, that is, "the voice of the poet addressing an audience, whether large or small." [36] Forceful words are addressed, conspicuously, to "you" at the beginning and the conclusion, but, for the rest, in fewer than threescore lines does the protagonist concern himself with his presumptive audience.

The implication of these numbers is confirmed by the poem's substance: it is almost exclusively self-centered, and the vast bulk of it is an often elliptic "interior monologue" by a man profoundly alone. It is, in fact, a meditation induced by what may be called an inner landscape and thus akin to the secular "meditation on the creatures" that M. H. Abrams has identified as the distinctive feature of the "descriptive-meditative poem" or "greater Romantic lyric." [37]

This meditation is conducted in three major attitudes. The predominant attitude or stance is controlled, almost detached, bemusement. The poet observes from it rather than lives the experiences of his consciousness and displays its powers by describing them, as if he were giving an outsider's account of not himself but his self. This "contemplative" angle of vision seems to put into rhetorical practice one of Whitman's most cherished insights: "I cannot understand the mystery, but I am always conscious of myself as two—as my soul and I: and I reckon it is the same with all men and women." [38] When, for instance, the poet articulates his sense of the elusive, he does so by describing it from the "outside" although to no audience besides himself:

> I dote on myself . . . . there is that lot of me, and
>   all so luscious,
> Each moment and whatever happens thrills me with joy.
>
> I cannot tell how my ankles bend . . . . nor whence the
>   cause of my faintest wish,
> Nor the cause of the friendship I emit . . . . nor the
>   cause of the friendship I take again.
>
> To walk up my stoop is unaccountable . . . . I pause to
>   consider if it really be,
> That I eat and drink is spectacle enough for the great
>   authors and schools,
> A morning-glory at my window satisfies me more than the
>   metaphysics of books.
>
>   (545–51)

These words not only describe their subject but obviously explain it, too: the "contemplative" attitude frequently veers into this curious kind of didacticism—curious because Whitman is preoccupied only with making things clear to himself—or into that equally curious, heightened intensity of vision which defines the "prophetic" manner noted earlier in the lines about the "loving bedfellow" and the bulging baskets. Although these didactic-prophetic overtones draw the statement toward a "dialogue" with "you," they cannot drown out its essentially reflective, "meditative" tone and character. In such lines the speaker seems to feel the need for a listener but does not remember that he has one.

The third attitude of meditation is in those passages in which the poet interrupts his train of thought, usually to address its object—the "sparkles of day and dusk," for instance, his "eleves," "priests," whom he does not "despise," "scientists," "sullen mopers," the "Listener up there," his soul, death, the "despairer," or, in all simplicity, "mankind" (1294; 964; 1092; 490–492; 1115; 1311; 1007; 1271; *passim*)—and on occasion to be addressed by it, as in his exchange with speech, "the twin of [his] vision":

> It provokes me forever,
> It says sarcastically, Walt, you understand enough. . . .
>   why don't you let it out then?
>
> Come now I will not be tantalized. . . . you conceive
>   too much of articulation. [. . .]
>
> My final merit I refuse you. . . . . I refuse putting from
>   me the best I am.
>
> Encompass worlds but never try to encompass me,
> I crowd your noisiest talk by looking toward you.
>   (568–71; 578–80)

The familiar lyric pose of the apostrophe makes this "histrionic" attitude the most conventionally "poetic" of the three meditative stances and also the one in which the poet seems closest to being aware of an audience. Paradoxically, the opposite proves to be true. The "you" in these passages has little to do with the listener, who is, to all intents and purposes, ignored by the poet in all three attitudes; rather, the object of the "histrionic" apostrophe is drawn into the private world of the speaker's self and loses its "otherness" entirely. This is the most self-absorbed among the three attitudes of meditation in the poem.

Finally, the meditative accounts of the adventures of the protagonist's consciousness are often accompanied by what amount to asides which, escaping him, seem to express how he feels while whatever he is describing is happening to him. For example, immediately after the lines explaining his bewilderment and perplexity at apparent commonplaces of everyday existence, he exclaims in wonder: "To behold the daybreak!" (552), and, as he continues, the meditative calm and the didactic touches are gone, to be replaced by an agitated, spontaneous murmur discovering sensations instead of articulating thoughts, as in the first excitement of the opening lines:

> The little light fades the immense and diaphanous
>   shadows,
> The air tastes good to my palate.
>
> Hefts of the moving world at innocent gambols,
>   silently rising freshly exuding,
> Scooting obliquely high and low.
>
> Something I cannot see puts upward libidinous prongs,
> Seas of bright juice suffuse heaven.
>   (553–58)

These "spontaneous" outbursts are virtually anterior to thought, and any purpose to communicate is incidental to them. They represent a complete turning inward, beyond meditation, so to speak. The words uttered in these passages are the closest to being "belched," instinctively, from the very core of the "Me myself."

It seems obvious even without any clear-cut statistical demonstration that the bulk of the poem consists of modulations among the three "meditative" attitudes between the extremes of "dialogue" and "spontaneous" "belches" or "yawps." [39] This state of affairs, however, plainly contradicts the expectations that have been raised by the poet's pronouncements about the all-pervasive functions of the "triplicate process." Whitman, quite simply, claims to be doing one thing while, in fact, he is doing something else. What first could only be suspected from the surprising imbalance between passages of "unitary" and "democratic" concern in the opening lines is thoroughly confirmed by the rest of the poem: there is nothing very "triplicate" about its poetic structure. Whitman may have found the essentially simple if often just facile dialectic of "bipolar unities" both intellectually and—as the discussion of the Preface has shown—psychologically congenial; the plan of the first *Leaves* as a whole and the composition even of its Preface reflect this habit of mind. But in this, his greatest and most characteristic poem, the intricate variety of ways in which the various parts, in James's phrase, "group together" cannot be adequately accounted for by the simple law of opposite equals advancing out of the dimness.

Not that the fundamental polarity discerned earlier disappears: the tension between the "unitary" and "democratic," self-centered and self-shunning extremes is the primary fact of the poem. Its force is felt steadily throughout, even if it is never again rendered in quite as pure and simple a form as in the first episode, and its poles are rarely attained. But the poem receives its distinctive character from that other, rather more complex tension which exists between this theoretical model and the persistent divergences from it both in the successive parts individually and in the manner itself of their succession. The "procreant urge" provides, indeed, the formula of coherence in the world of the poet's vision and thus of the poem's scope, but the poem's structure depends on this second type of tension, which recognizes the nature and possibilities of actual as well as theoretical continuity among its various modes of awareness.

Therefore, to account for the poem's structure, one must seek out the principle by which the poet's "bipolar" ambition of celebrating the self in rigorous balance with, and thus through, its "opposite equal" is transformed into the various degrees and forms of self-absorption that prevail in the poem. In practical terms, this effort, which is the next major portion of this study, consists of an examination of the patterns of transition both among the three attitudes of meditation dominating the poem and between the meditative passages in general and the lines explicitly addressed to the listener.

This examination, however, must begin with a kind of detour. The first characteristic pattern of transition can be discerned in the lines that F. O. Matthiessen has called Whitman's "vision": [40] the protagonist's dramatic reminiscence of his love affair with the soul and the subsequent free-associating meditations on the grass (73–139). Because of the results of these meditations, which are as startling as they are far-reaching, the passage is crucial to the whole poem. The introduction's impact of novelty and suggestiveness can easily obscure from latter-day readers—"listeners"—the fact that until the end of this episode, which is possibly the best-known and most-discussed portion of the poem, the "I" does not (indeed, cannot) assume the pose of boisterous self-assurance by which he has become familiar, not to say notorious. With this pose, the "I" for the first time behaves like the "great poet," assigning to himself some of the invigorating qualities by which the speaker in the Preface has identified his paragon. Implicit in this pose is thus the identity which is Whitman's chief concern, and a key to it is in these lines, for they give a dramatic and convincing account of its origins. Without first hearing out this account in detail, one cannot hope to identify rhetorical transitions in it; the next chapter, therefore, begins with a close reading of this passage before turning again to the argument about patterns of transition.

For the moment, then, the line of investigation that began with questions about the shifts in rhetorical address is suspended, with the provisional conclusion that the poem appears to be a meditative interior monologue that wants to be a dialogue of a loosely Platonic sort and fitfully mistakes itself for one. The exploration of the sources of this failure of intentions promises to uncover also the secret of the poem's success.

Chapter Six

"THE VERY HEART-BEAT OF LIFE"

I

Once the poet has explained that "apart from the pulling and hauling stands what I am" and by his description has identified himself, "in and out of the game," with the engraved portrait on the frontispiece, he can afford to turn to other things. For the moment the subject of what he is not and what he will not do seems to be exhausted. He settles back to "witness and wait" (72), with only the slightest hint of contempt in his voice for the impatient curiosity of whoever might be listening.

A pause follows which somehow asks to be longer than the simply redoubled spacing would indicate; when the poet begins again, his voice is changed because the subject has changed, too. He is speaking the much celebrated, exceedingly lovely lines in which the "I," like an affectionately insistent lover, "invites" his soul to "loafe with [him] on the grass" and, as if to reinforce his plea, describes their earlier sexual union, only to become so overwhelmed by the memory of it that, as he relives his ecstasy, he forgets even the very presence of his "beloved":

> Swiftly arose and spread around me the peace and
> joy and knowledge that pass all the art and
> argument of the earth;

And I know that the hand of God is the elderhand of
> my own,
And I know that the spirit of God is the eldest brother
> of my own,
And that all the men ever born are also my brothers
> . . . . and the women my sisters and lovers,
And that a kelson of the creation is love;

> (82–86)

His eyes begin to wander about the field; instead of the soul, he notices his surroundings—first "leaves," then "brown ants," then, in a lazy line whispered in pure indolence and tender amazement, "mossy scabs of wormfence, and heaped stones, and elder and mullen and pokeweed" (89), which in the next line lead him, with utter simplicity and perfectly hidden art, to grass: "A child said, What is the grass? fetching it to me with full hands" (90). The passage, thus, is an elaboration of the scene upon which the poem opened, for the poet, having begun by "loafing at [his] ease" and "inviting [his] soul," has all but imperceptibly drifted into "observing a spear of summer grass."

The ecstatic calm to which the ardor of his pleading gave way now changes to placid good humor as he repeats in mock exasperation the question of the child and begins to speculate, idly, without any hope of success, about an answer. He is merely toying with a few commonplaces, around which he weaves some homely embellishments (92–100). Then what Allen has identified as a Homeric echo [1] arrests his imagination: "And now it seems to me the beautiful uncut hair of graves" (101). He dwells on this suggestion, and at once not only his phrasing but his images themselves become forceful and original:

> Tenderly will I use you curling grass,
> It may be you transpire from the breasts of young men,
> It may be if I had known them I would have loved them;
> It may be you are from old people and from women, and
> > from offspring taken soon out of their mothers'
> > laps,
> And here you are the mothers' laps.

121

"THE VERY HEART-BEAT OF LIFE"

This grass is very dark to be from the white heads of
    old mothers,
Darker than the colorless beards of old men,
Dark to come from under the faint red roofs of
    mouths.

O I perceive after all so many uttering tongues!
And I perceive they do not come from the roofs of
    mouths for nothing.

                                    (101–11)

The vision of the dead, then, turns him to the thought of death itself, and the tone suddenly changes. The excitement that stole into his voice when he noticed the graves erupts in a series of ringing declarations, all of which, in effect, keep repeating that,

All goes onward and outward . . . . and nothing collapses,
And to die is different from what any one supposed, and
    luckier.

                                    (120–21)

One might suppose that, overcome by a sudden wonderful illumination, he is shouting for joy in happy confusion, except that whoever has listened to him carefully from the first has learned to tell when the excitement in his voice is due to a genuinely happy mood and therefore knows that this time it is not. Happiness loosens this speaker's tongue and prompts him to spellbinding eloquence: it can be heard in the Preface, for example, when he speaks of the "poetic quality" or when he declares that "the greatest poet forms the consistence of what is to be from what has been and is"; it can be heard in this poem time and again, from the first, lovely scene in the open air to the splendid conclusion; and its best example is in the incomparable lines just preceding his announcements about death. Until he understands, in a flash of insight that makes him exclaim, that the grass is "so many uttering tongues" sprouting from "offspring taken out of their mother's laps," his voice, though full of urgency and power, is never raised to a shout, and his emotions

122

and thoughts move with effortless persuasiveness from perception to new perception, easily finding their form in precise and detailed images of strong, immediate sensory appeal.

Now, however, when, his argument reaching its high point, one might expect him to be at his most convincing, he begins to sound hollow. He keeps repeating himself, and with every repetition his one abstraction—"there is really no death"—becomes more nebulous, while a lapidary stridency replaces the early lines' smooth, easy breathing:

> There is really no death.
> And if ever there was it led forward life, and does
>   not wait at the end to arrest it,
> And ceased the moment life appeared. [. . .]
>
> I hasten to inform him or her it is just as
>   lucky to die, and I know it. [. . .]
>
> [I] peruse manifold objects, no two alike, and every
>   one good,
> The earth good, and the stars good, and their adjuncts
>   all good.[. . .]
>
> Every kind for itself and its own . . . . for me mine
>   male and female.
>   (117–19, 123, 125–26, 130)

After immediacy, abstractions; after inventiveness, repetitions; after clarity, incoherence. Who would not want to believe what this speaker is so loudly proclaiming? Yet, listening to him, who can?

Most likely, he does not believe it himself. For precedents of the excitement in his purported vision of immortality one must return to his nervous rant about prudence, to his tirade about the erosion of liberty, and to the other shrill passages of the Preface, in which the volume of the voice is trying to make up for the conviction which is not there. These passages have shown that when the speaker's voice rises to a stentorian pitch and he starts talking faster then he can breathe, he is protesting too much, and his words conceal rather than reveal.

Much the same holds true here. Meditating, in "Adonais," on a spectacle similar to the one Whitman has outlined, Shelley comes to a similar conclusion: "Nought we know, dies." But then he continues in grief, which lasts until the end, and even in his consolation he is "borne darkly, fearfully, afar." [2] If Whitman's protagonist acknowledges no such fear, excess of it, not the lack, is the likeliest reason. As Kenneth Burke has shown, at times "it is" may be a "stylistic rephrasing" of "would that it were." [3] These shouted pronouncements on immortality bespeak not the exultation of the man assured that he will never die, but the anxiety of the man terrified that he will. The faster his words pour out, the firmer the impression that his mind is in the grip of this one overpowering fear. Frightened alone, among all the dead, he rediscovers his listener with a question in which the taunt cannot quite mask the real terror, nor can the torrent of self-addressed reassurances afterwards drown it out entirely:

> What do you think has become of the young and old men?
> And what do you think has become of the women and
> children?
>
> (114–15)

As if he were trying to shout himself free of the spell of a sight he was as helpless to avoid as he was to seek, he reasserts his share in the world of the living in half-articulate, self-hypnotizing phrases, declaiming wildly: "Every kind for itself and its own. . . ." (130; also 131–35).

But then, all of a sudden, he offers his audience the help he obviously craves himself, and the passage concludes on a robustly self-confident note:

> Who need be afraid of the merge?
> Undrape . . . . you are not guilty to me, nor stale nor
> discarded,

"THE VERY HEART-BEAT OF LIFE"

I see through the broadcloth and gingham whether or no,
and am around, tenacious, acquisitive, tireless
. . . . and can never be shaken away.

(136–39)

The images of the "merge" and of "undraping" turn these lines into a version of the scene in which the soul "parted the shirt from [the poet's] bosom" and sexually "merged" with him, except that this time, instead of being subdued, the "I" moves to subdue. His self-vaunting reassurances, unexpected and apparently illogical as they are, round thus out and frame the sequence that began with his memory of his ecstatic union with the soul.

Jarrell is right: this speaker "has his nerve" indeed! [4] In hardly so much as the blink of an eye, he has transformed himself from a submissive victim of his fear into a self-assured tower of inner strength. This new, aggressive, fearless, and assertive "I" is just about everything that the old, fear-driven one of less than a moment ago could never be. Boastful, arrogant, yet attractive for all that, he acts, for the first time and for all the world to see, like "the greatest poet" of the Preface. He brushes away all resistance to his approach with the authority of one who is "no arguer" but "judgment," and what he proposes with disarming impudence is nothing less than the fulfillment of the claim of the Preface that "if [the greatest poet] breathes into any thing that was before thought small it dilates with the grandeur and life of the universe" (v).

This transformation is all the more extraordinary because it is sprung upon the listener as a complete, dramatic surprise, although the new voice is so forceful, the power-happy "I" is so solidly *there*, that one submits to his presence without quibble for quite some time before noting that it is actually rather illogical. After his frightened, scarcely coherent shouting, the unbidden offer of the "I" to dispel guilt, insecurity, and fear is not only unexpected but, once in focus, difficult to trust, and it is not made more believable by the palpable incongruity between

125

the generous intent of the gesture and its aggressive form: what is meant to be an offer to help actually sounds like a combination of a threat, a command, and a jibe. Yet, if there seems to be no obvious connection between this gesture and the passages before it, there nevertheless has to be one, for the crisis that a moment before was threatening the protagonist has clearly been mastered by it.

To find the connection between the rest of the passage and this impressive pose, which is the last of the three major attitudes comprising the sequence, one must first of all examine the relationship between the other two, the protagonist's remembered union with the soul and his subsequent powerful vision about death.

The first of these is a sexual experience, which transcending itself becomes an ecstasy of life and affirmation that focuses in a moment of unparalleled intensity and beauty all the energy of living that the "I" is capable of. He learns from it that love is illumination, for above all it makes him see. Its light reveals for him the fullness and perfect harmony of the whole through illuminating every individual thing in sharp, crystal-clear detail.

This ecstasy, the wonderstruck poet reminds his lover, the soul, was brought on when "you plunged your tongue to my barestript heart" (80). The tender yet violent image marks the critical point in the entire episode and thus identifies the tongue as the central instrument of their resplendent, fundamentally life-asserting act. It is most significant, therefore, that the speaker's panic terror of death is also triggered by the tongue. His quiet fascination with the "beautiful uncut hair of graves" lasts only until he "perceives" after all the "guesses" that the grass is "so many uttering tongues." Something in this perception disturbs him, for he cries out with an unmistakable note of alarm in his voice. In a few lines, this agitation becomes plain fear, which blinds him as thoroughly as his ecstasy cleared his vision. His shouts reverberate in a world enveloped in darkness. Their hopeful self-assurance is made poignant by the absence in them of any sensuous certainty, of any distinct images. Having learned that love is illumination, he must now learn that death is blindness: of late the seer of splendid visions, he now cannot see anything.

Direct opposites of each other in most respects, the two states of mind embodied by the two scenes are alike in their intensity and in the passivity of the protagonist. His ecstatic contentment floods him as abruptly and irresistibly as his terror of death. He seems to have no will of his own: both experiences are, apparently, more fundamental and pervasive than anything his conscious will can control. His ecstasy and his horror [5] emerge, thus, as "opposite equals," but they do not advance from the darkness: the tongue's curious function in both suggests that the horror is the direct consequence of the ecstasy.

The extraordinary intensity and irresistible force of the latter postulate a commensurate urge toward it: the protagonist must have sought the sexual experience because it gratifies the most powerful desire he knows and because, in fact, he cannot help seeking it. Moving, astonishingly frank lines describe this experience, yet, for all their frankness, they reflect a form of shame, too. The precise arrangement of the scene simply cannot be made out, and the task of illustrating it accurately would defy all attempts even if a personification of the soul can be taken for granted. It obviously describes some sexual activity—probably an autoerotic fantasy of submitting to homosexual [6] fellatio—but this is by no means entirely clear. Curious transformations and a hybrid metaphor make for an opaque, indistinct picture. At the same time that a dauntless impulse to tell all produces partial images of minute and precise detail an equally powerful impulse to conceal seems to deflect these fragments as fast as they well up and thus prevents them from cohering into a single, lucid image. The key image of the plunging tongue not only points through its metaphoric intensity beyond the event described but manages also to obscure if not to hide it.[7] The "I" sounds somehow reluctant to acknowledge fully the starkly sensual element in his experience, and this impression is only strengthened by the rapid shift from an orgiastic to a procreative emphasis in his sexual references once the climactic scene is past.

This reticence of the speaker is not very difficult to understand once his performance in the Preface is remembered: he is considerably more shy, more worried, and more repressed in sexual matters than he likes to pretend, for, much as he would wish to, he is simply unable to disregard the conventional sexual morality of his land and age, with all its fears, anxieties, and superstitions. These cultural inhibitions alone are strong enough to insure a disastrous aftermath to his ecstatic happiness: he can no more help feeling guilty for what he has done than he can help doing it. This sense of guilt is the curious force that reasserts itself throughout the apparently aimless, placid musings of the poet, making their drift from contentment into morbid crisis seem inevitable in retrospect.

The tongue's transformation from the instrument of the speaker's joyful enlightenment through love into the herald of his blinding fear of death dramatizes, then, a tragic clash between impulses and inhibitions. He cannot allay his fears without increasing them, and he cannot satisfy his longing without frustrating it. What he must contend with is the terrible knowledge that, to paraphrase Stephen A. Whicher, to live is to love and to love is to die.[8] Unless he can find a way in which he can master this conflict by at least accommodating if not resolving it, it threatens to destroy him. His situation is explained by Whicher's argument about Whitman's "preoccupation with death," which "is evidenced in the early Leaves . . . in the very frequency with which [the poet's] victory [over death] has to be reenacted. The thought of death was clearly the chief threat his vision had to overcome." Speaking of a "demonic" mode of vision, "a nightmare confirmation of dread," which "shows its teeth everywhere in 'Song of Myself,' something like one-fifteenth of the whole being of this character," Whicher states:

> This dark element in the poem is by no means incidental; it is the enemy the hero exists to fight . . . . [His] appearance of invincibility is the true illusion, not the threat to it.

It is against this threat that the protagonist's sudden, startling pose of aggressive self-confidence and strength, his "appearance of invincibility," is assumed, in an almost instinctive, improvised gesture of self-protection. Eventually, the new, radiantly energetic attitude will prove to be the basis of his triumph over death by enabling him to become, as Whicher puts it, "one with a life-force to which death simply [is] not"; [9] at the moment, however, it is but the mind's last, desperate stand against forces that threaten to destroy it.

The speaker's mystifying and illogical self-renewal at the conclusion of the passage is thus accounted for. Only one question remains: if he is so riddled by sexual inhibitions, why must he seek his profoundest gratification and self-fulfillment in sexuality? Or, to turn it around, why does he take a sexual, physical release for the manifestation of his soul, that is, of all that is not physical in him, all that is not his body? Gay Wilson Allen says that the answer may be safely left to the psychoanalysts, implying that it does not—*should* not—concern the critic.[10] The present interpretation does not, indeed, depend on anything except the text itself; however, a psychological examination of some of its key points can clarify and reinforce it and therefore ought to be considered. "The main ideal of criticism," writes Kenneth Burke, "is to use all that there is to use." [11]

The conclusions reached earlier about the way ecstasy changes into horror as the speaker contemplates the grass are supported and made clearer by E. H. Miller's Freudian reading of the scene of the protagonist's reminiscence and especially of its central incident. A predominance of oral and tactile images, which Kenneth Burke was probably the first to recognize,[12] has led Miller to see the passage as essentially regressive. It is, he declares, a "regressive journey to the depths of [the artist's] being," during which "the fearful body is eroticized by the soul . . . in [a] consummation of frankly inverted sexuality." Since this view clarifies also the "childlike confusion of bodily organs" in the scene, Miller can interpret the plunge of the tongue as the most conspicuously regressive image in the passage, and he comments on it as follows:

[It] evokes the child at the mother's breast, "heart" being associated with the phallus and the breast. In "going under" Whitman, unconsciously, approximates the child's phallic picture of the mother. The tongue is the means of the child's earliest contact with the world, his bridge, in a literal and figurative sense, to something outside himself as well as a source of physical comfort. At the same time, for we are in the world of a child's associative processes, the tongue like the breast is phallic in its fecundating powers.[13]

One can very well understand now the reasons for the protagonist's mounting agitation as he muses over the "beautiful uncut hair of graves." If the experience which yields him his ultimate gratification, "the peace and joy and knowledge that pass all the art and argument of the earth," is a symbolic memory of the infant's contentment at the mother's breast, then separation between mother and child must signify the greatest calamity to him. And that is precisely what the "uttering tongues" finally suggest. Their frustrating "hints" culminate in a repetition of one of his elegiac "guesses" about the "curling grass": "It may be you are [. . .] from offspring taken soon out of their mothers' laps" (105). One innocent "guess" among others, this image could lead to another, completely reassuring one: "And here you are the mothers' laps" (106). Now, eight lines later, because the "uttering tongues" have transformed "guesses" into "perception," the reassurance disappears. The image emerges, in ominous finality, as a complete reversal of the one Professor Miller has shown in the tongue's earlier climactic plunge: having evoked "the child at the mother's breast," the tongue now "hints" about "offspring taken soon out of [their mothers'] laps" (113). With this "perception," the "I," apparently, has seen enough. He no longer scans the "uttering tongues" for further "hints" but turns to his listener with a pair of rhetorical questions and without waiting for an answer launches into his desperately self-serving prophecies of immortality.

Whitman was to "awaken" to death and to "welcome" it a few years after the first edition, but there is nothing "delicious" or "delicate" about it in these breathless prophecies. The speaker is temporizing against it, pretending that death is really not death at all, the dead "are *alive* and well somewhere." Death, here, is neither the ultimate reconciliation nor the "tragic Reason" that it is variously claimed to have become in the poems of Whitman's "tragic phase"; it is the supreme threat.[14] And the "I" fears it not simply because it is annihilation, the end of life, but specifically because it is the opposite of the reunion of "offspring" with mother and therefore the frustration of his efforts to satisfy his profoundest yearning.[15]

If the terms of the protagonist's dilemma and, indeed, his sense of it are blunter and cruder than the ones through which Whitman's own subsequent "awakening to death" could be described, his pain is not the less excruciating and intense. Miller's observation has led to a finer and fuller sense of the dimensions of the predicament of the "I." Confronted by death, the "I" feels threatened to the very core of his being. He is caught in a vicious, intolerable dilemma. Whistling in the dark does not help. As he keeps repeating his reassurances, his nightmare closes in on him again: his vision is locked within sexual and familial relationships. The list of all those he claims for himself leads up, once again, to the image of both his redemption and undoing, "For me children and the begetters of children" (135), and the terrible cycle threatens to resume. Literally at his wits' end he then throws himself into the pose of his own complete opposite, in a frantic game of bluff that the unconscious is forced to play on the consciousness to protect it from disintegration.

Much as this rereading on the basis of a psychoanalytical observation may have clarified and strengthened one's understanding of the passage, the interpretation proposed earlier has been only corroborated by it, not substantiated. What matters is the protagonist's anguish and his way of coping with it. His anguish may take a psychologist to explain, but it takes only careful listening to recognize, and his response to his predicament, though variously labelled, has always been familiar. Poets, in any event, seem to have known it for a long time. Ascribing to his audience the ills that beset him, Whitman's protagonist resembles Falstaff denouncing Hal and his gang as cowards after they have given him a chase and a scare for a lark, or the Pardoner castigating the avarice of his gullible listeners. And proposing to cure these same ills, he is a physician in no need of a rebuke: he is intent only on healing himself. He says what he wants to hear, doing unto others as he desperately needs others to do unto him, like Lear, who by "pardon[ing] that man's life" [16] appeals for the mercy that alone could grant him peace.

In any event, the expedient works. The pose struck in desperation has enabled the speaker to master his terrors. So great was the danger that he cannot be blamed if the outcome has him a bit stunned and disbelieving. It is a little too good to be true; besides, will it last? He pauses to catch his breath, knowing that he has said quite a mouthful, and when he begins to speak again cautious diffidence tempers his elation and, as Waskow put it, "his interest in the things around him is not quite the wild dance of merger," [17] for he is testing his newly-found device of survival, and his sanity is at stake:

> The little one sleeps in its cradle,
> I lift the gauze and look a long time, and silently
> brush away flies with my hand.
>
> The youngster and the redfaced girl turn aside up the
> bushy hill,
> I peeringly view them from the top.
>
> The suicide sprawls on the bloody floor of the
> bedroom,
> It is so . . . . I witnessed the corpse . . . . there
> the pistol had fallen.
>
> (140–45)

Deceptively simple: birth, love, death—the cycle of life. At closer look, however, these are also the crucial images of his crisis. Now he faces them from his new pose, like someone who has just awoken from a nightmare and rehearses his dream only to convince himself that he is happily out of it. The speaker is, indeed, in full control. His transformation has brought with it also the reversal of the roles played by his old self. The new "I," having proposed the "merge" as aggressively as the soul had gratified the old, can now bend over the infant with the maternal gesture and affection the old "I" was yearning for. Viewing "from the top" the lovers rushing toward the "peace and joy and knowledge that pass all the art and argument of the earth," this time he is also above the guilt and inhibitions burning on the girl's cheeks. And in the suicide—hardly just a conventional representation of death in the life cycle—he finally confronts the culmination toward which his despair was driving him and which he scarcely managed to elude. There is the alternative to his imposture. The corpse, in a sense, is that of his old, untransformed self, and he can "witness" it and live! He must persuade himself that what he sees is true: "It is so. . . ."

That pistol makes one even wonder whether Whitman, who never read *Moby-Dick*, might not have at least seen the book and perhaps browsed in it, glancing at the first few pages at least or just the first page of the first chapter. Probably not. Meanwhile, the only surviving manuscript fragment of trial lines for this passage indicates that this suicide had hanged himself first, and only later was it decided that he "went to a lonesome place with a pistol and killed himself." [18] At any rate, "the substitute for pistol and ball" of one Ishmael is an undertaking quite similar to the one Whitman's protagonist faces. "It is still too little realized," writes Whicher, "that, with the possible but not obvious exception of Melville, no American author has ever engaged in a more daring or eventful voyage of the mind than Whitman." [19] Amen! and here is its point of departure, for it is clear now that if the "I" wants to preserve his mastery over the forces threatening him he must maintain the pose that makes it possible. He must, therefore, strengthen and solidify his pose until it becomes permanent, no longer a pose but an identity, and to do so means to continue "testing" it under the widest variety of conditions, to explore it in a veritable voyage of discovery into its powers and limitations. When he has understood that he could "witness" the suicide's corpse instead of being it, the speaker has found his specific task and, consequently, his poem its program.

That this exploration will be conducted within the particular context of the individual's relations with his community is indicated by the company the "I" has begun to keep when he assumed his self-creating pose of self-defense. Whitman's new "I," like Lear, Falstaff, or the Pardoner in the situations described earlier, has become an *alazon*. This is the label Northrop Frye gives to the character "who pretends or tries to be something more than he is" in response to his sense of being painfully isolated from society because of "a conflict between the inner and the outer world." [20] The *alazon* pretends to be more than he is because, like Whitman's terror-stricken protagonist, he must escape from what he actually is; consequently, he may often deceive others, but he must always deceive himself. By freeing him from the strain of having to acknowledge the real or imaginary inadequacies which would force his withdrawal from society, his ploys of deception provide him with the illusion through which he can maintain mutually acceptable relations with his world. Clearly, the practical result of the psychological predicament of Whitman's "I" is the type of conflict that the *alazon* responds to: while he is alone with his "soul" he can be idyllically happy, but as soon as he looks away from himself, however innocently, into the "outer world," the guilt and terror lurking in the "grass" inexorably creep up on him.

Truth, however, which is bound to crush him, usually catches up with the *alazon* sooner or later; his vital reliance on self-delusion, therefore, makes him, as Frye has shown, not only the logical subject of most comedies but very often a tragic hero, too. [21] But, to anticipate a conclusion that remains yet to be substantiated, Whitman's protagonist is an *alazon* with a difference, an American *alazon*. Burning all bridges behind himself, he must try to make good his pretensions and not just act out but become his pretense. His self-delusion is not merely the conventional *alazon's* inevitably losing stratagem to stay the defeat of "imaginative reality" by "the sort of reality which is established by social consensus," [22] as Frye at one point defines the "outer" world, but an audacious effort to graft the "imaginative reality" of the individual upon "social consensus" and thus force the "outer world" to make room for the "inner." The "I" 's new self, therefore, must prove itself through surviving any number of confrontations with the "outer world" or, in the terms of the poem's symbolic structure, through reconciling "soul" with "grass."

Thus, "the fullest expression of the sources from which Whitman's poetry rose" is to be found not so much in his "vision" (that is, the protagonist's invitation to his soul) as in the longer, self-contained sequence which it initiates. Although close enough to the traditional view of the matter, which Matthiessen, in effect, elaborates,[23] this conclusion thus rejects the special "mystical" status usually accorded the vision itself. In discussing this passage, and, indeed, the whole book, to speak of mysticism has proved both unwarranted and unnecessary.

Whitman, of course, has been hailed from the first by many of his readers as a "mystic"; only it has never become quite clear just exactly what they mean by the term. It would be convenient indeed if the issue could be resolved by declaring that mysticism is such-and-such, and the poem or passage in question is—or is not—mystical because there is—or is not—such-and-such in it. Mysticism, however, has come to mean such-and-such and many other, often contradictory, things besides. One man's "altered state of consciousness" is another's divine inspiration in the traditional Christian sense, and all too frequently the same man will begin speaking of the one thing only to end up speaking of the other.[24] Consequently, by calling a given passage or emotion in *Leaves of Grass* mystical, one may rightfully claim to be telling the truth and yet say nothing much at all. That much of Whitman's poetry and especially the lines discussed in this chapter reflect rare and elusive states of mind is beyond question, naturally. At the same time, it would seem prudent to attribute only such events to divine intervention that cannot be accounted for in any other way.[25] As the argument of this chapter has endeavored to show, Whitman's lines can; there is nothing in them that the agnostic need feel baffled by.

As the speaker lifts his eyes from the dead form of what he might have been, his new, self-proposed self, the "greatest poet," stands ready to face his trial, to confront his world in a quest to prove and thus to create himself. He does what he does, not because he chooses to do it or because he was commanded in a mystical revelation to do it, but simply because he must do it. He has no choice, for the alternative is annihilation and therefore, to Whitman, who has not yet "awakened" to death, no alternative at all.

II

An examination of the rhetorical attitudes in this passage can establish now a distinctive pattern of continuity among them. The protagonist's invitation to his soul and his reminiscence, at the beginning of the sequence, are spoken in the "histrionic" attitude of meditation, as an address to an imagined listener (72–81). The "contemplative" voice takes over (with some "prophetic" overtones) when, forgetting his imaginary interlocutor, the speaker proclaims what he "now" knows (82–86). Toward the end of this lovely list, his voice trails off into a spontaneous murmur of admiration; then, the child's question eases him back into detachment as he begins "guessing" about the grass (90–101). Perhaps to emphasize its special power, a solitary line introduces the metaphor of the "uncut hair of graves," and the discourse shifts into the "histrionic" attitude again (102–0). The "perception" of the "uttering tongues" hits home and wrings a spontaneous exclamation from him, and he goes on to explore their "hints" in the same spontaneous voice until he fully recognizes the menace they present and turns, dramatically, to his listener (110–13, 114–15). The next lines consist of losing efforts to maintain a dialogue while slipping helplessly back time and again into a spellbound sort of meditation, the "contemplative" attitude, modified by "prophetic" shrillness (116–35). This desperate declamation, however, cannot ward off his terrors, and to perform his final, spectacular and frenzied act of transformation he must turn full face to his listener again (136–39).

These shifts, then, follow quite regularly the speaker's changing sense of security and self-confidence. His "contemplative" detachment, well displayed in his report of the child's question and his response to it, reflects a mind in pronounced if moderate estrangement from his surroundings, that is, in a position of approximate equilibrium between self-assurance on the one hand, and on the other an awareness, though not yet a fear, of the "world outside" as a disturbing and potentially destructive force. In this attitude the speaker is wary of what might happen but unworried by it. When his self-assurance increases, as in his "guesses" about the "uncut hair of graves," he dares to ignore all that is "other," substituting instead, in his "histrionic" attitude, make-believe replicas of it, figments, as the saying goes, of his imagination. He is letting down thereby his guard: his imaginary conversations usually lead to uncontrived and unselfconscious musing in his "spontaneous" stance, which in turn is often followed by a terrified awakening to danger, as after the last "hint" of the "uttering tongues." When, however, the speaker's awareness of potential danger increases instead of his self-assurance, his voice acquires a "prophetic" or "didactic" quality reflecting an anxiously aggressive posture assumed in self-protection, as in the fatuous lines asserting that he is "not an earth nor an adjunct of an earth" but the "mate and companion of people" (127–28). He turns "outward," to his audience, only as a last resort in moments of greatest insecurity and crisis. On these occasions his words, especially at their most arrogant, are in effect a desperate cry of fear. In a sense, he strikes up a dialogue because he is terrified of what he would have to tell himself next. Against the menacing forces that he has released with his complacent obsession with himself to the almost

137

complete exclusion of the "outer world" he can in the end find protection only in seeking out the community. The "centripetal" excess must be mitigated by a "centrifugal" effort; to protect himself against being destroyed by "pride" he is forced to show and, indeed, to learn "sympathy." Since his direct statements to his listener are, therefore, devices of self-preservation first and only afterwards attempts at straight communication, they are, as noted earlier, usually the most cryptic and elusive portions of his poem, while the words spoken in disregard of all audience can reveal his state of mind with lucidity and power.

The pattern of rhetorical modulations in the lines discussed above operates without any major exceptions throughout the poem, although the poet will rarely deal again with a comparable range and intensity of emotions. Toward the conclusion of the poem, for example, when the renewed "I" has "tramped" a long way the "perpetual journey" (1199) of exploring his self-assigned powers, he faces the same crisis in basically the same way but in a calmer, more self-assured manner. After asserting that "no array of terms can say how much [he is] at peace about God and about death" (1273), he settles into unhurried meditation:

> I hear and behold God in every object, yet I
> understand God not in the least,
> Nor do I understand who there can be more wonderful
> than myself.
>
> (1274–75)

As he expatiates on this, he even echoes his "guess" in the earlier passage that the grass is perhaps "the handkerchief of the Lord," "designedly dropped" and "bearing the owner's name" (93–95): "I find letters from God dropped in the street, and every one is signed by God's name" (1279). Warming up to his subject, he drifts into apostrophes, the "histrionic" attitude— "And as to you death," "as to you corpse," "as to you life," and "O stars of heaven, / O suns . . . . O grass of graves . . . . O perpetual transfers and promotions. . . ." (1281, 1285, 1288,

1290–91)—interjecting, in the spontaneous tones of total self-absorption, a lovely and startling vision of death as birth; one of his images recalls his ecstatic discovery that "the hand of God is the elderhand of my own" (83), and he can still confront death only by insisting that the "dead are alive":

> To his work without flinching the accoucheur comes,
> I see the elderhand pressing receiving supporting,
> I recline by the sills of the exquisite flexible
>   doors . . . . and mark the outlet, and mark the
>   relief and escape.
>
> (1282–84)

Then, juxtaposing in an astonishing metaphoric *tour de force* sensuality and decay,[26] he denies death by treating it as if it were life as he "tenderly uses" the "uncut hair of graves" again:

> And as to you corpse I think you are good manure,
>   but that does not offend me,
> I smell the white roses sweetscented and growing,
> I reach to the leafy lips . . . . I reach to the
>   polished breasts of melons.
>
> (1285–87)

As he continues, however, he gradually switches from talking of death as if it were birth to talking of birth as if it were death. Again, the horror steals up on him unawares while he is apostrophizing the "sparkles of day and dusk" (1294). Although the lines are, as E. H. Miller observes,[27] a "development" of "the birth motif," the music of the words drowns out their meaning. The "moaning gibberish of the dry limbs" (1295) is too loud to allow one to admire tossing sparkles at length or even to notice them at all. The histrionic attitude then yields to the spontaneous, self-centered one, in which the poet first records an illusion of flight and release (1296–98), then wrestles with an elusive mystery. Whether it is a threat or a boon is impossible to tell, but the struggle for it fills his voice with anxiety and ends in failure:

139

"THE VERY HEART-BEAT OF LIFE"

There is that in me . . . . I do not know what it is
. . . . but I know it is in me. [. . .]
I do not know it . . . . it is without name . . . .
it is a word unsaid,

(1299, 1302)

A form of nothingness is upon him again, but he extricates himself from jeopardy with the gesture that has given him his identity: turning "outward" again he addresses directly his audience, his "brothers and sisters." He asserts *for their sake* the opposite of the "chaos or death" which in fact threatens to engulf his utterance, if not his senses: "It is not chaos or death . . . . it is form and union and plan . . . . it is eternal life . . . . it is happiness" (1308).

One may conclude, therefore, that Whitman's poetic discourse moves in a characteristic fashion along a sort of scale upon which the rhetorical attitudes distinguishable in it arrange themselves. This scale stretches from the protagonist's highest contentment, attained in the "spontaneous" voice of total self-absorption, to his greatest fear, recognizable in the voice of the "dialogue," its intermediate stages being formed by the "histrionic," "contemplative," and "prophetic-didactic" modulations as they range in order from the self-centered extreme toward the one representing insecurity. Along this scale the discourse is steadily and gradually drawn by a "centripetal" force toward extreme introversion, but upon reaching this point it is hurled abruptly and vigorously back *toward* the opposite end by the "centrifugal" power of the imperative of preserving the "self" through the "other."

III

Through this pattern of rhetorical movement, the poetic statement is found to evolve in a fashion capable of order beyond the purely improvisational, haphazard kind, which alone is usually held to obtain in it. That in this order a principle or organization is also implied needs, however, further arguing.

To the good common sense of the earliest readers Whit
man's poem in its form—or formlessness, rather—resembled a
chance conversation as it rambled along from image to image,
line to line, idea to idea by the most primitive chain of spontaneous association, without any discernible plan or, for that matter,
purpose besides perhaps passing the time of the day. Since
then, it has been generally allowed that the conversation the
poem resembles was most likely Whitman's own, but otherwise
the possibility that the poet may have had any but the lowest
degree of conscious control over his material has not found
much favor. "The plan of ['Song of Myself']," Davidson, for example, suggests, "may have developed in the way that [Whit-
man's] conversation is said to have developed," [28] that is, as a
contemporary of the poet described it, "after he had got a
thought stated in definitive terms—terms which suited him—
then he would go on and link it with another, and so his talk
would progress." [29] Whitman himself said as much to Traubel:

> The surprise to me is, how much is spontaneously suggested which
> a man could never have planned for. I sit down to write: one seem-
> ingly simple idea brings into view a dozen others: so my work
> grows. . . .[30]

Most readers have been content to let the matter rest at that.
Kenneth Burke noted once that, "it is possible that, after long
inspection, we might find some 'overarching' principle of development that 'underlies' his typical lists. . . . . [And] some critic
might also discern a regular canon of *development* in such 'turbulent' heapings". Then he went on to a penetrating and
suggestive analysis of some patterns of verbal association in
Leaves of Grass, demonstrating in exemplary fashion how the
"long inspection" might begin, but few have followed his lead.[31]
It is, at any rate, generally agreed that, "[Whitman] seems never
to have been sure of *how* his poetry was made." [32] The dilemma
that this assumption forces especially upon the critic approaching Whitman's first and probably best poem is impressively illustrated by Harold W. Blodgett's rueful concession that the "orga-

nization [of 'Song of Myself'] is intuitive rather than logical," although "we must believe that Whitman knew where he was going in this poem." [33]

At first glance, Whitman's own pronouncements seem no help at all in dispelling the dilemma. Late in his life he prided himself that he "rounded and finished little if anything" [34] and "never fooled with technique more than enough to provide for simply getting through," [35] and once he declared to Traubel that "the secret of it all" was "to write in the gush, the throb, the flood of the moment—to put things down without deliberation," adding: "I always worked that way." [36]

He was rather reticent about the history of the first edition, but some casual remarks he is reported to have made a few years after its appearance suggest that his reliance on the "gush and throb" of the moment was never more complete than during its composition. Charles W. Eldridge, in a letter to John Burroughs, claims to have heard Whitman compare his own reaction to "Song of Myself" in later years to that of a somnambulist when he is shown in his waking hours the perils he passed through while asleep,[37] and when John T. Trowbridge, in the spring of 1860, asked the unexpectedly subdued poet—"I found him the quietest of men," Trowbridge notes—how his first poems struck him upon rereading them in preparation for the new edition of Leaves of Grass, Whitman's startling reply was: "I am astonished to find myself capable of feeling so much." [38]

He also told Trowbridge, a few years later: "I do not suppose I shall ever again have the afflatus I had in writing the first Leaves of Grass." [39] Although Trowbridge quotes the remark from memory almost thirty years after it was spoken, it sounds quite authentic. Many others besides Trowbridge have noted and the poet himself had time and again suggested that, as Furness put it, "the quick of his creative process" was "a certain trancelike suspension of ordinary mental processes" in which he could be possessed by "a sense of illumination from the 'Inner Light.' " [40] Furness's Quaker term is justified, since Whitman himself liked to remind his readers that he was "at least half of

Quaker stock" [41] (even though this was not, strictly speaking, true),[42] and, according to Traubel, he once even considered joining the Society of Friends.[43] Furness concludes, rather apologetically, that "we are forced to accept ["afflatus," "inspiration," in the traditional sense] as Whitman's trusted guide, in default of any evidence of a more scientifically accurate mentor," [44] and that the poet conceived of it as obeying a "Voice—the invisible demon of Socrates and the *voices* of Joan of Arc." [45]

That Whitman himself should prefer a "still small voice" figure to "inner light" is not surprising. Throughout his work, his sense of perfection, of fulfillment, of "satisfaction," is usually expressed as an auditory rather than a visual experience. For him, truth is harmony; he does not see it quite so well as he hears it, and in most cases his ecstatic perception of it, be it induced by his own "belched words," "the orbic flex of [the] mouth" of the "tenor large and fresh as the creation," "America singing," or "the word up from the waves," is not so much an illumination as an "entunement."

Whitman's metaphor is also appropriate in another sense. Along with his insistence on spontaneity, his methods of composition display a strong concern with design as well. Years could pass before he would shape into a finished work the various fragments that "the gush, the throb of the moment" produced. He notes himself in *Specimen Days* that he "commenced putting 'Leaves of Grass' [1855] to press . . . after many MS. doings and undoings," [46] and, of course, his surviving notebooks and manuscript pages supply a number of ideas, images, phrases, and even complete passages, which found their way into the first printed version yet antedate it by sometimes as many as seven years.[47] His constant revisions of his book and even the appearance of his manuscripts, full of hesitations, second thoughts, false starts, and deletions both before and after the first *Leaves,* also indicate that he may have "put things down without deliberation," but he certainly did not put them down automatically, as they came.

Spontaneity and design are not, however, irreconcilable

once one extends to Whitman's creative method the assumption frequently held about his creation: it has the character of musical composition. He writes his poems as if he were composing not a reasoned argument but music, organizing them through tonality and rhythm, like someone striving to capture a melody by transcribing it as faithfully as possible into notation. Obviously, he will not be able to do it at the first attempt, and obviously he can do it only when he can hear the tune, for it must be heard and cannot be recollected: Whitman, apparently, had to rely on his moments of inspiration for the combination of the several fragments into a finished poem as much as he had to for the composition of the fragments themselves.

By speaking of his inspiration in auditory and musical terms Whitman shows a more precise understanding of his creative processes than he is usually credited with. Whether he was a Quaker at heart or not, he seems to have had a remarkably sound idea of what made his poetry happen, even if he did not know how it was made. He knew that he had to depend on a specific state of mind for it, his "entunement," which he learned to use, although, apparently, he had no power to bring it on. He had to "invite" it, and Waskow is not far off the mark when he notes that the speaker's call to his soul before his reminiscence of their ecstasy—"only the lull I like, the hum of your valved voice" (77)—may, in effect, be taken for an equivalent of the traditional invocation to the muse.[48]

In all this Whitman resembles any number of artists, but if he is just another "aeolian harp," what are the winds that fill him with sound? What is the music itself of his inspiration that comes and goes as it pleases and that the poet can only recognize but not command? Because of the very nature of the question one can only speculate about an answer, but the conclusions reached so far make it possible to do so with some assurance.

IV

"Whitman has let himself go," John Burroughs remarked, "and trusted himself to the informal and spontaneous, to a degree unprecedented": [49] this extraordinary capacity to lower his guard, to "let himself go," was an essential part of Whitman's creativity, for it has enabled him to listen to the sounds that floated up from within. His moments of inspiration seem to have been those in which he managed to become as fully aware as possible of the contention of drives which constituted his very being.

Jean Catel has advanced a similar view, seeing the source of Whitman's creativity in the occasions of the poet's rediscovery of a near-forgotten, truer, inner self (*"identité intérieure"*), which leads to "the illusion of a more intense life." "In 1855," he adds, "we find this in its dionysiac disorder"; however, he does not seem to be telling the whole story when he explains this experience as "a phenomenon which leads either to madness or to poetry: the sudden emergence of the unconscious into the luminous domain of the mind." Perhaps the phrasing is inexact, but if Catel attributes Whitman's poetic energies solely to the operation of the unconscious (the inner self is clearly Whitman's "soul," and "one may assume," Catel claims, "that 'Soul' is the equivalent of 'Unconscious' "), he seems to be quite wrong, however eloquently so:

> The soul is the reality of the unconscious, the light of this shadow, the melody of this confusion, the order of this chaos. It is both the ideal which Whitman's entire past life had been seeking and the force which has thrust him, irresistibly, upon the open road onto which he calls all others. [50]

According to this, all Whitman has to do is surrender to his unconscious the way the protagonist in his first poem surrenders to his soul in lines 78–89, and he has become the poet of *Leaves of Grass*. One has already seen, however, that the ecstasy is only part of an involved sequence: similarly, the function of the unconscious does not account for all of Whitman's inspiration. [51] In his "grim yet joyous elemental abandon" [52] Whitman was not simply yielding to his unconscious; he was submitting rather to the complex dynamism of the relationship among the forces, conscious as well as unconscious, that made up his awareness; he was listening to and trying to capture in words the curious rhythms and harmonies of what D. H. Lawrence called IT, "the deepest *whole* self of man, the self in its wholeness." [53]

Although Whitman never fully articulated a conception of his creative processes as they are suggested here, he does seem to have suspected often enough that while he was trying to catch in his verse "the very heart-beat of life" and especially while he was "taking it up again after some time and reading it afresh" to make sure that "there [was] no jar in it" [54] he was actually responding to the ineluctable motions of his deepest self. Throughout his later life he insisted that all of *Leaves of Grass* and especially "Song of Myself" were meant to express above and beyond anything else his "own physical, emotional, moral, intellectual, and aesthetic Personality," [55] and Personality, for him, was always an essentially psychological concept, "the eternal bodily composite, cumulative, natural character of one's self . . . a character, making most of . . . the passions, in all their fullest heat and potency, of courage, rankness, amativeness, and of immense pride." [56] Thus, in *Democratic Vistas*, for example, the traits distinguishing "the model Personality" whose "formation" is "the spinal meaning" of "the programme of culture" Whitman is proposing "for the purposes of these States" are rooted in the instincts and the affections: "The best culture will always be that of the manly and courageous instincts, and loving perceptions, and of self-respect," and it must ever rely on "the simple, unsophisticated Conscience, the primary moral element . . . that old, ever-true plumb-rule of persons, eras, nations." These alone can insure, Whitman implies, "The quality of BEING, in the object's self, according to its own central idea and purpose, and of growing therefrom and thereto." [57] The same, essentially psychological, concept of the self has been inscribed, after all, at the head of all of *Leaves of Grass* since 1871. Setting out to sing "One's-Self," he promises to sing of "not physiognomy alone nor brain alone," but "of life immense in passion, pulse, and power," "of physiology from top to toe." [58]

One may safely assume that "physiology" here means not

so much physiological processes in themselves as the variety of ways in which they are related to consciousness and thus allow the "soul" to manifest itself in the qualities and behavior of the body. This is the sense implied by the following lines, too, as Whitman steers cautiously clear of the conventional meaning of the word:

> Something there was and is in Nature immeasurably beyond, and even altogether ignoring what we call the artistic, the beautiful, the literary, and even the moral, the good. Not easy to put one's finger on, or name in a word, this something, invisibly permeating the old poems, religion-sources, and art. If I were being asked to suggest it in such a single word, I should write (at the risk of being quite misunderstood at first, at any rate) the word physiological.[59]

Since he never made a secret of his ambition to see his own poetry become a poem, "religion-source," and art for the new world, what he has to say here of these achievements of antiquity applies implicitly to his own work as well: its deepest roots issue from elemental processes in the primordial dimness where conscious and unconscious merge. This is true, of course, of all human creativity, as Whitman must have known very well; his remarks about his own inspiration show, however, that he also knew that few others could allow these forces to surge into poetic vision as completely and directly as he could, "without check with original energy," and that therein lay the gift which distinguished him as a maker.

This awareness is, then, the measure of Whitman's conscious control over the structure and form of his poetry, especially of the most elusive pieces. In his best and most characteristic poems he knew how to keep his extrinsic, received notions of poetic order far enough out of the way of the "original energy" welling up in him.

The form, therefore, of his "first poem" reflects the form of his consciousness. Consciousness, like poetry, being a temporal phenomenon, form in both cases means, in Pound's phrase, "form cut into time," [60] that is, rhythm. That there is to the

poem a manner of rhythm, which creates the only convincing
sense of order in it, much as this order may resist analysis, has
long been a commonplace of Whitman criticism. Thus, Roy Harvey Pearce speaks of "the intensely personal pulsations and
periodicities" controlling "the movement . . . of the hypnagogic meditation . . . which gives 'Song of Myself' its quality
of process, not form." "Such pulsations and periodicities," he
adds, "are expressions of the energy of the creative self; and
they cannot be plotted in advance; they can only be released
and followed out to their transformative end." [61] This same
rhythm appears to be the basis of the various musical analogies
offered in explanation of the poem's structure; [62] all of these attest to an impression of an order in the poem that is not less
firm for obeying no rules other than its own. A fundamental
rhythm is the basis of, for example, Malcolm Cowley's account
of his sense of the poem's coherence:

> The true structure of the poem is not primarily logical but psy-
> chological, and is not a geometrical figure but a musical progres-
> sion. As music "Song of Myself" . . . comes [close] to being a
> rhapsody or tone poem, one that modulates from theme to theme,
> often changing in key and tempo, falling into reveries and rising
> toward moments of climax, but always preserving its unity of feel-
> ing as it moves onward in a wavelike flow. . . . There is no line in
> the first edition that seems false to a single prevailing tone. There
> are passages weaker than others, but none without a place in the
> general scheme. The repetitions are always musical variations and
> amplifications. [63]

The regularities that rhetorical transitions have revealed in
the text point toward the same conclusion. The characteristic
rhythm in which the "centripetal" forces gradually engulfing the
statement are counteracted and rebuffed, at the last moment, as
it were, by sudden explosions of "centrifugal" energy appears to
be the direct expression of the rhythm that defined and sustained Whitman's "self in its wholeness," for this pattern in the
poem's rhetoric clearly corresponds to what the analysis of the

Preface has established as the essential pattern of Whitman's processes of consciousness: elemental impulses of self-assertion invariably followed by compulsive gestures of self-denial. One can venture to propose, therefore, that this fundamental, all-pervasive, *primary rhythm* is the basis of the various impressions of an order of periodicities or musical progression in the poem and, further, that its pulsations, the "diastole and systole in the poet's relation to external reality," as Christopher Collins put it,[64] provide the only structure intrinsic to the poem.[65]

In the primary rhythm—let it be called the "heartbeat," after Whitman, who strove to capture, he said, "the very heart-beat of life" [66]—is thus the principle of continuity found that can make sense of the rhetorical modulations established in the previous chapter. It also furnishes the resolution of the apparent paradox that Whitman's poem owes its success to the failure of his announced intentions. The speaker's loud promises and insistence on a thoroughgoing, uncompromising, rigorously "symmetrical" mutuality—"what I assume you shall assume"—is a "centrifugal" gesture against the overwhelming "centripetal" drift in the manner, diction, voice, and, indeed, the entire imaginative effort through which he attempts to fulfill those very promises.

For the moment no detailed demonstrations other than the two offered earlier in this chapter need to be given of how the primary rhythm organizes a longer passage. Several instances will emerge, in any event, from the discussion of the question that must be the subject of the following chapter: how are the other, "geometrical" or "phasal" possibilities of structure in the poem to be reconciled with the ordering function of the primary rhythm, which is neither very phasal nor geometrical? This question must yet be answered before a satisfactory conclusion can be reached about the poem's significant form and before its final evaluation can be undertaken.

Chapter Seven

POSSIBILITIES OF A PHASAL STRUCTURE

I

Various readers have attempted to show, over the years, that "Song of Myself" moves in some manner of linear order, from beginning through middle to end, even if the poet himself may not have been aware at all of constructing such an order. That only widely divergent and often contradictory conclusions have been reached so far has not diminished either the conviction of most readers that some such order exists or the determination with which the search for it is renewed time and again. "The nagging suspicion persists," says one critic, "that, in a poem of such magnitude and force Whitman *must* be moving to some end," [1] and, though the phrasing may vary, the substance of this view is among the very few items of something approaching broad critical agreement on the poem. Thus, for all that he has to say about the "true structure of the poem," which is "not a geometrical figure but a musical progression," Cowley goes on to argue that one can, nevertheless, discern a "geometrical figure" as well in the poem:

150

POSSIBILITIES OF A PHASAL STRUCTURE

The form of the poem is something more than a forward movement in rising and subsiding waves of emotion. There is also a firm
narrative structure, one that becomes easier to grasp when we start
by dividing the poem into a number of parts or sequences. . . .
The parts, however defined, follow one another in irreversible
order, like the beginning, middle, and end of any good narrative.[2]

More cautious perhaps but equally persuaded, Pearce declares
that

the studious reader of Song of Myself must be somewhat diffident
about the detailed precision of any outline of the phasal structure
of the poem. Yet he must insist on the validity of the theory of
phasal structure itself,

because, he adds further on, "the new heroic poem, the specifically American epic [that is, "Song of Myself,"] is one of ordering, not of order." [3]

This "nagging suspicion," needless to say, is scarcely unfounded. In spite of the rather disjointed, chaotic first impression of the poem, many of its lines evidently belong together,
clustering around a major gesture or statement; the rest of the
lines may be seen as held within the sphere of attraction of one
or another of these clusters; and there is no obvious reason not
to assume that the order in which the clusters follow one another is, in some sense, necessary or, to cite Cowley, "irreversible." In what sense, though? That is the crux of the matter. How
can a phasal structure be reconciled with the ordering function
of the primary rhythm, the "heartbeat"? For an answer one must
examine the nature and possibilities of continuity among the
several clusters or sections into which the poem can be divided.
This examination clearly must begin with the establishment, if
only for argument's sake, of a plausible sequence of sections.

It is, of course, impossible to offer a scheme of this sort
without feeling intensely aware of how tentative most of it must
be and how familiar much of it must sound. Though probably no
two readers have arrived at exactly the same division of the

poem, most readers recognize in it the same major line-clusters, loosely defined, nor would too many people care to define them with anything resembling exactitude. High precision here could only be pedantry: imprecision of the worst sort. For much the same reason, as Cowley explained, "the exact number [of divisions in the poem] is not important." [4] Need one add that nobody would dare to foist still another of these schemes on a patient world and reject the arrangement of another critic unless he saw firmer justification in the text for his own? [5]

As seen in the previous chapter, with the momentary victory of the poem's protagonist over the forces that threaten him, his task and the poem's direction have become clear. If his victory is to last, he must become as invincible as he pretends to be; he must strengthen and solidify the powerful and exuberant self-assurance through which he has overcome his fit of mortal anguish until it is transformed from a pose struck in an instantaneous, instinctive gesture of self-defence into an identity. He must do so by exploring, testing, and finally mastering its powers, that is, by relearning the use of his faculties from this radically new vantage point. One can, therefore, assume, provisionally, that the development initiated by these lines will be a narrative of a rudimentary sort, dramatizing the involvements of the "I" with the infinite possibilities of being that lie beyond it. This narrative can be divided into seven major phases, which would thus make, with the introductory lines and the passage of the protagonist's crises and transformation, for a nine-part structure. What follows is an account of the seven phases of the narrative.

II

First Phase (146–352). It takes the "I" a few dazed, uncertain moments, as he turns away from the suicide's corpse, before his task of firming up his pose into an identity becomes plain to him. First, he just looks around himself, hardly believing his success, and only gradually does his bewildered stare at what terrified him change into a quietly jubilant survey of all that he can "merge" with. The first major cluster of lines is based on this long, slowly brightening glance, on his endlessly repeated declaration: "I see." [6] Introduced by his boast that appearances cannot deceive him—"I see through the gingham whether or no"—the passage itself begins with the image of the babe in the cradle and concludes with the speaker's amazed whisper: "The palpable is in its place and the impalpable is in its place" (352).

When, having "witnessed the corpse," he looks up, he finds himself in the midst of a crowded, turbulent city and launches into a short, excited catalogue. It starts out as the first among the many exuberant celebrations Whitman was to write of the city, but it soon becomes a menacing vision of vice, pain, violence, and death:

> What groans of overfed or half-starved who fall on
>   the flags sunstruck or in fits,
> What exclamation of women taken suddenly, who hurry
>   home and give birth to babes,
> What living and buried speech is always vibrating
>   here . . . . what howls restrained by decorum,
> Arrests of criminals, slights, adulterous offers
>   made, acceptances, rejections with convex
>   lips.
>
>   (155–58)

The morbid spell of the preceding crisis, apparently, is not entirely broken yet, but the speaker can at least face this time his visions of anguish; he then spells out again, in astonishment, his success, just as he did after viewing the suicide's corpse: "I mind them or the resonance of them . . . . I come again and again" (159).

Still, this nightmarish city-scape is obviously not the safest place for him, even if he has managed to remain in control of it. He looks another way, to pastoral scenes, and the move calms him. As the swarming, feverish rush of images slows down they expand into a series of rural vignettes, beginning with a lovely scene in which the "beautiful uncut hair of graves" changes into a fragrant symbol of the harvest and thus of life. "Stretched atop of the load" of "the dried grass of the harvest-time" in the "slow-drawn wagon" the speaker seems the embodied spirit of the season itself, like Autumn in Keats's ode, which these lines resemble in the delicacy of their diction and the peculiar enchantment of the moment they create:

> I jump from the crossbeams, and seize the clover and
>   timothy,
> And roll head over heels, and tangle my hair full of
>   wisps.
>
> (164, 161, 166–67)

Several vignettes of the same kind follow. Each of them is a carefully composed and neatly framed, self-consciously typical picture of *the* trapper, *the* runaway slave, *the* butcher-boy, and the rest. The protagonist steps from one picture into the next: [7] he is a hunter "alone far in the wilds and mountains" (168), the helmsman of a "Yankee Clipper" (173), the companion of "boatmen and clamdiggers" (175), and a wedding-guest at the "marriage of the trapper in the open air in the far west" (178). He is, however, evidently much too insecure yet in these involvements with what lies outside himself. He cannot really assume these identities; he can only dress up in them. As the series progresses, his participation grows less and less active in it, and after the episode with the runaway slave (183–92) he is merely watching, from a distance, the lonely woman (193–210), the butcher-boy (211–12), the blacksmiths (213–18), and "the negro that drives the huge dray of the stoneyard" (220).

A masterful expression of the mood that explains this paradoxical, reluctant aggressiveness is in the wistful, lovely idyll of "the twenty-ninth bather," "handsome and richly drest aft the blinds of the window" (197), who yet came "dancing and laughing along the beach" (202) to see and love the "twenty-eight young men [bathing] by the shore" (193). That the episode is one of the most naturally self-contained portions of the poem and makes for a splendid poem in itself has been often recognized; so has its elusiveness. It is a happy poem, although its subject is frustration. It owes much of its immediate appeal to the delicate equilibrium that Whitman, seemingly without effort, establishes between the joy and beauty of imaginative experience and the profound pain of vicarious experience. Whatever else these lines may mean—and interpretations are not few [8]—a major part of their significance in the larger work is that the plight of the twenty-ninth bather is the plight also of Whitman's protagonist. Like the woman hidden in the house, he feels the dejection of actual separation all the more sharply because of the poignant beauty of the contact he has come to know in imagination. Seeming to withdraw to observe the observer, the "I," in fact, comes to the heart of the matter, for by showing the pathos in the delight that the unseen bather has contrived out of the pain of her frustration through "twenty-eight years of womanly life, and all so lonesome" (195) he is also revealing his own predicament.

He retreats even further, "backward as well as forward slueing, / To niches aside and junior bending" (226–27), as he looks at animals for a while. [9] This delightful catalogue of animals (228–47) leads up to his proud announcement that in all he looks at he can recognize himself:

> What is commonest and cheapest and nearest and
>   easiest is Me,
> Me going in for my chances, spending for vast
>   returns,
> Adorning myself to bestow myself on the first that
>   will take me,
> Not asking the sky to come down to my goodwill,
> Scattering it freely forever.
>
>   (252–56)

He has been forced to dare to impose himself on the world outside himself, to scatter his "goodwill" "freely forever," and his effort is beginning to reap its rewards. His growing exhilaration speeds up again the sequence, which slowed down with the pastoral scenes. A splendid, long catalogue follows: he is celebrating—naming, like Adam—a multitude of occupations, only to recognize himself in each of them (257–352). Only once does he interrupt the wonderful torrent of images to catch his breath and to state the law of "opposite equals" as it applies to the moment:

> And these one and all tend inward to me, and I tend
> outward to them,
> And such as it is to be of these more or less I am.
>
> (324–25)

He goes on to elaborate this notion, and in the lines that follow, this last "I am" replaces "I see" as he discovers himself in paradoxes:

> I am of old and young, of the foolish as much as
> the wise, [. . .]
> Stuffed with the stuff that is coarse, and stuffed
> with the stuff that is fine.
>
> (326, 329)

These, not illogically, lead to thoughts of his nationality, and he soon identifies himself first as the native of just about every state in the Union he can think of and then as "Not merely of the New World but of Africa Europe or Asia . . . . a wandering savage" (344).

When he finally stops, with one last flourish of incongruous selves he can "be" ("A prisoner, fancy-man, rowdy, lawyer, physician or priest" [346]), the vision his words have induced goes on expanding. He may have run out of breath but not of things to say. After a moment's pause he begins again, and the pell-mell torrent of substantives is replaced by syntactically complete, parallel statements in evenly spaced, precise stresses in each of the six lines that follow, as if, overcome by his own enthusiasm, he were speaking much more slowly and calmly in a changed, low voice.[10] This passage concluding the phase is not a resounding, aggressive declaration but the moment of the awestruck protagonist's discovery that by acting out his pretense of self-assurance he has come to possess the strength he thought he had to fake. His voice is that of total, self-absorbed amazement and admiration, not unlike the voice that spoke of "the peace and joy and knowledge that pass all the art and argument of the earth" (82), for the moment it records is itself not unlike that earlier, ecstatic one:

> I resist anything better than my own diversity,
> And breathe the air and leave plenty after me,
> And am not stuck up, and am in my place.
>
> The moth and the fisheggs are in their place,
> The suns I see and the suns I cannot see are in their
>   place,
> The palpable is in its place and the impalpable is in
>   its place.
>
>   (347–52)

Second Phase (353–80). Although the cluster they form is very short in comparison with the rest, the lines of this phase are clearly distinguished from either of the phases that enclose them. In a series of metaphors the speaker attempts to give a name to what he is doing, much the same way as he tried to explain what grass was.

All these lines depend on "This is . . . ." He is no longer "guessing," of course, but the variety itself of his metaphors qualifies his certainty. As he clarifies to himself and to whoever might be listening what it is that he is doing, oral and musical images predominate, that is, images that usually express the orgiastic, self-assertive emotions that precipitate his crises of morbid anguish. It is no longer surprising, therefore, that the sequence drifts again toward a preoccupation with failure, isolation, and pain. At the end of the section, metaphors begin to yield to explicit statement, and what was implied by the conjunction of orality and music with elements of Whitman's nightmare is now spelled out:

This is the press of a bashful hand . . . . this is the
float and odor of hair,
This is the touch of my lips to yours . . . . this is
the murmur of yearning.

(377–78)

I reach you, he might add, the way the twenty-ninth bather has reached the twenty-eight young men—"float," "hair," "bashful" (cf. "unseen"), and "hand" recall directly the earlier episode—and for the same reason. Thus, for all the excitement of joyful anticipation in them, these lines are aware also of the darker moods and guilty anxiety they portend for the speaker. The last line finally arrives at as precise a definition of what the "I" has been doing as any of Whitman's critics have been able to produce: "This is the thoughtful merge of myself and the outlet again" (380).

Third Phase (381–546). This phase contains some of the most admired and most often discussed passages in the poem. Its core is the question, "What am I?" (390), and the answer to it (perhaps the oldest lines in all of *Leaves of Grass*): [11]

I am the poet of the body,
And I am the poet of the soul.
(422–23)

Perhaps because the preceding phase concluded on an exceedingly private note, the speaker introduces his question with a flourish of resonant declarations that what he is doing is no more unusual or elusive than any other natural process (381–85); then, reminding himself and his listener alike of each other's presence, he adds:

This hour I tell things in confidence,
I might not tell everybody but I will tell you.
(386–87)

This good-natured teasing will rarely disappear from his voice through most of the phase and may be taken for a measure of his self-confidence that no longer has to be based on bluff.

POSSIBILITIES OF A PHASAL STRUCTURE

As the main question is asked, the fondness of the "I" for contrasts and paradox—"opposite equals"—becomes ever more pronounced, both in imagery and diction. "Hankering, gross, mystical, nude" (388) is only the first of splendid phrases in this group which owe their vitality to the endlessly startling, inventive juxtaposition of the stolid, earthy, and coarse with the delicate and disembodied. And "hankering" as a contrast to "gross" introduces a series of purposefully unwashed, bathetic colloquialisms through which the speaker reinforces his defiance of snobbery in self-inspection.

> I have pried through the strata and analyzed to a hair,
> And counselled with doctors and calculated close and
>   found no sweeter fat than sticks to my own bones,
> (399–400)

he announces, then goes on to put into words the peculiar law of mutual reflection by which, from the moment of his transformation, the new, self-assertive, death-defying "I" has maintained himself in all his imaginative confrontations with the world beyond the scope of his ego:

> In all people I see myself, none more and not one a
>   barleycorn less,
> And the good or bad I say of myself I say of them.
> (401–2)

He then recapitulates, so to speak, the articles of his faith of self-assurance (388–421), by way, possibly, of justifying his assertion that he is not a but *the* poet. He is, obviously, the poet by the fundamentally Emersonian decree that the Preface has elaborated. He is enabled by the "poetic quality" in him to perceive the "poetic quality" in all else, and the consequent gesture of the "merge" gives him his rank, for by "indicating" through it "the path between reality and [the] soul" he but "re-attaches things to nature and the Whole." [12]

It is only apt, therefore, that he goes on to prove his poethood by enacting the merge in scenes of metaphoric sexuality.

159

He becomes the "lover," in turn, of the night, the earth, and the sea (434–60). His exuberance, not to say frenzy, of delight leads, however, to emotions that prompt him to declare that he does not "decline to be the poet of wickedness also," adding, in pungent slang: "Washes and razors for foofoos . . . . for me freckles and a bristling beard" (467–68).[13] Like the shift from ecstatic toward disturbing subjects, this veering from the self-absorbed toward the public, didactic voice, too, follows in a manner that has by now become quite familiar: the pattern of the primary rhythm of the "heartbeat." Only after a sequence of self-consciously grandiloquent rhetoric has compensated with its deliberate extroversion for the ecstatic self-absorption of the lines of the merger can he take his next major step.

The lines that have been heard so far since the protagonist's transformation have expressed the renewed, desperately willed self of the "I" as it can be known through the senses. This self-in-the-senses can now be given a name; it can now assume a social identity:

> Walt Whitman, an American, one of the roughs, a kosmos,[14]
> Disorderly fleshy and sensual . . . . eating
>   drinking and breeding,
> No sentimentalist . . . . no stander above men
>   and women or apart from them . . . . no more
>   modest than immodest.
>
> Unscrew the locks from the doors!
> Unscrew the doors themselves from their jambs!
>   (499–503)

Needless to say, any other name would do just as well. Walter Whitman, of Brooklyn, New York has managed to mark out just the proper distance between himself and his creation, and it bespeaks Emerson's astuteness that on reading the poem he did not "trust the name as real & available for a post-office." [15] "Walt Whitman" is the "greatest poet" of the Preface, realized in the "I" Walter could conceive.

POSSIBILITIES OF A PHASAL STRUCTURE

The phase concludes with the newly named poet's proud recital of what he does and what he is; the list has been heard before, but this time it is presented from a somewhat modified, social perspective (507–46). The voice is that of didactic-prophetic meditation, but it is neither shrill nor offensive. He claims, in effect, that he is the "liberator god" Emerson said the poet was: through him "many long dumb voices" (509) become "clarified and transfigured" (520), and he is "divine [. . .] inside and out" (526).[16] The peroration of this phase is the "I"'s sensuous hymn of praise to his body as a landscape of splendid vegetation dominated by the plants symbolizing the genitalia, the organs whose gratification ensures the ecstasies of his imagination and gives form to them.

The limits of sensuous self-realization have been reached. The pose of self-assertion has been realized as an identity in the senses. The senses have made good the "I"'s bluff: "I exist as I am" (413).

Fourth Phase (547–706). The theme of this phase may be described as the intellecutal uncertainty contrasting the sensory certitude of the previous sections; its keynote is the phrase "I cannot tell" (547). In his senses the "I" can possess the mystery, "the puzzle of puzzles / [. . .] that we call Being" (609–10), but he can neither articulate nor, quite simply, understand it.

Yet another account of the merge opens the phase. In metaphors that Chase, among others, finds "astonishing," the poet shows the dawn merging with the sky much as he has learnt to merge with the world outside himself:

> Hefts of the moving world at innocent gambols,
>   silently rising, freshly exuding,
> Scooting obliquely high and low.
>
> Something I cannot see puts upward libidinous prongs,
> Seas of bright juice suffuse heaven. [. . .]
>
> Dazzling and tremendous how quick the sunrise would
>   kill me,
> If I could not now and always send sunrise out of me.

161

POSSIBILITIES OF A PHASAL STRUCTURE

We also ascend dazzling and tremendous as the sun,
We found our own my soul in the calm and cool of the
daybreak.

(555–59, 562–65)

The mystery outside is set off by the mystery within: "My knowledge my live parts . . . . it keeping tally with the meaning of
things" (576). After this, the way the "I" scorns the taunts of his
speech because he cannot articulate his happiness is scarcely
surprising. He does not "let it out" (570) because he does not
have to:

My final merit I refuse you . . . . I refuse putting
from me the best I am. [. . .]

Writing and talk do not prove me.
I carry the plenum of proof and every thing else in my face,
With the hush of my lips I confound the topmost skeptic.

(578, 581–83)

As if to prove his point, he launches into a catalogue of what he
hears (584–610). By the time its ecstatic conclusion is reached not
only does he know again that he can "exist as he is"—the earlier
experiences of seeing have already done this much for him—he
also knows that this awareness, though he can always feel it, will
always remain "the puzzle of puzzles." He elaborates this paradoxical, non-rational form of knowledge in the much-discussed
episode of the touch (618–51).

This clearly autoerotic experience is still another merge, in
this one phase the third enactment of essentially the same scene
of self-realization conceived and expressed through analogies of
sexual gratification. This time, however, the self-realization is
described as unwilled and anguished. Each time he looks at this
scene, the voice of the "I" is filled with the bewildered and excited astonishment characteristic of him in this phase, and each
look is closer, harder, and longer than the one before. He has
been leading up, perhaps unwittingly, to a confrontation with
his arch-fear: the horror in the ecstasy. Now that this third, clos-

162

est look is taken, the erotic metaphors have the peculiar coloring of his own—the "I" 's, not necessarily Walter's—narcissistic, compulsive, and guilt-ridden sexuality. Instead of more or less aggressively imposing himself, as in the "merges" recounted before, on the world around him, he must be teased out of himself by all that is not "I." His fulfillment thereupon becomes a full-blown crisis, complete with confused guilt and frightened protestations that he has been seduced by "prurient provokers" (622). Or has he?

> I am given up by traitors;
> I talk wildly . . . . I have lost my wits I
> and nobody else am the greatest traitor.
> (636–37)

The question is left unresolved. He is not, after all, up to looking directly at the sources of the curious dynamism of gratification and guilt that defines his whole being; he compromises instead by shutting his eyes again and accepting it for a fact without comprehending it intellectually. The becalmed and again affectionate and happy tone of the lines of sexual release attests to this acceptance; for the full force of the change the preceding couplet should be heard, too:

> You villain touch! what are you doing? . . . . my
> breath is tight in its throat;
> Unclench your floodgates! you are too much for me.
>
> Blind loving wrestling touch! Sheathed hooded sharp-
> toothed touch!
> Did it make you ache so leaving me?
>
> Parting tracked by arriving . . . . perpetual payment
> of the perpetual loan,
> Rich showering rain, and recompense richer afterward.
> (639–44)

Nor is this effort of the mind to catch up with the senses entirely without a reward. Having learnt through sight—and sympa-

163

thy, the sight of the spirit—to recognize himself in all that is, the "I" has now stared long and hard enough at the moment of the merge to recognize *in* himself all that is. The narrowly egocentric perspective of the moment when the splendor of the sunrise could remind him only of his ejaculating sperm is balanced now and compensated for by the expansive, dilating vision whereby his ejaculation becomes the metaphor of a whole triumphant world:

> Sprouts take and accumulate . . . . stand by the curb
> prolific and vital,
> Landscapes projected masculine full-sized and golden.
> (645–46)

He may not be able to tell how or why the merge works, any more than he can tell how his ankles bend, but, without quite comprehending it, he has begun to live the fact that "what I assume you shall assume," the fact that in his self is implicit all experience: "All truths wait in all things" (747).

The certainty he attains this way, though an intellectual compromise, is different, possibly fuller, than his earlier convictions, and he is careful to indicate the difference. Earlier, he first "guessed" about the world around him, then "knew" in his bones that he was "august" and the rest; now, in a moment similar to the one in which the child asked him what the grass was, he announces a knowledge that is firmer than the previous modes, though it also bypasses the intellect: he "believes."

> Logic and sermons never convince, [. . .]
> And a compend of compends is the meat of a man or woman,
> And a summit and flower there is the feeling they have
> for each other, [. . .]
> I believe a leaf of grass is no less than the journey-
> work of the stars.
> (652, 658–59, 662)

In the familiar serenity of these lines (662–83) one can hear the poet's sigh of relief too that, grave as it was, he could ride out the crisis. He then turns toward the animals again, as he did on a previous occasion (226 ff.), as if to take a rest and catch his breath in a congenial, untaxing atmosphere (684–707). There is a touch of self-reproach in his praise of the beasts because "they do not sweat and whine about their condition, / They do not lie awake in the dark and weep for their sins," (686–87), and he delights again in finding in them "tokens of myself" (692). Having been forced to merge with the world beyond him, he discovers again that in himself he possesses the key to all that seemed in it secret, forbidden, or threatening; having become, in the desperate transports of the imagination, a self, an identity, he has, paradoxically, become more than just a person. The concluding gesture in this respite among the animals points beyond the personal and social identity that the might of his senses could provide him and that his intellect could not deny in his stance of imaginative self-assertion. Dismissing the splendid stallion with which he took his last turn (702–6),[17] he exclaims:

> I but use you a moment and then I resign you stallion
>   . . . . and do not need your paces, and outgallop
>   them,
> And myself as I stand or sit pass faster than you.
>
> (707–8)

He has begun to comprehend the sense in which his faith— only his fond wish at first!—that his experience is all experience and all experience is his experience is no more than sheer fact: "Now I know it is true what I guessed at" (709). This last proposition is the one he must go on now to test and prove.

Fifth Phase (707–963). This last discovery frees the "I" of a strictly individual identity, and filled with an exhilarating sense of liberation he plunges ahead into what is no longer just the single self's imaginative effort to secure his place in a personal world but a visionary realization of the generic self in the midst of all human experience. The fifth phase is an elaboration of the protagonist's announcement: "I am afoot with my vision" (714). Its substance is "the flight of the fluid and swallowing soul"

165

(799), "speeding through heaven and the stars" (790) and "below the soundings of plummets" (800). The "I" soars and expands, "dilates," until he feels that he has enclosed all that is and that whatever has happened happens to him. Earlier, when he absorbed into one sweeping glance all that came within his ken, he could declare:

> And these one and all tend inward to me, and I tend
> outward to them,
> And such as it is to be of these more or less I am.
> (324–25)

Now, after an even more masterful survey, he reaffirms and significantly intensifies his statement:

> These become mine and me every one, and they are
> but little,
> I become as much more as I like.
> (939–40)

Possibly because this vision performs for the generic self what the transformed protagonist's first long look around himself does for the personal self, this fifth phase of the narrative resembles the first in its basic structure and shape. Like the first phase, it is, fundamentally, one immense list of the events and sights, "identities," that make up his vision. It begins fast, with a catalogue proper (715–96), in which each line presents a new situation; then, in its midsection (797–932), it slows down and expands as each item in the list is worked out in ever greater detail into self-contained episodes; and at the end it speeds up again when almost "mastered" by his "fit" the "I" rushes into another crisis, which is followed by another self-absorbed and then defiantly extroverted conclusion (933–68).

In the catalogue—one of the longest Whitman ever wrote, an exuberant and overwhelming testimony to his all but inexhaustible gift of inventiveness and precision—the "I" describes where and how his flight is performed. Next, short episodes

(797–863) explain what he does: by becoming the protagonist in each scene and event that he conjures up he "take[s] part" (856) and thereby both discovers and proves that he can "become any presence or truth of humanity here" (941). His realization is not as boastful as it sounds. These "presences" are, after all, challenges for the generic self because they all bear for him the threat of mortality in that they might entrap him into their own limitations. The "I" must both assume and "survive" these "identities." As he soon finds out, that is not always easy.[18] The generic self thus shows himself capable of fuller identification than the personal self, which, in the corresponding situation, rarely dared to move beyond simply observing the life around him. Moreover, this time his "participation" puts the "I" to a very severe test indeed, for as the images of the catalogue gradually grow into longer episodes, human experience at large is soon narrowed down to suffering.

Strangely enough, although they perform their function in the poet's scheme very well, these episodes aiming to show human experience at its most tragic seldom rise above sentimentally conceived "human interest" stories in pulp magazines, where Whitman, in fact, seems to have "lived through" most, if not all, of them.[19] Perhaps he intended to demonstrate with his choice of material the potential for greatness in the commonplace; all the same, the banality of the conception tends to weaken the effect of the scenes he evokes.

It is, however, their growing obsession with morbidity that is truly distinctive about these episodes. One gruesome scene follows another: the drowned man (816–17), the shipwreck (818–27), "the mother condemned for a witch" (829), the "hounded slave" (830–39), the "mashed fireman" (843–50), then the scenes of war, "some fort's bombardment" (853–63), the massacre in Texas (869–89), and the naval battle (890–933). The poet is aware of the morbid turn his vision has taken, but at first he does not seem to be unduly disturbed by it. He even suggests that in these scenes of suffering and destruction, far from being threatened with defeat, he participates in the human triumph over death that heroism and martyrdom in blood can gain. "Agonies are one of my changes of garments" (840), he declares, evidently not a little proud that he can remain in control of the frightful vision even if he does not seem to be able to dispel it.

Soon, however, it becomes obvious that what detains him, possibly in spite of himself, in these disturbing sights is not the triumph but the price in anguish and pain at which it is bought. He may envy "the large hearts of heroes" (818) and the "disdain and calmness of martyrs" (828), but what preoccupies him is the "irretrievable" (932) in physical and mental suffering, which he expatiates upon inexhaustibly. As when he "guessed" that the grass was the "uncut hair of graves," the sight of failure and death seems to fascinate him to the point of obsession, and, in spite of his earlier self-confidence, his vision begins to run away with him. The episodes grow longer and more lurid until, in the last two, they become fully rounded narratives of pain and destruction.

Finally, as the poet is winding up the story of "the old-fashioned frigate-fight" with a particularly oppressive image (made more shattering by the rigorous objectivity of the presentation)—"The hiss of the surgeon's knife and the gnawing teeth of his saw, / The wheeze, the cluck, the swash of falling blood . . . . the short wild scream, the long dull tapering groan" (930–31)—the horror becomes more than he can bear. "O Christ! My fit is mastering me!" (933), he exclaims, his self-centered, self-absorbed voice of anguish all but erupting from beneath the prophetic-contemplative tone of his recital. The vision has turned into a nightmare again, and the poem regains its headlong speed as, no longer in control of his flight but swept along by it, the spellbound "I" enumerates in an unruly catalogue the sights that crowd in upon him (934–52). Image after image of pain, exclusion, shame, and humiliation draws him into a vortex of despair, and he is left in the end wholly rejected and deprived, a beggar:

POSSIBILITIES OF A PHASAL STRUCTURE

Askers embody themselves in me, and I am embodied in
    them,
I project my hat and sit shamefaced and beg.

(951–52)

A masterful combination of the alliteration of the sibilants with
the tongue-breaking sequence of terminal stops slows down and
breaks up the last line into three distinct parts, creating an extraordinary effect of emphatic finality.

All but crushed by his "fit," the "I" must cry out: "Somehow I have been stunned. Stand back!" (955). The vision of his
"dilation" is now only "dreams and gaping" (956), and it will not
just go away at his command. The old crisis is upon him again.
Death has caught up with him in his universal, generic self just
as it caught up with him in his personal self, and to the familiar
predicament he must respond in a familiar way. As in his personal scope he had to find the posture that could save him, he
must do so now in his generic scope, and he does. From the
welter of human experience he "remembers," just in time,
Christ's resurrection, which thus becomes his, and he can move
on in his enterprise. He leaves behind his nightmare of agonies,
which thus proves to have been, in the totality of human existence, but one "fraction" that by a "usual mistake" he "over-
stayed." Death is defeated and eluded again:

That I could look with a separate look on my own
    crucifixion and bloody crowning!
I remember . . . . I resume the overstaid fraction,
The grave of rock multiplies what has been confided
    to it . . . . or to any graves,
The corpses rise . . . . the gashes heal . . . . the
    fastenings roll away.

(960–63)

Sixth Phase (964–1308). This is the last major phase in the
narrative; it is also the longest and most complex. Its keynote is
in "Eleves" and "troop forth" (969, 964), its backbone being a

169

long sermon that the "I" "risen" from death and thus confirmed under his generic aspect addresses to the "average unending procession" (964)—all humanity (though, oddly enough, not to "you," his presumed listener). This sermon comprises, more or less precisely, lines 964–73, 984–1054, 1092–1132, and 1198–1261. The rest of the lines, interspersed with increasing frequency, are taken up by an unselfconscious meditation in which the "I" reflects upon what the orator does and says. Toward the end of the phase these two strains are gradually fused and, in the concluding lines, only the pedant would attempt to tell them apart.

In his recovery from his last and perhaps gravest crisis the limits of the "I" 's capacity for visionary self-realization have been reached and thus the same moment in the representation of the generic self that the naming of "Walt Whitman, an American, one of the roughs, a Kosmos," (499) marked in the representation of the personal self. The "I" has acquired the social identity commensurate with the visionary mode of his being, just as earlier the name signified the social form of the identity realizable in the senses.

Now as before, the limit to the "I" 's power is set, quite starkly, by death. For one who has managed to keep himself from utter dissolution in despair only by insisting that he "cocks [his] hat as [he] pleases, indoors or out," (397), to have become a beggar is indeed, as one critic remarked, "the last straw" and the very death of his self-assertion.[20] Again, his salvation must be, like that of his personal self, illogical, miraculous. Of course, the generic self must be saved by a generic miracle—the resurrection. The "I" overcomes his ultimate crisis by the ultimate triumph of making his personal myth of salvation coincide with all mankind's pre-eminent myth of salvation.

The strictly religious significance of the gesture, whether it can be construed as some manner of testimony for biblical Christianity, has been a matter of much debate, and, like Whitman's mysticism, it has become by now an unrewarding issue to argue, one way or the other. In this poem, at any rate, the religious references and especially the references to Christ seem consistently immanent, and the scene of resurrection itself, far from being the supreme infusion of supernatural grace into the destiny of all creation, emerges as the realization of the ultimate resources of the self and therefore as man's greatest achievement. After proclaiming his remembered resurrection, "The grave of the rock multiplies what has been confided to it" (962), the "I" hastens to add "or to any graves," and his "replenish-[ment] with supreme power" only makes him "one of an average unending procession" (964). Christ's humanity, not His divinity, is emphasized by the image of the poet "walking the old hills of Judea with the beautiful gentle god by [his] side" (789), and even when the "I" announces, somewhat unctuously, that he accepts "him that was crucified, knowing assuredly that he is divine" (1102), he is only announcing his equality with Christ, having already declared of himself that he is "divine [. . .] inside and out" (526): for him, "divine" means but mankind at its fullest, nature in its plenitude. Undoubtedly, he has a special fondness and preference for Christianity; witness, for example, the careful gradation in, "In my portfolio placing Manito loose, and Allah on a leaf, and the crucifix engraved" (1026), or the remark about his "replenished" troop: "The blossoms we wear in our hats are the growth of two thousand years" (968).[21] It seems, however, an exaggeration to claim—on the basis of this poem, in any event—that "the 'God in man' idea is the dominant theme in *Leaves of Grass*" and the whole work "Whitman's attempt to express the Christ idea once and for all." [22]

On the other hand, it is true that, as J. Albert Robbins has noted,[23] the poet assumes here an attitude of "bestowal" much more openly and consciously than before. Whether this attitude makes a Christian or even in the loosest sense a simply religious man out of him is a different matter. There is, in the passages in question, no more of a sense of self-sacrifice, which would make him essentially Christ-like, than there is a sense of a supernatural order of being, which would make the poem itself, in some form, religious. Besides, the "I" does not *do* any more "bestowing" than he did before. The gesture is but another expression of his original self-assertive transformation from one who needs help into one who provides it, as its moment's resemblance in situation, manner, and tone to his call to "undrape" (136–39) clearly shows:

> I am not to be denied . . . . I compel I
>   have stores plenty and to spare,
> And any thing I have I bestow.
>
> I do not ask who you are . . . . that is not important
>   to me,
> You can do nothing and be nothing but what I will infold
>   you.
>
> (995–98)

Now as then, he is intent primarily on his own needs, and his bestowal is merely an effort to find his way to community, to "fetch you whoever you are flush with myself" (1081).

Perhaps it is unwise ever to hold Whitman completely to his word. In any case, the "I" of this poem seems to be telling only the simple truth when he declares that "nothing, not God, is greater to one than one's-self is" (1264), that he does not "understand who there can be more wonderful than [himself]" (1275), and that "In the face of men and women [he sees] God, and in [his] own face in the glass" (1278). Meanwhile, the generic "I" 's resurrection and his subsequently assumed identity of teacher-redeemer reflect, in fact, the protagonist's familiar ambivalence in his relations with the world outside himself: he must seek it because he is relentlessly drawn in the opposite direction. To evade the finally excessive "centripetal" risks in the splendors and nightmares of his lone vision, he must say "we" and "our" for a few moments and respond to the "centrifugal" force of "trooping forth" as a part of a multitudinous "procession" (964 ff.), but soon enough the drift toward self-absorption begins anew as he ingenuously remarks, no longer "we" but "I," "that my steps drag behind yours yet go before them" (972).

The teacher-redeemer identity must be understood, then, in

this light. As noted above, this identity signifies for the generic "I" the social form that his self-realization could take. The next step of the protagonist, therefore, is much the same as after the naming of the personal "I" and leads to a similar result. The mind attempts to comprehend that which has been realized in the visionary imagination and eventually contains the inevitable failure of rational understanding by learning to submit to prophetic understanding. The subject of the entire phase is this final triumph of vision over intellection; the sermon itself tends to represent the doomed efforts of reason left to its own devices, whereas the meditation gradually expands intuition into prophecy.

This arrangement explains why the sermon, long as it is, says so little. The "I" begins by greeting briefly but rather grandiloquently his "Eleves" (964–73).[24] The first meditative interruption follows (974–83), in which the "I" wonders about the apparition of the teacher-redeemer much as he wondered earlier about the grass:

> The friendly and flowing savage . . . . Who is he? [. . .]
> Behavior lawless as snow-flakes . . . . words simple as
> grass . . . . uncombed head and laughter and naivete;
> (974, 980)

His comments foreshadow the listener's conclusion about the sermon: the chief argument of this orator is his presence:

> Slowstepping feet and the common features, and the
> common modes and emanations,
> They descend in new forms from the tips of his fingers,
> They are wafted with the odor of his body or breath
> . . . . they fly out of the glance of his eyes.
> (981–83)

The orator "I" then resumes his greeting, and if his extravagant promises can bring to mind a huckster hawking his wares, one cannot help admiring him all the same, for his "spiel" is superb—comic, unusual, invigorating, and irresistible:

POSSIBILITIES OF A PHASAL STRUCTURE

Earth! you seem to look for something at my hands,
Say old topknot! what do you want? [. . .]
You there, impotent, loose in the knees, open your
        scarfed chops till I blow grit within you [. . .]
On women fit for conception I start bigger and nimbler
        babes,
This day I am jetting the stuff of far more arrogant
        republics. [. . .]
I dilate you with tremendous breath . . . . I buoy you
        up;
Every room of the house do I fill with an* armed force
    . . . . lovers of me, bafflers of graves [. . .]
                     (986–87, 1001–2, 1009–10)

There he goes "merging" again! And his audience is "sold," although it is hard to tell what he is selling besides himself:

I have embraced you, and henceforth possess you to
        myself,
And when you rise in the morning you will find what I
        tell you is so.
                     (1013–14)

After introducing the orator through describing what he can do the sermon now goes on to explain his intentions. His purpose is no less than completing the work begun by his "predecessors": Jehovah, Kronos, Zeus, Hercules, Osiris, Isis, Brahma, and every other name and title by which supreme divine power has ever been known, the list being limited, presumably, only by the extent of Whitman's knowledge of the history of religions. The poet is "accepting the rough deific sketches to fill out better in [himself]," and, with his "centrifugal," "democratic" impulse at work, he also "bestows"—that is, recognizes—"them freely on each man or woman [he sees]" (1031).

Glimpses of the common man's "human face divine" follow to make good this claim. This short catalogue is one of Whitman's most magnificent passages (1031–49). Small wonder that

---

* In the 1855 text "am"—an obvious misprint (*Facs*, p. 45).

the orator disdains "special revelations" (1034): his ardent vision transforms into a revelation of glory each of these four moments of the humble, matter-of-fact pain of everyday existence. The firemen emerge from their work, like the three youths from the fiery furnace, "Their brawny limbs passing safe over charred laths . . . . their white foreheads whole and unhurt out of the flames" (1037), and the same biblical, mythical light shimmers around the other scenes as well, so that, though telling their common story, they yet seem parts of a timeless legend. Rushed along by his enthusiasm, the preacher finally exclaims in rapt admiration of his multifariously divine self but with a touch of humor in his voice, as if gently winking at his audience:

> The day getting ready for me when I shall do as much
> good as the best, and be as prodigious,
> Guessing when I am it will not tickle me much to
> receive puffs out of pulpit or print;
> By my life-lumps! becoming already a creator!
> Putting myself here and now to the ambushed womb of
> the shadows!
>
> (1046–49)

Amid all this exuberant abandon suddenly another voice is heard. Its speaker identifies the voice of the orator as his own, but by doing so he effectively disengages himself from it:

> . . . . A call in the midst of the crowd,[25]
> My own voice, orotund sweeping and final.
> (1050–51)

The preacher's call to his "children" (1052–54) is only a reminder that the sermon continues while this bemused and at first somewhat sardonic voice has its say. It begins with a remark on the oratorical performance itself, then reaffirms the impression created by the change of tone a few lines earlier: whoever this voice belongs to feels that he has little in common with the spectacle and its participants. His words are a direct repudiation of the preacher's address to his "household and intimates" (1053):

> Music rolls, but not from the organ . . . . folks
>   are around me, but they are no household of
>   mine.
>   (1057)

Then, while the orator "I" presumably goes on with his boisterous, self-confident assertions and assurances, this meditative "I" quietly reminds himself that the "old inexplicable query" (1061) is just as "inexplicable" as before. Though he may be "aware who they are" (1074), he is just as estranged from the city and its citizens (1070) as he was when he recognized them for "trippers and askers" (58) and learned to hear their "living and buried speech" and "howls restrained by decorum" (157). Let his teacher-redeemer self triumphantly "promulge" all the answers he may; his own words "are words of a questioning" (1082). His questions can at least keep him from confusing the accidental with the essential:

> The panorama of the sea . . . . but the sea itself?
> The well-taken photographs . . . . but your wife or
>   friend close and solid in your arms?
>   (1085–86)

The meditation eventually fades out with a last question, the most "inexplicable" of them all:

> Sermons and creeds and theology . . . . but the
>   human brain, and what is called reason, and
>   what is called love, and what is called life?
>   (1091)

The echo of this curious, short catalogue (1083–91) and especially of its conclusion provides an insistent, ironic counterpoint of restraint once the teacher-redeemer takes over again: he is delivering a "sermon" which announces his "creed," and, after another fairly long interruption by the meditative voice, explains his "theology" (1092–1134 and 1198–1261). His creed is based on "the greatest of faiths and the least of faiths" (1093) and his theology on the notion of the "perpetual journey" along "a plain, public road" (1198, 1206). To arrive at his faith, the orator reminds his audience, he had to fight off, like Jonah—or Ishmael?—the leviathan of doubt (1109–14):

> How the flukes splash!
> How they contort rapid as lightning, with spasms and
> > spouts of blood!
>
> > > (113–14)

Having become "already a creator!" (1048) he claims now to have also become a prophet of himself, "one of that centripetal and centrifugal gang" (1107), one of "the winders of the circuit of circuits" (1106): a sort of cosmic circuit rider, preaching his message of trust—which is but a bold restatement of the familiar self-encouragement of the protagonist of the poem:

> I do not know what is untried and afterward,
> But I know it is sure and alive and sufficient.
> > (1120–21)

The earlier impression is reconfirmed. For all his transformations, the "I" has still not been able to elude his old bane. He still fears death, and because he does—how those flukes are splashing still!—he "launch[es] all men and women forward with [him] into the unknown" (1134).

The meditative voice then interrupts the sermon again, as if continuing his series of questions: "The clock indicates the moment. . . . but what does eternity indicate?" (1135). This time, however, the speaker chooses to attempt an answer. He begins in his usual manner, guessing, but the panorama soon spreads out to cosmic proportions. In possibly the most expansive and enraptured lines, in this poem full of moments of rapture and "dilation," he unfolds his vision of the self as the focus and pur-

177

pose of all existence and of its life as an endless, soaring ascent (1135–98). "I am an acme of things accomplished, and I an encloser of things to be" (1148), he declares, and from this vantage point he surveys his past "below" him and his future "above" him:

> My feet strike an apex of the apices of the stairs,
> On every step bunches of ages, and larger bunches
>   between the steps,
> All below duly traveled—and still I mount and mount.
> (1149–51)

Life has the same phases in this vision as in those first hesitant glances that the transformed "I" cast at the infant in the cradle, the lovers on the hillside, and the suicide's corpse: birth, love, death. The generic self's "life," however, means the life of all mankind: the "I" looks back into "the vapor from the nostrils of death" (1153), the "lethargic mist" (1155) from which he emerged to be born, and attempts to peer ahead, beyond "the rim of the farther systems" (1183), into the mysterious "condition" his death will "promulge" (1180). What he is now is the product of all that has come to pass:

> All forces have been steadily employed to complete
>   and delight me,
> Now I stand on this spot with my soul.
> (1167–68)

The present of this generic "I," however, looks much the same as that of the personal "I." Every moment of it is filled with the tension of the forces that shook the "I" when he made love to the atmosphere, invited his soul, or contended with his "prurient provokers." It is "the procreant urge of the world," at once threatening and enticing, furtive and ubiquitous, a shame and a joy, and some of the poem's most poignant lines describe it:

POSSIBILITIES OF A PHASAL STRUCTURE

My lovers suffocate me! [. . .]
Calling my name from flowerbeds or vines or tangled
        underbrush, [. . .]
Lighting on every moment of my life,
Bussing my body with soft and balsamic busses,
Noiselessly passing handfuls out of their hearts and
        giving them to be mine.
                                                (1170, 1174, 1176–78)

Having momentarily reduced himself to his personal scale, the "I" is no more up to facing his terror now than before, and when he has to consider the next phase in the scheme he is recounting, he must shut his eyes and plunge through death, "the dark hush" (1181), with as few words as possible. Once amid "the far-sprinkled systems" (1182) again, he recovers his generic identity and with it his capacity for vision unencumbered by limitations of time and space. Though the imagery has the scope and speed of a galactic explosion, the lines resound with the same quiet certainty as in the "I" 's sudden comprehension that "the sun I see and the suns I cannot see are in their place" (351):

Wider and wider they spread, expanding and always
        expanding,
Outward and outward and forever outward. [. . .]
There is no stoppage, and never can be stoppage; [. . .]
A few quadrillions of eras, a few octillions of cubic
        leagues, do not hazard the span, or make it impatient,
They are but parts . . . . any thing is but a part.
                                                (1184–85, 1189, 1193–94)

Reason, obviously, can do little to prove or disprove such certainty, just as earlier it had nothing much to do with what his senses taught the "I": "I exist as I am" (413). The illogic, therefore, of the image concluding the meditative passage is not as confusing as it possibly should be: the soaring is "limitless," and "God will be there" (1197) at its end. It is an image of arrival, es-

179

sentially, and the "I" 's point seems to be that the eternal departure that he envisions is so glorious that it is itself an arrival. To
the question with which he interrupted the sermon—"what does
eternity indicate?"—he has thus found an answer that he can
"know" though cannot understand: "I have the best of time and
space—and [. . .] I was never measured, and never will be measured" (1198).

Then it is the orator's turn again (1199–1261). "I tramp a perpetual journey" (1199), he declares, and he urges his listeners to
understand that they may have been doing the same thing without quite knowing it. Awakening them to the fact is all that the
teacher-redeemer can actually do for them:

> Not I, not any one else can travel that road for you,
> You must travel it for yourself. [. . .]
>
> Long enough have you dreamed contemptible dreams,
> Now I wash the gum from your eyes, [. . .]
>
> It is you talking as much as myself . . . . I act as
>   the tongue of you,
> It was tied in your mouth . . . . in mine it begins
>   to be loosened.
>   (1207–08, 1225–26, 1244–45)

Here, then, is the first full formulation, and also one of the
strongest and most memorable, of what has come to be known
as the theme of "the open road." It will have an eventful life of
its own both in Whitman's poetry after 1855 and in virtually
countless critical discussions. One might note, however, that at
this point it is not yet "the heroic message of the American future" D. H. Lawrence could grow rhapsodic about.[26] It has a
well-discernible function within the world the poem has made
for itself, but as an ethical proposition or a moral program independent of the moment in which it appears and of the voice
that utters it little more sense can be made of it than of the
various earlier versions of the motif of leavetaking (e.g., the out-
doors episode in the opening lines or "My ties and ballasts leave

me" or "I resume the overstaid fraction," etc.) out of which the open-road theme has evolved.

With this passage about his "perpetual journey," the preacher has finally gotten around to revealing his message; by the time he finishes, the misgivings that the meditative voice has expressed about his performance and even presence will also have been dealt with. At first, however, his words may even sound ironic, for they obviously aim at "measuring" the "I," which the preacher's sceptical observer has just declared impossible to do. The two voices, nevertheless, have just begun to draw closer to each other.

The meditative voice has "split off" the main utterance at the beginning of this phase because the protagonist must somehow resist all purely social identity, be that even the loftiest, even that of a messiah. As seen earlier, the central tension in the "heartbeat" makes it inevitable that any one identity means death to the generic "I": though only in the community can the protagonist finally seek the stay against the desperate perils of his turning too far inward, he would wind up running the same risks of mental or spiritual destruction if he settled into any one social identity long enough to be marked by a role as a "simple separate person" in all his singleness and separateness. The meditative voice, therefore, has undercut and contradicted the orator as long as the latter could threaten to entrap the "I" in the function of teaching the unenlightened. To counter, so to speak, the orator's *stasis* in having one and only one social role and thus identity, the meditation has reaffirmed the protagonist's ceaseless *motion:* "There is no stoppage, and never can be stoppage" (1189).

Now, however, the meditative "I" can begin to believe his orator self, for the latter elaborates the same notion. He repeats, in effect, the other voice's account of the cosmic voyage in which one can "see ever so far . . . . there is limitless space outside of that, / Count ever so much . . . there is limitless time around that" (1195–96); only he recasts it in an "earthbound," commonplace setting and rephrases it as a social function:

181

"Shoulder your duds, and I will mine, and let us hasten forth; / Wonderful cities and free nations we shall fetch as we go" (1212–13). In this way does the generic "I" discover the compromise by which he can enact a role that gives him a social identity while protecting the sovereign power of the self over his existence. Although the teacher-redeemer, by definition, has an exclusively social identity, what he teaches is the constant severing of all ties that could make for a community. The "perpetual journey" is, in fact, a perpetual going away. It is the same endless and profoundly lonely departure that the meditative voice has suggested is the only fit arrival for the "I":

> My right hand points to landscapes of continents,
>   and a plain public road.
> [. . .] When we become the enfolders of these orbs
>   and the pleasure and knowledge of every thing
>   in them, shall we be filled and satisfied then?
> And my spirit said No, we level that lift to pass and
>   continue beyond.
> [. . .] As soon as you sleep and renew yourself in
>   sweet clothes I will certainly kiss you with
>   my goodbye kiss and open the gate for your egress
>   hence. [. . .]
> Now I will you to be a bold swimmer,
> To jump off in the midst of the sea.
>   (1206, 1218–19, 1224, 1229–30)

Along the way to this conclusion the preacher's manner has gradually changed from reasoned rhetorical persuasion to visionary assertion. The invitation itself to the "perpetual journey" is rather carefully "staged" to give it a thoroughly matter-of-fact, realistic and rational air: "My signs are a rain-proof coat and good shoes and a staff cut from the woods" (1200). When the time comes, however, for the preacher to announce the purpose and destination of the journey, he seems to become impatient with reason, for he entrusts his sermon, instead, to the strength of his intuitive conviction that what he urges his listeners to believe is true even if he cannot explain or understand

why. What proves him right is his vision of the fulfillment, harmony, "satisfaction," in the community of those who live by
"resuming" his "lesson." He conjures up this world with the
same prophetic power through which the meditation has en-
compassed the "few quadrillions of eras" (1193) and more that
make up the cosmic version of the "perpetual journey":

> If you would understand me go to the heights or
>   water-shore,
> The nearest gnat is an explanation and a drop or
>   the motion of waves a key,
> The maul the oar and the handsaw second my words.
>   (1248–50)

During all this time the two voices, meditative and messianic, have been converging, and in the end they coincide. The
sermon begun by a self-conscious orator is concluded by the unselfconscious protagonist, who is talking, again, mainly to himself. In the concluding segment of this phase (1262–1308), which
has already been discussed in detail in an earlier chapter, the
protagonist is back, in effect, where he began. He is assigning
the questions that agitate him to a make-believe audience so
that he can reassure himself through reassuring them, giving
them the answers he needs to hear himself. What happened earlier happens again. As he throws out question after question to
lead himself to a glimpse of the unendurable, he is drawn into a
barely articulate, self-absorbed spell, which he can break only by
wrenching himself away, toward his "brothers and sisters"
(1306), the Other.[27] He is going through the same all but spontaneously evolved process by which he has learned to keep himself mentally alive and to keep his fear of death at bay.

Seventh Phase (1309–36). Whitman not so much argues as
orchestrates a conclusion to his poem, and an astonishingly effective conclusion it is, too. It leaves no doubt in the reader's
mind that there is no more to say and that the poem has been
brought to an end, not just left off, although nothing that came
before has prepared him for this ending. Neither the "heart-

beat" nor the story of the transformed "I" 's explorations of its powers provides a thematic structure in which the conclusion must come where it does and can be anticipated; the former is a kind of never-ending, vicious circle, and the latter, as it has just been shown, is a *perpetual* journey. The individual phases have developed a characteristic and predictable "curve" from self-control to self-absorption, but there is no reason why, theoretically, their sequence could not be continued indefinitely. When, for example, in the preceding phase the protagonist begins his meditative address to the corpse (1285 ff.), his gradual sinking into a self-absorbed exacerbation of his fears no longer comes as a surprise because he has done it before, and one has learned to expect afterwards the precipitate, near-hysterical flight back to the audience, too, which will signal the completion of yet another major cycle of the "heartbeat." There is, however, no indication at all that the possibilities of repeating the same cycle have been exhausted; the series, in fact, could go on endlessly.

"One of the most obvious ways," writes Barbara Herrnstein Smith, "in which a poem can indicate its own conclusion thematically is simply to say so." [28] Whitman does just that. The announcement that,

> The past and present wilt . . . . I have filled
> them and emptied them,
> And proceed to fill my next fold of the future [,]
> (1309–10)

has the air of "fresh woods, and pastures new" about it. Then the protagonist reveals that he is to disappear soon: he will be enwrapped in invisibility by darkness, he will go away to keep an appointment he would not miss, and he will dissolve into the elements. Each successive statement is begun before the preceding one is finished, the whole developing in a fugue-like fashion into the cumulative statement: the day is going—I must go—I am gone.

First, he declares that the day is done; it is time for him to "snuff the sidle of evening" (1312). He begins with an ironic evening prayer of sorts. If the "Listener up there" has anything "to confide" to him (1311) or wants to "look in [his] face" (1312), he does not mind, provided no time is wasted, but, for his part, he has nothing in particular either to say or to ask. The night which is to fall is no "mad naked summer night" (438) but the onset of darkness, something like the "dark hush" (1181) mentioned in the preceding section: "The last scud of day holds back for me, / [. . .] It coaxes me to the vapor and the dusk" (1324, 1326). Like the daylight, the "I," too, wants to leave:

> [. . .] I stay only a minute longer, [. . .]
> Will you speak before I am gone: Will you prove
>   already too late?
>
> The spotted hawk swoops by and accuses me . . . . he
>   complains of my gab and my loitering.
>   (1313, 1320–21)

Not only must he go; he must go *out* ("I wait on the door-slab. / [. . .] Who wishes to walk with me?" [1317, 1319]), and when he goes, he goes both *up* ("I sound my barbaric yawp over the roofs of the world. / [. . .] I shake my white locks at the run-away sun" [1323, 1327]) and *down* ("If you want me again look for me under your bootsoles" [1330]). In his going "soul" ("I depart as air" [1327]) and "grass" ("I bequeath myself to the dirt to grow from the grass I love" [1329]) are finally reconciled as complementary aspects of the same motion. And hardly has the notion of the "I" 's going away sunk in when one realizes that he is already gone: he says his farewell, makes his last "bequest," and, ever the one who has plenty of help to offer but will never acknowledge that he might use some himself, offers his audience a last reassurance: don't worry, "I'll stop some where waiting for you" (1336).

In the last four lines the verse settles into a simple pattern of two strongly marked, brief half-lines which combine with the syntax—short declarative and imperative sentences—to slow down the pace and then bring it to a halt with calm authority.

The reader's—listener's—final impression is made up of muted, elegiac emotions and a sense of the complete appropriateness and inevitability of the moment.

The finality of this ending is not that of the silence after a story has been told; it is the finality of parting. The listener cannot tell for certain what story he has heard or whether what he has heard was a story at all, but he knows that he has met someone whom it has been good to know and impossible not to heed. After all, no one who has listened to the poet and watched his performance this long can fail to have yielded him at least a degree of that "personal affection" which Whitman was to describe in 1876 as "endless streams of living, pulsating love and friendship, directly from [my present and future readers] to myself" and which he always "yearned" for and held indispensable for the realization of his poems.[29] What marks the poem finished now is the reader's sense of loss over his disappearance and the corresponding hope of meeting him again.

The last six lines encourage this hope even as they aid substantially in bringing the poem to a convincing close. Though they no longer ask, "Who wishes to walk with me?" (1319), they urge the listener to follow, one way or the other: possibly by striding down the "open road" or beyond the "dark hush," possibly by becoming a disciple and attaining "an esthetic-religious experience of his own," [30] possibly by learning to face down his own nightmares, and possibly also by looking across the page, at the next "leaf of grass." Coming at the end of the first and crucial poem, these last injunctions, by their very position, provide a smooth enough transition, in this first edition, to the rest of the poems. No one will ever know for certain, of course, but this practical function of the last lines is conceivably not quite accidental.

There is another source of a marked transitional effect, at the very end, and that is most likely an accident, though not the less effective for that: no punctuation mark of any kind concludes the last line. The omission is probably a typographical error, yet it does not weaken the total effect of the passage at all. On the contrary, the way it allows the last words to reverberate and then die slowly away, so that they all but beckon the listener on, has seemed so appropriate to some readers that they have speculated very persuasively that Whitman omitted the punctuation mark on purpose "to reinforce the idea that until the reader catches up with the poet, the poem is incomplete." [31] Whether inadvertently or not, the omission also helps to dispose of the problem of "[providing] closure without resolution," which Barbara Herrnstein Smith has shown to be characteristic of "associative structure," [32] an accurate enough label for the structure of Whitman's poem.

In fact, since the appearance of Professor Smith's admirable study "of how poems end" these concluding lines of Whitman's poem have seemed, at least to the present writer, much less mysterious and elusive in their effect than before, though, of course, every bit as convincing and, indeed, as Chase would have it, "incomparable." [33] Virtually every device that Whitman employs to allow his poem to "know that it is finished" [34] fits the description of one item or another on her list of "special terminal features" through which "closure must be secured . . . when"—as in Whitman's poem—" a principle of sequential structure does not imply its own termination point." [35] The most important among these are two kinds of "closural allusions." The first group includes "words and phrases . . . which, while they do not refer to the conclusion of the poem itself, nevertheless signify termination or stability." Whitman's lines have "through" (as an adjective), "filled," "emptied," "done," "gone," "last," and "stop." The other group consists of

references not to termination, finality, repose, or stability as such, but to events which, in our nonliterary experiences, are associated with these qualities—events such as sleep, death, dusk, night, autumn, winter, descents, falls, leave-takings and home-comings. [36]

As seen earlier, the entire conclusion of Whitman's poem is built around the dusk and the night and two successive phases of leave-taking. Another observation in *Poetic Closure* goes a long way to explain why one accepts without surprise or protest the "I" 's departure, even though nothing has prepared it.

> In general, [Professor Smith writes] it appears that the conditions which contribute to the sense of truth are also those which create closure. . . . Certain utterances which neither conform to our expectations nor confirm our experiences (verbal or otherwise) may nevertheless have the ring of truth because of a quality that we might call the *tone of authority*.

Whitman's lines certainly seem to fit this description, and one gets some further suggestions why: "The *unqualified* assertion . . . conveys a sense of the speaker's security, conviction, and authority." [37] Whitman, of course, does not need to go next door for unqualified assertions throughout the entire poem and, indeed, volume; this much, however, is clear: the assertions in the last sixteen lines are at least as unqualified as in the rest, and that is what, presumably, makes them "ring true." The "closural effect" of the last six lines' settling into a regularity of their own making is also clarified somewhat:

> One of the most common and substantial sources of closural effects in poetry is the terminal modification of a formal principle. . . . In Whitman's poetry, where lines are characteristically quite long, terminal modification frequently takes the form of an unusually short final line.[38]

The poem thus finishes on an extraordinarily strong note. The ending is convincing and "final," even if it does not follow from any thematic necessity. Unless . . . One cannot conclude the discussion of these lines without mentioning a speculative possibility. The protagonist's words after he has declared that he is "to grow from the grass I love" (1329) would not be inappropriate if spoken from "beyond the grave." The listener is assumed, then, to be in the same position in which the protagonist was before, trying to "translate the hints" (112) of the grass, and the "I," instead of "guessing," as he did earlier, at the grass that "transpired" from the dead, is now one of the dead himself,

188

talking through—"growing from"—the grass "transpiring" from him. His message, however, is not what, judged by his reaction, he himself must have "heard" the grass reveal but what he *wanted* to hear: he is "alive and well somewhere" (116), and he is waiting for his listener-disciple to catch up, fortifying him meanwhile with his reassuring disclosure.

According to this reading, the protagonist concludes his performance with the most dazzling of his feats: after exploring a wide range of possibilities of being to defy and thus contain his terror of annihilation, he now confronts death itself and explores the possibility of being dead by assuming the identity of the dead. It would make for a neater interpretation if this reading could be convincingly proven, for then thematic necessity could head the list of features bringing the poem to such an effective and memorable close: the indomitable young hero finally corners the evil monster in its lair and slays it.

There is enough that is plausible in this reading to make it worth mentioning; there are, however, some major flaws in it, the most serious of them being the discrepancy between the dead "I" 's message and what he must have "heard" the "uttering tongues" say earlier. These reassurances could not have produced the crisis which is the motive force of the poem. Also, the different directions in which body and soul "depart" do not impair the integrity of the "I" 's self if he only "disappears"; if he "dies," however, consigning the body to the "dirt" while releasing the soul "to the vapor and the dusk" would contradict his first and foremost, cardinal tenet of faith that body and soul are one. He can no more afford to be trapped by the identity of being dead than by all the other identities he has tried out. The echoes and associations of the central crisis in the last six lines cannot add up, therefore, to a thematic continuity between the two scenes, although by alluding to death (a "terminal event" if ever there was one) they do function very forcefully as motifs of closure.[39]

Wherever the listener will begin looking for the poet, whether under his bootsoles or on the next page, he is most likely in the end to remember his disappearance by the image of the "spotted hawk swoop[ing] by" and calling to him (1321). The image provides Whitman with an occasion to end his poem with the same reminder with which he began it: his words are but a translation of the "untranslatable" (1322). The essence of what he has had to say is in "the sound of the belched words of [his] voice" (17), not in the words themselves; it is in the "barbaric yawp" he "sound[s] over the roofs of the world" (1323), not in its articulation. The degree to which his listener is persuaded that, Whitman's claim notwithstanding, the elusive substance has become apprehensible through the form it has acquired in the poem is the degree of the success of the poem itself in the terms of I. A. Richards' observation that "a poem begins by creating a linguistic problem whose solution by language will be the attainment of its end." [40] The "linguistic problem" or challenge in this case has been nothing more or less than putting the "untranslatable" into words. Finally, the distinction Whitman makes between his words and what they struggle to encompass serves as a powerful clue, both in itself and in the way it frames the entire poem, for first resolving then interpreting the paradox of the poem's structure, which rests on the "heartbeat" yet discloses a plausible phasal arrangement of its parts.

III

At first glance, the foregoing survey may well appear an elaborate exercise in futility, for it has obviously led to the same conclusion that others, like Gay Wilson Allen, Malcolm Cowley, or Richard Chase, have reached by briefer and less laborious routes: there is no consecutive narrative thread and no dramatic development in the poem.[41] What there is *instead*, however, is another story, one that does not seem to have been told yet, and to vouch for it the trek which had to pass through some tedious patches of the familiar was the only safe course to take.

According to the assumptions which allowed, provisionally, for a narrative context, the poem, indeed, seems to end where it began. The forces mounting the threat against the "I" 's integrity and thus precipitating his metamorphosis have been neither destroyed nor defeated; they are being merely held in check. The poem has not told the story of a dramatic struggle to challenge and to overcome them because no such struggle has occurred and therefore there is no such story to tell. Instead, the poem has articulated, for the benefit of speaker and listener alike, the manner in which the threat has been contained.

The "I" seems to wind up where he started not because he has gone around in a circle but because, in a sense, he has never budged. The context and dimensions are different in each section, but the story is always the same. The initially self-possessed "I" gradually gives in to his centripetal "hankering" and allows it to lead him, by associations he cannot control, to the edge of a world composed entirely of himself. Even when his path becomes more desolate the closer he gets, lined as it is with visions of frustration, suffering, or death, he rushes toward the moment of attaining that world as if he expected ultimate gratification and fulfillment there, and even when he is swept along by joyful ecstasies he manages to stop half a step short of it as the horror of the annihilation which actual attainment would bring suddenly stares him full in the face. In each phase the protagonist begins calmly and finishes overcome, mostly by fear, sometimes by awe; he begins in robust self-confidence, firmly in control of all that comes into view, and finishes wholly at the mercy of his terrors—or of the ecstasies which will inevitably disclose them. Only a squarely centrifugal gesture can save him then: at the last moment he reaches out toward the listener.

This thematic reading, although established without direct reliance on the "heartbeat," is fully borne out by the rhetorical modulations, which in their broader, general movement follow the same pattern throughout each phase. They begin rather close to the extrovert extreme, never further away from direct dialogue than the cautious, restrained notes of the "contemplative" mode, and from there they gradually draw toward the introverted "spontaneous" manner of self-absorption. At the start the "I" never raises his voice; at the end he is always shouting—or whispering, as the case may be—in frantic excitement. A cursory glance at the transitions from phase to phase will show how the pattern operates.

The first phase ends in a "spontaneous," introverted, ecstatic whisper (347–52), which is followed by the completely centrifugal lines of the "dialogue" that opens the next phase (353–54).

The second phase ends with the "spontaneous" lines that the "I" has been led to by his efforts to define metaphorically what he is doing (377–80).[42] They are halting, undecided lines and are probably followed by a longish pause, for they have led the speaker very near his "forbidden country," and the next line should thrust him into it. Self-conscious rhetorical questions follow instead (381, 383), striking up a "dialogue" with the listener: the "I" is safe again, and another phase, the third, is begun.

The third phase ends as the "I," overcome with excitement, runs out of breath and interrupts his enraptured paean to the "spread" of his body (530–44), which by then has passed far beyond his anatomy to incorporate, literally, the sun, the air, the landscape, and the speaker's past. Two rather embarrassed, humorous lines follow (545–46), then a full pause, then "contemplative" lines detailing what he, for a change, cannot do (547 ff.). Though the shift toward the "other" is not as pronounced as the shift away from the "self," the pattern is clearly the same as in the previous phases.

The transition from the fourth to the fifth phase unquestionably strains the argument presented here but does not quite break it. The protagonist, wrought up by the disturbing transports that make up most of the fourth phase, has tried to take refuge among the animals and in a wistfully "contemplative" manner (684–701), but the gesture does not prove strong enough to pull him entirely free of his centripetal whirling, and he is soon "merging" again, "spontaneously," with the "gigantic beauty of a stallion" (702): "His nostrils dilate. . . . my heels embrace him. . . . his well built limbs tremble with pleasure.

192

. . . we speed around and return" (706). The next lines do not emerge from this ecstatic self-absorption beyond the "histronic" (707–8) and then, for a brief moment, the "contemplative" (709–11) mode; then they soar away again, with a protagonist entranced by another vision of a world that has become but an extension of himself (712–14). Only in the long catalogue which follows does he recover a less self-engrossed, firmly "contemplative" attitude, slowing down, so to speak, from "skirt[ing] sierras" (713) in his flight to "tread[ing] day and night such roads" (796). By this time, of course, another phase has begun; the transition occurs in those few lines in which the "I" momentarily breaks the spell he is under (707–11), even if it is only a quick glance cast at himself, as it were, from the outside. Admittedly, the rhetorical parallel to the thematic shift here is at best vestigial; it nevertheless supports the present argument by being there at all.

As discussed in another part of this chapter, the fifth phase ends with another scene of absolute self-involvement. The "I," who is usually driven to ecstasy which suddenly changes into horror, is now reduced by an obsessive series of nightmare-images to sheer terror, in which, helpless and "spontaneous," he still discerns the ecstatic dimension (951–54). He then rapidly fights his way back to the "other" with a few "histrionic" lines (955–57), followed by excited prophecy and, finally, the complete turn outward: "We walk the roads [. . .]" (965).

In the last transition, as seen earlier, the thematic shift coincides fully with the characteristic modulation of the "heartbeat" from barely coherent, all-oblivious "spontaneity" (1299–1306) to lines of "dialogue" meant to reassure the speaker by reassuring others.

The rhetorical modulations thus point toward the same conclusion that the thematic analysis has produced: from first to last the poem enacts the same crucial moment of crisis and recovery, the several phases of the "narrative" being but refractions of that one moment in various contexts. What is one to make, then, of the unmistakable indications of a phasal progression throughout the poem? Whitman's protagonist himself speaks on occasion as if he were involved in a timebound series of events, as when he announces, "I think I will do nothing for a long time but listen" (584), or when he exclaims, "Now I know it is true what I guessed at" (709), although such remarks are altogether too rare and irregular even to suggest, let alone define, any co-herent time scheme in the work. There is, however, evident order of a progressive kind in the way the focus changes from phase to major phase as they have been established in this chap-ter. The "I" perceives through his senses in the first three phases, through his intellect in the fourth, and through his imag-ination in the fifth and sixth. Both his senses and his imagination lead him first to direct, then briefly to metaphoric, and finally to social perceptions (in the first phase and part of the fifth [715–932], in the second phase and part of the fifth [933–63], and in the third and sixth phases, respectively). Curiously, perhaps the most emphatic shift in perspective occurs between phases four and five, where the rhetorical transition proves the least perceptible. Not only do the passages of the imagination begin here, here is where the generic "I" takes over from the personal "I," and here is where the poem begins to range as freely through time as it did over space before.

Needless to say, these changes do not mean that no refer-ence to time occurred before this point or that in no subsequent line can one possibly hear the personal "I," just as the typical pattern of the rhetorical transition between phases does not exclude the appearance of an occasional "spontaneous" passage or even a line or two of "dialogue" within a phase. There just are no such clear-cut lines of demarcation in the poem. One can, however, establish with reasonable accuracy the tone, point of view, attitude, theme, or concern prevalent in any given pas-sage. On this basis the conclusion is inescapable that, even though there is no narrative continuity in the poem, there is quite plainly some sort of phasal development in it. The shifts in focus reflect more or less the same progression that has been described as the poet's "movement away from the self and toward the universe or cosmos" [43] or the poem's expansion of "lyrical impressionism into epic design." [44] The statement moves from the individual toward the generic, from the palpable toward the abstract, from the One toward the Many, from self toward community, and thus, in the broadest sense, from the "I" which is the poem's first word to the "you" which is its last.

IV

Two distinct structures can be thus recognized in the poem, one founded in recurrence and one founded in change. The two should be incompatible, yet they are not, and the catalogues in the poem can help to explain why, for they display the same structural paradox in a more conspicuous and also simpler way. Each major catalogue in the poem operates through a sort of dichotomy, like some religious formulas such as litanies or blessings,[45] implying rather than excluding that which it has not listed. What have been named serve as "committees," as the Preface has it (vi), for all that have not. The seemingly endless repetition of a given syntactic and rhetorical pattern induces, like an incantation, a mode of perception which persists beyond the list itself and adumbrates a vision of wholeness.[46] As Santayana noted more than sixty years ago, with this "mass of images without structure" Whitman "fills us with a sense of the individuality and the universality of what he describes—it is a drop in itself yet a drop in the ocean." [47] Santayana's verdict on Whitman's entire achievement may have been too harsh, but few people could quarrel with this observation. It is generally agreed that "the total effect of [the] catalogues is not complexity but simplicity" [48] so that "each catalogue results in a single image because the reader has been forced to condense"; [49] most readers, however, sense in the catalogues some degree of progressive organization as well, and they are hard put to reconcile the two.

The difficulty can be cleared up by admitting a distinction

between what the catalogue strives to express and the effect of that expression on the audience. The two are not the same even if they happen to coincide, for the "heightened sense not only of reality but of the variety and abundance of its manifestations" [50] is an experience of a different shape for the poem and for the reader. The subject of the catalogue is a perception in a single instant; the reader's experience consists of a perception gradually attained.

This distinction seems implicit in parataxis itself, especially in its transcendental variety. Poetry, like music, can be perceived only in time, but—just as painting can represent three-dimensional subjects on a two-dimensional surface—it can, and of course often does, represent subjects in which the temporal dimension is suspended, discontinuous, or simply lacking. Among the various means that can contrive the particular kind of willing suspension of disbelief by which the reader will credit his illusion of no duration even while he knows that what he confronts takes time to read, paratactic structures, in which "coherence . . . will not be dependent on the sequential [i.e., logical, temporal, or otherwise serial] arrangement of . . . major thematic units," [51] are by definition pre-eminently suited to deal with temporal discontinuity, that is, with simultaneous or instantaneous events.

Parataxis does not represent duration even when its component parts do. In the paratactic lists in which Swift describes a city shower, Chaucer describes the chase after the fox, and Whitman describes the long "committee" of all that "tend inward to [him]" (324; 257–325), each item consists of a distinct action. These snippets of time are not coordinated by any time scheme, thematic plan, or any other principle of serial organization. Nevertheless, "the desire to present details, individuals, parts as parts of a whole," [52] the gravitation toward a single core of meaning, or, as John B. Mason has it, "a single image," [53] which has been shown time and again in Whitman's catalogues, is unmistakable in all three lists, in Chaucer's and Swift's lines as well as in Whitman's. Their coherence is in the artist's synoptic view of all the parts that make up the scene. Each passage, therefore, represents the instant in which the items constituting it are perceived to coincide. When the items in the catalogue have no definite temporal dimension of their own, as in the conclusion of the "oldfashioned frigate-fight" (890; 919–32) or in the beginning of the meditative commentary on the orator's sermon, their coincidence is even plainer.

For Swift or Chaucer, the paratactic list was only an occasional technique; for Emerson, however, and for those whom he had "brought to a boil," it reflected, as a number of scholars have shown, a favorite mode of vision, their perception of "unity in diversity." In Whitman's catalogues, as Lawrence Buell has put it, "the method of the song mirrors the complex unity of the singer." [54] The graceful phrase sums up neatly the prevalent critical view of the catalogues; the present argument seeks not to dispute but merely to reinforce this view by clarifying and perhaps slightly adjusting its perspectives.

All that this entire adjustment amounts to, after all, is some extra emphasis on the temporal aspect of the transcendentalist microcosm, which is the ultimate subject of Whitman's catalogues. The matter is not one of replacing spatial terms with temporal ones but of conceiving and speaking of "unity in diversity" in its temporal as well as spatial dimensions. [55] "Whitman's usual poetic method" is accurately described "as an analytic spreadout, an itemized unpacking, of certain large, parallel categories," [56] but one must add that the categories are parallel in time as well as in space, that is, they are parallel and simultaneous. Whitman's sense of "the principle of microcosm," like Emerson's, indeed consists "in the disclosure of identity in variety, that is, in the concurrence, the *running together*, of several distinct images or ideas," [57] but one must add that the identity is temporal as well as spatial, not just concurrence but also coincidence.

That the catalogues have been usually analyzed in predominantly spatial terms is perhaps only a manifestation of the phenomenon J. Hillis Miller has noted:

POSSIBILITIES OF A PHASAL STRUCTURE

> Our language and our imaginations are strongly spatialized, rich in
> spatial terms and poor in temporal terms. It is much easier to talk
> about a work of literature as if were a spatial mosaic than to do jus-
> tice to its temporality.[58]

There also seems to be another, more direct reason: virtually all
discussions of the catalogue deal with the process by which the
reader grasps its purport, be that process "reciprocating," "con-
densing a single image," allowing oneself "to get caught up," [59]
or whatever else. They address themselves to the reader's experience, and that is, of course, always subjective and involves duration; it cannot be simultaneous or instantaneous. It is invariably described by way of some linear structure because it consists
of a linear, gradual process of perception. The various reasoned
accounts of subjective responses to the catalogues are always
fascinating and often enlightening, "valid," in a way, even at
their most wildly contradictory. As a matter of fact, what is perhaps most remarkable about them is not that they all disagree
but that they all arrive at essentially the same conclusion, and
not that they chart a different course but that all of these are
highly plausible and convincing, even those that point in diamet-
rically opposed directions. Nor can there be much doubt that
some of the familiar landmarks along the various routes of comprehension have been "designedly dropt," not to mark out any
specific path for the reader, but to help him to hack one out for
himself. With all due respect to both texts, the practice is as old
as biblical catalogues.

On a number of occasions the reader's timebound, subjective experience of responding to the catalogue has been mistaken for the poet's experience of conceiving it, and that experience, in turn, for its own subject. Whitman himself is not quite
free of blame in this compound confusion, since he had called,
time and again, as Thomas J. Rountree has shown, for "reciproc-
ity between the poet and the reader," which his "indirection"
was to promote.[60] Those who confuse their own experience with
the poet's take his command, "What I assume you shall as-

sume," a touch too literally and wind up telling *him* the same thing. The often elaborate and ingenious structures of the reader's perception are then ascribed to the catalogue itself, disturbing and undercutting the very sense of unity in time and space which they have led to; in the end the reader is forced to distrust either the order through which he perceives the catalogue or his sense of its impact.

The elementary distinction, therefore, that "a poem can be known only through individual experiences, but it is not identical with such an individual experience" [61] cannot be discarded even if the poet himself urges the reader to do so. Instead of choosing between the two types of perception in the catalogue and making the one chosen stand for both, one should admit the distinction between them and accept each in its own sphere of validity. The critic in this case is entitled to have his cake and eat it, too. The catalogues present a structural paradox only if the "unstructured" oneness which is their subject is allowed to be confused with the reader's structured perception of it.

V

The argument about the catalogues can be extended now to the entire poem itself, which is, after all, a grand catalogue of versions of the protagonist's crisis and recovery. Instead of an identical pattern of syntax, grammar, or rhetoric, its units—the major phases—are defined by the "heartbeat." Just as in a transcendentalist catalogue each line ultimately implies all the others, each phase of the poem implies all the others; theoretically, they can also be changed around, and any one or two of them can even be left out without any structural damage to the whole, as in all paratactic schemes. Naturally, the present arrangement of the parts is far too familiar to allow a realistic test of this last proposition; besides, even if such a test were possible, excisions would undoubtedly modify the total impact, paratactic structure notwithstanding. [62] Still, as the study of its conclusion has shown, there is nothing in the poem to impose a strong sequential structure on it. "It has passages which present dramatic scenes, but it has no plot; such narration as it has is episodic, and this only in a few spots," Allen has observed.[63] There is, one might repeat, no consistent time scheme, no sustained, gradually evolving argument, and no single dominant thesis or "message" in it, either. Its coherence, like that of the catalogues, rests, as V. K. Chari has explained, in "a unity of impression and gesture rather than a contrived unity of structure." [64] Finally, the subject of the poem, like that of the catalogues, is a perception which is, as Mason has shown, "perpetual and instantaneous," [65] whereas the reader's perception of it is necessarily an affair of duration.

Because of these fundamental analogies between the catalogues and the poem itself, the same distinction by which the apparent confusion of the structures discernible in the catalogues could be sorted out will also resolve, at long last, the problem which is this chapter's main concern. The ordering function of the "heartbeat" can be reconciled with the potential for phasal or sequential order in the poem without forcing either into the Procrustean bed of the other, because the two continuities represent two distinct experiences. The sequential structure reflects the growing understanding of the listener, and the "heartbeat" is the form through which the experience which is the poem's subject is expressed.

This latter is the synoptic perception of the story of the "I" 's renewal in all its versions. The catalogue-like gravitation toward oneness, a single center of meaning, is evident, however, not only in the poem as a whole but in each individual phase as well. Within each phase the stages of the protagonist's transformation follow according to a more or less fixed sequence but not at measurable intervals of duration except in the sense that, as the angel Raphael explained it to Adam,

> Time, though in Eternitie, appli'd
> To motion, measures all things durable
> By present, past, and future.[66]

The "I" 's story, therefore, is best understood as a single, undivided and indivisible event, occurring outside of real time and infinitely fast, that is, instantaneously. One may conclude, then, that the subject of the poem is not the process whereby the protagonist has attained the perception that saves him but the moment of the perception itself, the instant that reconciles the forces whose strife constitutes his being into a configuration that allows him a mastery as spectacular as it is precarious over them.

Thus, in one sense, what John B. Mason has established about the catalogues holds true of the entire poem: it represents "processes which occur outside of time and space." [67] Put another way, the poem, theoretically, demands that the reader respond to all its parts at one and the same time. One may have the illusion, perhaps, of responding that way to short lyric poems; however, to adapt a comment by J. Hillis Miller to Whitman's poem, "a simultaneous possession by the reader of all the words and images" in its 1,336 lines "may be posited as an ideal, but such an ideal manifestly cannot be realized." Instead, the reader perceives the poem as "words follow[ing] one another in time and establish[ing] in their sequence a temporal rhythm of connections and relationships." [68] This response is the subject articulated by the poem's phasal structure, which every reader sees but no two readers ever find the same.

Like the similar accounts of the catalogues, almost every single version of the phasal structure is all but unassailable. Given their premises, all of them are logical, perceptive, and most enlightening, contradict each other as they may—and, being by definition subjective, they of course often do. Beyond their individual merits, however, these interpretations are highly significant because, taken together in all their variety, they represent the manner and degree of the poem's assimilation into the culture of human community whose complex challenge provoked it and whose approving protection it sought. Most readers are not content just to read the poem but insist on distilling the "lesson" it must be teaching. Implicit in every phasal account is the effort not only to integrate the poem into a shared frame of rational reference but also to establish the ethical basis of the human triumph embodied in it.

This, of course, is just the response that Whitman himself

always called for. The evidence has often and very convincingly been presented [69] that he meant every word of it when he declared that "no one will get at my verses who insists upon viewing them as a literary performance." [70] The "greatest poet's" didactic ambition is one of the keynotes in the Preface to the first edition, and the listener is periodically reminded of it through the rest of the volume. The command that opens the first poem—"What I assume you shall assume" (2)—is repeated at its end:

> Failing to fetch me at first keep encouraged,
> Missing me one place search another.
>
> (1334–35)

And lest the directions about indirection in the Preface prove insufficient, some lines near the beginning of the poem even spell out how the "fetching" is to be done:

> Stop this day and night with me and you shall possess
> the origin of all poems, [. . .]
> You shall not look through my eyes either, nor take
> things from me,
> You shall listen to all sides and filter them from
> yourself.
>
> (25; 28–29)

It is, however, a major paradox in this poem scarcely wanting in paradoxes that, though it is full of didactic attitudes, it never really teaches anything much outright, except for a pervasive optimism, which only becomes diffuse and rather trite when articulated:

> I do not know what is untried and afterward,
> But I know it is sure and alive and sufficient. [. . .]
> It is not chaos or death . . . . it is form and union and
> plan . . . . it is eternal life . . . . it is happiness.
>
> (1120–21; 1308)

As the poet himself admits with disarming grace in one of the shorter poems in the volume:

202

POSSIBILITIES OF A PHASAL STRUCTURE

I lie abstracted and hear beautiful tales of things
    and the reasons of things,
They are so beautiful I nudge myself to listen.

I cannot say to any person what I hear I
    cannot say it to myself . . . . it is very
    wonderful.

("Who Learns My Lesson Complete," 10–12)

Besides, the didactic element, as some earlier chapters have shown, is not an independent, self-justifying phenomenon in the poem but, through the centrifugal gesture inherent in it, performs a function integral to the "heartbeat," the rhythm pervading and sustaining the entire work.

As a result, the "lessons" the poem inspires are much more sophisticated intellectually and spiritually than the ones it actually teaches. It is like some magic mirror in a fable: whoever looks into it can discover his noblest ethical ambition or metaphysical hope, which he then articulates into a story and thus provides the poem with a phasal structure. Chase has spoken of "Whitman's unsuccessful attempt to be an Emersonian or Wordsworthian moralist" and to " 'promulge'. . . the normative self"; [71] however, his critics seem to have done much more "promulging" than Whitman himself. As the reading of the text has proved so far, no such "normative" intentions can be laid at his doorstep, except in what might perhaps be called an "inductive" sense, and in that sense his attempt does not seem to be unsuccessful at all. As he puts it further on in the volume, "It is no lesson . . . . it lets down the bars to a good lesson" ("Who Learns My Lesson Complete," 5): he does not set the norm, but he induces his readers to seek norms. This poem has been described in its time as, among other things, the comic drama of the self, the mystical revelation of truth in an Eastern or Western, direct or inverted manner, the proto-epic appropriate to the American imagination, the simmering of a metaphysical teapot, and—this chapter's contribution—the journey of exploration into the powers of the self-redeemed "I"; except for some sort of scheme of duration, the only common denominator of these phasal interpretations is the determination of their proponents to isolate in the poem the moral grounds on which alone could—nay, should—its protagonist be as buoyant, self-assured, and strong as he is. The unabated proliferation of these ostentatiously pragmatic, subjective responses, which refuse to view Whitman's verses as "a literary performance," is a measure of the "affection" with which "his country [has absorbed] him" (xii) and thus of his success on his own terms.

The phasal structures thus reflect Whitman's own theory of poetry, according to which, as Feidelson sums it up, "a poem, . . . instead of referring to a completed act of perception, constitutes the act itself, both in the author and in the reader." [72] Obviously, it is impossible not to respond in this fundamentally subjective fashion not just to Whitman's poem but, to some degree, to all poems, nor should anyone want to give up the rich rewards it can yield. No poet can restrict by decree, however, the way his work may be approached, not even Whitman, and one does not have to ignore the subjective approach altogether to be also able to conceive of a poem as being no more in the reading than in the writing of it. What J. Hillis Miller remarks about the critic of the novel holds evidently true for the critic of poetry as well: "The critic must, as far as possible, dispossess himself of his own mental structures and attempt to coincide, in an act of pure identification, with the mental structures of the novel." [73] As this chapter has endeavored to show, the reader of Whitman's poem can find particular rewards in each approach, and the results of both can be accommodated in a single view. One need not choose between phasal structures and the "heartbeat." The question, to paraphrase a remark by Northrop Frye, is not "Which one of the two seemingly incompatible structures is correct?" but, "What follows from the fact that both are possible?" [74]

The answer is in recognizing the proper function of each in the interaction between poem and reader. In constructing a phasal structure each reader has become a Raphael to his own

Adam, telling of "Acts . . . more swift / Then time or motion," which,

> to human ears
> Cannot without process of speech be told,
> So told as earthly notion can receave.[75]

The "heartbeat," on the other hand, reveals what the poem is about: the endless instant in which the ominous cycle of ecstasy and horror is both recognized in its full complexity and mastered by a single percipient act of the will to become, which embodies the awareness that is "the greatest poet." The apparently spontaneous, improvised meditations of the protagonist provide, in fact, an inventory of the moment in which he had to become the hero he had not been, to resist the threat of destruction he perceived in the grass because he had to seek to stay alive through joy with his soul. The poem is thus the translation into time of the protagonist's single, desperate and triumphant gesture of mastery.[76]

In a sense, one cannot even accuse the poem's speaker of being too devious about his business. If his subject has taken a touch too long to recognize, he is perhaps not the one to blame. He does, after all, begin by stating:

> I loafe and invite my soul,
> I lean and loafe at my ease . . . . observing a
> spear of summer grass.
>
> (4–5)

And that is "all" he does. The poem is but that soul-enthralled and grass-obsessed "loafing" writ large.

Chapter Eight

THE METRE-MAKING ARGUMENT

I

It has taken three chapters to identify the poem's subject by establishing that its form is an open-ended meditation in which a fundamental and distinctive rhythm of awareness is elaborated. It will not take nearly so long, however, to reach some reliable assumptions about the poem's meaning as a statement of an individual in a community. The "metre" finally known, one should not have much difficulty in discovering the argument which makes it. "My form has strictly grown from my purports and facts," [1] Whitman maintained, and, as it turns out, he was right, for his "purports and facts" are, indeed, revealed in his form, although probably not under the aspect in which he would find them easiest to acknowledge. The following attempt to identify such "purports and facts" in the poem does not propose to refract a full-fledged survey of American culture, past, present, and future, through Whitman's lines; such a survey would be beyond the scope of this study as well as the powers of its writer. Its purpose, instead, is to conclude the discussion of the poem by developing an interpretation of the cultural character of the gesture it makes.

THE METRE-MAKING ARGUMENT

There is a contradiction implicit in all of Whitman's work, especially its earlier portion, which was not brought into sharp focus—faced up to, really—until quite recently. Although Whitman insisted from the beginning that "I am your voice—It was tied in you—In me it begins to talk," [2] and has held the popular reputation of being the poet of fellowship, community, and democracy, Quentin Anderson has shown, in a highly provocative and illuminating argument, overwhelming evidence that it is essentially "unrealized in Whitman's imagination . . . that one exists in one's relations to other persons" and that in the "world suggested by [Whitman's] poetry, the responsive, the antiphonal, the other is absent." [3] Dismaying news to sensibilities that live by Ishmael's discovery that "it's a mutual, joint-stock world" and cherish "the intuition of human solidarity as a priceless good," [4] yet all that the present inquiry has so far established about the poem verifies it. As the previous chapters have demonstrated, the poem's didacticism and its moments of splendid altruism and democratic sentiment are all part of the process by which the cornered will of the "I" manipulates the tensions that make up his awareness into a balance it can control. When he calls out, "O despairer, here is my neck, / By God! you shall not go down! Hang your whole weight upon me" (1007–8), he has produced out of thin air a "despairer" whom he can save in order to save himself, and when he admonishes "Have you outstript the rest? Are you the President? / It is a trifle . . . . they will more than arrive there every one, and still pass on" (432–33), he is reassuring "them" only to reassure himself. And not just the versions of the "histrionic" "you" but, as the discussion of the Preface has shown, the interlocutor in the "dialogues," too, is the product only of the poet's creative imagination and lives only so long and so far as the protagonist needs him. Indispensable as the sense and the idea of the "other" are to the poem's scheme, nowhere in the poem does the listener appear to possess an autonomous, objective existence, independent of the protagonist's concern. The final "you" toward whom the poem was found to gravitate is no more "real" to Whitman, after all, than the skipper of the sinking ship (820–23) he read about in the newspapers or the trapper's red bride (178) he saw in Alfred Jacob Miller's painting. The "I" is preoccupied entirely with himself, and the "you" is allowed into the poem only to assist in that preoccupation.

Obviously, Whitman would dispute this interpretation vehemently, for he forestalled it vehemently all his life. He wanted to be viewed as Professor Anderson views him: as "first [a] figure . . . in the culture, then [a] maker. . . ." [5] He would have protested rather indignantly, however, against the suggestion that his work ignored the "other," for he wanted all to see that, on the contrary, it was undertaken for the "other's" sake. The keynote of his ceaseless efforts to insure the proper response to his work was that by "put[ting] a *Person,* a human being ([him]-self, in the latter half on the Nineteenth Century, in America) freely, fully and truly on record" he was contributing "to the effectual and moral consolidation of our lands." [6] The point needs no detailed elaboration, since it refers to probably the most thoroughly discussed and most familiar aspect of Whitman's work.[7] In his pronouncements about the first two volumes, his insistence on the political, public significance and intentions of his undertaking is, if possible, even stronger than in the prefaces and statements after 1860.[8] Although the poems of 1855 deal with an essentially private concern, his anonymous reviews of this edition and the letter to Emerson which served to introduce the next one strive to assert that the poet represents a group, his identity being unmistakably American, and that in *Leaves of Grass* a new literature commensurate with the triumphant new world is born. "An American bard at last! one of the roughs," he declares; [9] his work is "an attempt . . . to cast into literature not only his own grit and arrogance, but his own flesh and form, . . . regardless . . . of all except his own presence and experience, and all outside the fiercely loved land of his birth. . . ." [10] It demonstrates that "America, having duly conceived, bears out of herself offspring of her own to do the workmanship wanted." [11]

Since the poems themselves do not seem to justify these claims, the frequency and the intensity of the latter are at least as noteworthy as their substance. Whitman's apparent reluctance to permit his poems to speak for themselves suggests that, although he had a remarkably sound idea of how his poems came into being, he perhaps did not know very well why he wrote them. It shows both insecurity about what he was doing and anxiety about what he might be doing. His prose explanations of his purpose, especially in his early reviews, often read as if he were trying to enlighten first of all himself. His key sentences are usually inconclusive and often unfinished, endlessly qualifying their modifiers and multiplying their examples, like the speech of someone struggling to find out what he is thinking.[12] That the chief burden of these statements, even in 1855 and 1856, is his concern for the community and the representative character of his inspiration seems an attempt either to camouflage somewhat the self-absorption predominating in the poems or to compensate for it. Whitman, apparently, suspected that he did not "speak the password primeval" and did not "give the sign of democracy" (507) nearly as often as he wanted or perhaps felt he should. Perhaps he had become frightened by the jinn that surged out of the bottle and attempted to talk it into seeming smaller or at least fitter for human society. In any case, his commentaries on his first volume in particular indicate a most anxious awareness of "the imaginative priority of communal life"; they show that while the idea that "one exists in one's relation to other persons" [13] may go largely unrealized in it, the first *Leaves of Grass* was its author's desperate bid to enter or to be allowed into such a relation, to be accepted into a community.

II

Of course, Whitman is an "American bard," no "bard" could ever be more "American" than he, and the appearance of his book was a momentous event in the cultural history of the nation, even if not quite for the explicit reasons he himself proposed in his anonymous reviews of the volume. The tension between what Whitman did and the name by which it came to be known is simply the first clue toward a new, possibly more accurate, perspective upon his achievement. The next clue is in the thoroughgoing and unembarrassed eclecticism that characterizes his performance.

His poem declares itself to be a "new chant of dilation and pride" (429) and warns from the first that what it does has never been done before: "You shall no longer" respond to poems as before (25–28), because "the gum" has been "wash[ed] [. . .] from your eyes" (1226). Of course, it lives up to its word admirably in many ways; in the heat of "close analysis" one can easily forget just how admirably. A periodic rereading, rhapsodic embellishments and all, of Randall Jarrell's splendid piece on Whitman should be compulsory for all those engaged in detailed investigations of *Leaves of Grass,* just so they can remind themselves of the beauty of the forest in which they are tagging the trees. Tried against Jarrell's "touchstones," Whitman's achievement makes some critical views, those that sport "some doubt of Whitman's greatness" and hold his "stature" unproven,[14] seem simply fatuous. The cornerstone in that achievement is this poem. It is new, however, not just because it frequently displays Whitman as "a poet of the greatest and oddest delicacy and originality and sensitivity, so far as words are concerned"[15] or because through it "more than anyone else . . . Whitman made the city poetically available to literature" and "made sex a possible subject for American literature";[16] it is new, first of all, because, as the preceding chapters have shown, it has found a form—the emergence of "Walt Whitman," the triumphant, "dilating," "greatest poet" the protagonist contrives out of the conditions of his defeat—through which a radically new awareness, one that originates in an almost exclusively "physiological" sense of identity, could manifest itself. As Quentin Anderson put it, describing this new awareness as the "imperial self," Whitman's "novelty lay in his mode of apprehending the world." [17]

The nature of this "novelty" is further clarified by Whitman's choice of the means to realize it. All the studies of his craft reach essentially the same conclusion: the "greatest poet" "does not repel the past" any more than, as he explained in the Preface (iii), "America" does. In his style conventions and originality, tradition and innovation, old and new are freely combined. In the successive editions of Leaves of Grass conventionality gradually began to get the better of Whitman as he "became increasingly mindful of form" [18] and kept adjusting his texts generally to bring them closer to what readers could traditionally expect from poems. Floyd Stovall could see a cause for rejoicing in this development because it reflected the poet's "drift from love of freedom toward love of law," [19] and Asselineau, while acknowledging that Whitman's poetry was "thinning" as his concern with form grew, insists that "the patient labor of revising his work which [Whitman] undertook from 1856 to 1881 was not in vain." [20] The fact is, however, that even in 1855 Whitman's craft was neither as artless nor as lawless as Asselineau and Stovall suggest. It was "heteroclite and disparate" [21] from the first. Along with its many innovations and "lawlessness," the first edition clearly shows the traces and influence of conventional poetic diction and prosody, in spite of the "great trouble" Whitman later claimed to have taken to "[leave] out the stock 'poetic' touches" from it.[22]

His work was to display "the renovated English speech in America," [23] yet, as Rebecca Coy has shown, "aside from the liberal introduction of technical and commercial terms, Whitman made no radical changes in conventional poetic diction." [24] If Whitman's language is wrong, Ezra Pound observes, "it is wrong NOT because he broke all of what were considered in his day 'the rules' but because he is spasmodically conforming to this, that or the other; sporadically dragging in a bit of 'regular' metre, using a bit of literary language, and putting his adjectives where, in the spoken tongue, they are not." [25] In that case, Whitman's language was never more "wrong" than in the first edition, since there are proportionately more slang expressions, coinages, colloquialisms, and other "offences" against poetic decorum in it than in any subsequent edition and therefore the disparateness of the elements making up the manner is bolder and more conspicuous. When a phrase like, "To me the converging objects of the universe perpetually flow" (404) is heard within ten lines of "life is a suck and a sell, and nothing remains at the end but threadbare crape and tears" (395), it sounds much more "poetical" in the sense one would not expect from "one of the roughs" than after 1881, when "suck and a sell" is deleted, presumably for the same reason that "I cock my hat" (397) is changed, in 1867, to "I wear my hat." [26] Similarly, when the "extoler of amies" (463) declares, "I am he attesting sympathy" (464), the stilted grandiloquence of the lines is not quite as startling in 1881 and after [27] as in the earlier editions, where he adds, virtually in the same breath: "Washes and razors for foofoos . . . . for me freckles and a bristling beard" (468).

The prosody of the first *Leaves* reveals the same characteristic admixture of the conventional and the regular to the various ways in which the "greatest poet" undertakes to flaunt traditional rules and expectations. Whitman's verse in 1855 is undoubtedly looser, wordier, and more casual than in later years. The lines have a lighter and perhaps faster, livelier music; the difference seems summed up in the revision of "And mossy scabs of the wormfence, and heaped stones, and elder and mullen and pokeweed" (89). From 1856 on Whitman kept rearranging—though never changing—these words until, in 1881, he came up with the final version: [28] "And mossy scabs of the worm fence, heap'd stones, elder, mullein and pokeweed." [29] The transformation of the unstressed *and*'s into pauses slows down the line and breaks its three graceful periods into four terse and ponderous phrases. Besides the higher number of unstressed syllables between stresses, the prosody of the first *Leaves* is also distinguished from the prosody of later editions by the undifferentiated pauses within the lines, which the peculiar, four-dot ellipses indicate, and by the absence of any subdivisions within each poem beyond stanzas of varying length marked off by double-spacing. Finally, as noted in another chapter, the volume possesses a carefully designed and purposeful "visual prosody," [30] which Whitman, because of practical difficulties of publication, could never again impose upon his book. In general, the prosody of 1855 allows the reader greater flexibility in construing the verse; it is more open and thus closer to Whitman's professed intentions than in any of the revisions that follow it.

Even in this first and freest version, however, Whitman's prosody clearly shows its several links with the mainstream of tradition, for, as Fred Newton Scott put it, even "when he thinks he is uttering tufts and tussocks of grass, [Whitman] is in reality building the lofty rhyme." [31] Gay Wilson Allen's demonstration—that despite the poet's ambition "to start a new 'school' of American versification," Whitman's " 'new' and 'free' rhythms" are "at least as old as Hebrew poetry" and only about as free—is based, in large measure, on texts found in the first edition. [32] The same holds true of Sculley Bradley's theory—by all odds the soundest, most comprehensive, and most convincing elucidation of Whitman's prosody—of the "fundamental metrical principle" in *Leaves of Grass*. [33] A careful and detailed analysis of two long passages (434–48 and 193–210) from the first poem of the first edition provides the final and most persuasive proof of his conclusions that Whitman "did not completely reject any device of the older poetry" and that his success in developing an "organic" form "to shape his words to the exact surface and movement of the spirit in nature or in truth" is due to "his conscious rejection of syllabic meter in favor of that more ancient and native English meter based on the rhythmic 'period' between stresses." [34]

What at first sight could seem so unique, "irregular," and brazenly contemptuous of conventions, thus turned out to be a much more complicated and also much less unusual affair, be-

213

cause, as Asselineau puts it, "the victory which [Whitman] thought he had won over tradition in 1855 was not as complete as he had imagined." [35] When Frank B. Sanborn first looked into the copy of *Leaves of Grass* Emerson lent him in the summer of 1855, he thought that "it was unlike anything," but recalling the event more than forty years later he concluded that there was "a great deal of affectation in Whitman's poetry; a great deal that he borrowed." [36] It is hard to decide which of his two observations was more ruefully made. The first may have been disturbing, but the second plainly registers a disappointment that has since become quite familiar in the criticism of Whitman. The "greatest poet" was "not using anything like a folk-speech," [37] after all, and, persuaded that he should have been, some readers feel called upon to apologize for him or strain to explain away the "deficiency." What else but blind affection could have induced Kenneth Rexroth, who knows better, to insist that "much of [Whitman's] strange lingo is not the stilted rhetoric of the self-taught, but simply Quaker talk"? [38] Rexroth probably wished to defend Whitman's idiom against such descriptions as Matthiessen's, who called it a "curious amalgamation of homely and simple usage with half-remembered terms he read once somewhere, and with casual inventions of the moment" and would not deny that it can often serve as an unwitting example "of the confused American effort to talk big by using high-sounding terms with only the vaguest notion of their original meaning." [39] It is an unblinking and rather uncharitably worded view, but it is also an accurate one, and Whitman needs no protection against it. For all that his effects can sometimes resemble the incongruous sight of London Bridge in the middle of the Arizona desert, his craft is all his own. "His language," runs Matthiessen's conclusion, "is . . . the natural product of a Brooklyn journalist of the eighteen-forties who had previously been a country schoolteacher and a carpenter's helper, and who had finally felt an irresistible impulse to be a poet." [40]

Emerson himself said as much by telling Sanborn that *Leaves of Grass* "is a remarkable mixture of the Baghvat Ghita and the

New York Herald," [41] and he can hardly have meant to censure Whitman with it, for he spoke in the summer of 1855, when he still found "incomparable things said incomparably well" in "the most extraordinary piece of wit and wisdom that America has yet contributed." [42] Some critics who came after Emerson seem to have wished that *Leaves of Grass* had been either more of the Gita and less of the *Herald* or the other way around because the character of the one or the other was surely a flaw in the representative poem of democracy; Emerson, however, understood, apparently, that the book was a great and thoroughly American achievement *because* of the mixture it was, not in spite of it. Whitman was simply doing the best he could. The spectacle of his inglorious experiments in conventional verse [43] reinforces the impression created by his evident willingness to resort at random to traditional prosodic devices [44] in developing his characteristic style: the manner of the first *Leaves of Grass* is unconventional and heterogeneous not so much by design as by necessity. Whitman could not claim to have invented a style for the express purpose of challenging the tastes prevalent in his day, like Wordsworth, for example, who could assert that with the studiedly unadorned style of *Lyrical Ballads* he wanted to cure the public of its "degrading thirst after outrageous stimulation." [45] In Whitman's case, the style came first, and his realization that it could, in fact, be regarded as such a challenge came afterward.

The thoroughly eclectic character of Whitman's craft in 1855 is but another manifestation of what Quentin Anderson has called "the brilliant inversion that made apparent weakness strength." [46] Like everything else in the poem, the form, too, demonstrates that Whitman could not help being an Antaeus of sorts; thrust back upon only his own resources, he made them do and even compelled them to yield him occasions of triumphant self-assertion. In the end, the protagonist of the poem has made what he is and what he possesses appear to be not only enough but *all* there is. His insistence in his style upon the sovereign right to pick and choose among the available materials and to reject or observe conventions as it seemed both possible and fit to him implements the substantive gesture of the poem: the demand of its protagonist to be acknowledged as sufficient in and unto himself. As noted earlier, the poem cannot sustain the cultural nationalism of Whitman's own anonymous reviews of the volume or the several doctrinaire commitments labelled American that have been variously attributed to it over the years. In the heroic self-sufficiency of the "I," however, the state of mind projected by the Preface as "the greatest poet" is realized; and with it the potential for the "spiritual democracy" of the "unnumbered supremes," the collective state of mind the Preface calls "America," is also fulfilled.[47] "I resist anything better than my own diversity" (347): through this gesture alone the poem is centrally and essentially "American."[48]

III

Spectacular and exhilarating as the victory of the poem's protagonist may be, it is not without substantial risks as well. Quentin Anderson has spoken of the poem's display of "the cost and glory of being enough for oneself";[49] one should also note the direct dangers involved. The poem itself proves, by the prodigious expense of creative and psychic energy it absorbed, how precarious and vulnerable is the self-reliance its protagonist has achieved. The distance between the "great poet" and a confidence-man is all but incalculably great, yet it can be travelled in the blink of an eye; resisting anything better than one's own diversity is not proof against being cheapened into positive thinking; "I exist as I am, that is enough" (413) can all too easily be vulgarized into a slogan of secular revival meetings. Also, the "I" born in the poem is clearly a difficult fellow to have around in a society dedicated to any proposition other than himself. His vision of a future of "unnumbered supremes" is undeniably naive; he will not fit into schemes of "purposive change" and cannot conceive of occasions when it is the individual's duty, not choice, to serve his community and to subordinate himself

216

to it. (On the other hand, no Grand Inquisitor will ever get the better of him, and that may make all the risks seem worth running.)

Against all these dangers the only defence of the "I" is in the integrity of his emotions: perhaps the greatest risk of all but, as it turned out, the source of his greatest victory. The immitigable condition of the success of his desperate "scheme" to fend off the forces of his destruction is that he surrender himself to the pose that is to save him. If he is to be Walt Whitman, he cannot afford to be Walter Mitty. He must not simply deceive himself with his pretense; he must believe in it. One false note, and he is lost—objectively, to seedy vulgarization or puerile solipsism, and subjectively, to the horrors within. But there are no false notes. There is, instead, "a unity of feeling," as Cowley has put it, throughout the poem, and "no line . . . . that seems false to a single prevailing tone." [50] What has begun as the deliberate self-deception of an *alazon* concludes with his complete metamorphosis: the *alazon* no longer acts—he has *become* his pretense and thus disappears in it. The crisis that precipitates the transformation is not forgotten—the stature of the heroic "I" could not be fully surmised unless measured against the destructive forces over which he is prevailing—but the earlier, hard-beset identity of the protagonist has wholly receded from view.

This transformation fuses the private triumph of Whitman's hero with the vision of national identity by which America has known itself. It substantiates both the poet's boastful allegation that in his blatantly self-centered, apolitical, and unprogrammatic poem "the United States have . . . taken measure and form" [51] and his public's suspicion, strong from the first and often uneasy, that, all appearances to the contrary, he is right. This suspicion has led to the anxious concern with the moral imperatives that circumscribe the heroic self of Whitman's poem: if the "I" is, indeed, as he is felt to be, the representative American, he had better be living by the principles Americans profess. Democracy should make "the greatest poet" possible. The reconciliation, however, has never been entirely successful, and Whitman himself suggests the reason why. In his prose, which may at first seem to go a long way toward making his protagonist measure up to democratic expectations, he argues at length, especially in *Democratic Vistas*, their exact opposite, that "the greatest poet" makes democracy possible.

The contradiction does not invalidate the nation's intuitive recognition of the poet as its own but points up the error of attempting to justify it as a coincidence of ideals and convictions. "The greatest poet" and "America" recognize themselves, each in the other, not because they profess to share any given set of ethical or political assumptions but because poet and nation alike account for themselves by an essentially identical myth of self-realization. "The nation that has sprung from its 'Platonic conception' of itself" [52] cannot help perceiving that the birth of Whitman's "I" is analogous to its own, for "the United States themselves are essentially the greatest poem" (iii) only by the same token that the speaker of the Preface can become, "essentially," "the greatest poet." It is a melancholy though hardly surprising corrollary of the case that, in spite of the compelling evidence, the "trial of the poet" is not over yet and his "absorption" by his country is not the joyous occasion of mutual affection he envisioned but a rather reluctant affair. There is little reassurance in the fact that the "Platonic concept of himself" was not freely elected by the "I" but forced upon him by an oedipal crisis. The kinship between him and "America" is too great for the country to reject him outright, yet what buried and murky compulsions must the nation unearth from itself to accept him the way he demands to be accepted? It does not seem to help much to be reminded that the more painful the ordeal the more glorious the victory. To face its poet on his own terms America must heed Lawrence's instructions: "You have got to pull the democratic and idealistic clothes off American utterance, and see what you can of the dusky body of IT underneath," [53] and so far America has by and large preferred not to. Through the birth of Whitman's "greatest poet" "the interior American republic" is "declared free and independent"; [54] the "exterior" re-

218

public has heard and understood the declaration but has not quite learned yet to be proud of it.

IV

To speak of a "myth" of self-realization means inviting trouble, for, as Socrates told Phaedrus, "this sort of crude philosophy can take up a great deal of time" to little avail; [55] it must be done, nevertheless, because the examination of the dimensions of myth in the poem provides, Socrates notwithstanding, the conclusions with which the present interpretation of it can at last rest its case.

However the ominous concept may be phrased, it is appropriate to the poem not so much as narrative category but as "ideational form." [56] With its Protean hero and its "symbolic actions amid symbolic objects" in an "[embodiment of] some form of the conflict between human wishes and nonhuman forces" the poem fits Newton Arvin's description of myth.[57] The transformation through which the "I" can hold death at bay is an "action . . . near or at the conceivable limits of desire" and thus a myth according to Northrop Frye's definition.[58] The essentially unified vision of the transcendental parataxis displayed in the catalogues and in the catalogue-like organization of the poem itself reflects "the myth-making consciousness," for which, Cassirer writes, "separate elements are not . . . separately given, but have to be originally derived from the whole." [59] Cassirer also describes a "mythico-religious protophenomenon" in words that apply with remarkable accuracy to the poem's central event, the protagonist's triumphant resolution of his crisis of mortal fear in the emergence of his superhuman, transfigured self :

> When external reality is not merely viewed and contemplated, but overcomes a man in sheer immediacy, with emotions of fear or hope, terror or wish fulfillment: then the spark jumps somehow across, the tension finds release, as the subjective excitement becomes objectified, and confronts the mind as a god or a daemon.[60]

When Whitman, years later, began to insist that from the very inception of his work "one deep purpose underlay the others . . . and that has been the religious purpose," [61] he may well have been recording his awareness of this mythic dimension in his first poem. Although by this time he had heard O'Connor describe him as a Modern Christ,[62] and he was well along in his efforts to live up to the image his disciples had created of him, he went on to explain that his religious purpose was not simply to instruct or edify and had nothing to do with "conventional pietism, or the sickly yearnings of devotees," but it was "aiming at the widest sub-bases and inclusions of humanity." [63] A much more explicit indication of his view of religion around the time of the publication of the first *Leaves* is in the volume itself. In one of the shorter poems he affirms a paradoxical, immanent faith: "The sun and stars that float in the open air . . . . the appleshaped earth and we upon it . . . . surely the drift of them is something grand" ("A Song for Occupations," 57); then he goes on to explain the strictly subordinate, secondary role that any discursive account of such a faith can have:

> We consider the bibles and religions divine I
>   do not say they are not divine,
> I say they have all grown out of you and may grow out
>   of you still,
> It is not they who give the life . . . . it is you who give
>   the life;
> ("A Song for Occupations," 78–80)

This is the view corroborated by some random notes for a lecture on religion, which he projected in the mid-1850s but never completed. A typical fragment reads:

The fact that concealed beneath the ostensible life which is celebrated in forms, politics, society, conversation, the churches and what is called knowledge and amusement, is the deep silent mysterious never to be examined, never to be told quality of life itself, to which all those ostensible things ceaseless tending—the eternal life which active or passive, will not let a man ever entirely rest, but in

220

one way or another arouses him to think, to wonder, to doubt, and often to despair.[64]

Clearly, when his first poem was written religion for Whitman meant feeling, not precept.

Should his comments on the subject not be convincing enough, his poem itself leaves no doubt that if it has any religious significance at all, that significance is sacral, not homiletical—myth, not doctrine. Throughout the volume Whitman displays an easy familiarity with the conventions of religious and particularly biblical expression, and it soon becomes obvious that he uses them in a purposeful and effective manner. These biblical influences on the prosody and imagery of the poem have been analyzed in several excellent studies,[65] and there is no need to review all their findings here; two of them, however, call for special attention: the effect of the allusions to the biblical myth of creation in the imagery, and the often incantatory, spell-weaving character of the verse.

Although never very loud and at times scarcely audible, this biblical undertone runs through the entire volume and provides a particularly impressive manifestation of Whitman's indirect ways. In a subtle, all but surreptitious manner he accumulates the slightest hints and the faintest echoes into a background of tonality and allusion against which single images and image-clusters acquire a perspective they could not possess on their own. The effect is virtually subliminal: the listener is barely aware, if at all, of the background and registers only the curious resonances that make many of the lines sound somehow more familiar than their words entitle them to be.

Thus, as noted earlier, the echoes of the King James Version release in the Preface an analogy to the opening verses of Genesis in the passage where "the soul of the poet" "swells" "cleaving and circling" over the "fathomless and therefore calm" "depths of qualities and things" (vii). The memory of this image, reinforced by the continued biblical intonation, activates in the first poem, in turn, a number of likewise dormant allusions to

221

the myth of creation. Out of this mythical "dimness" "advance," then, the "opposite equals" through which "the procreant urge of the world" (38, 37) is satisfied; the oracular tone of the preceding lines, which announce that "there was never any more inception than there is now" (32; 33–35), underscores the reference. More distant perhaps but still discernible is the parallel between the contented stock-taking of the "I" ("Clear and sweet is my soul . . . . and clear and sweet is all that is not my soul" [44]) and the contentment of God, equally satisfied in His discreteness and in His creation as He "saw that it was good." [66] The effect of this perception lingers on: after this moment the several subsequent occasions of the protagonist's joyful contentment (e.g., 350–52, 661, 1167) are illuminated by the mythic glow, faint though it may be, of the creator's delight in what he has wrought. Similarly, when the "I" asserts that he can "now and always send sunrise out of [himself]" (563) or when he declares, "I dilate you with tremendous breath" (1009),[67] and, "Now I will you to be a bold swimmer" (1229), he evokes biblical gestures of creation and thus wraps himself, so to speak, into myth. In the end, as he concludes his impassioned enumeration of "the rough deific sketches" (1031) that he comes "magnifying and applying" (1020) "to fill out better in [himself]" (1031), he exclaims:

> The supernatural of no account . . . . myself waiting my
> time to be one of the supremes, [. . .]
> By my life-lumps! becoming already a creator!
> Putting myself here and now to the ambushed womb of the
> shadows!
>
> (1045; 1048–49)

and only his sublime comic arrogance is startling, but the substance of his declaration is not. It simply confirms what has been hinted all along: the poem consistently invites an analogy between its subject and the mythic moment of creation.

This perspective makes good sense out of the poet's suggestion that his poem is merely the "translation" of his "belched words" or "barbaric yawp." In this mythical light, his "yawp" can be seen as doing for the world of his self what God's creative Word does for Creation—it is the Logos of *Leaves of Grass*. According to the biblical analogy, it is "the source and origin of all the means by which [he] reveals [himself] to [his] creation," [68] and it is timeless: as the Creation is the manifestation in time of God's "continuous creative act" performed "in and through his word," [69] so is the poem the temporal articulation of "the greatest poet's" proto-verbal gesture of timeless self-creation. It is very doubtful, however, that Whitman himself had theological subtleties in mind as he conceived of the function of "the sound of the belched words of [his] voice" (17). The biblical allusions themselves and the mythic perspectives they erect are much too consistent and purposeful to have reached the poem without design, by mere coincidence or impulse, but "sermons and creeds and theology" (1091) as such only provoke "the greatest poet's" contempt. "The philosophical or religious idea of the Infinite," Cassirer explains, "is *above* the possibility of exact verbal determination, [whereas the Indefinite] is still *below* such fixation." He goes on:

> Language moves in the middle kingdom between the "indefinite" and the "infinite"; it transforms the indeterminate into a determinate idea, and then holds it within the sphere of finite determinations. So there are, in the realm of mythic and religious conception, "ineffables" of different order, one of which represents the lower limit of verbal expression, the other the upper limit; . . . [The] emergence from the vague fulness of existence into a world of clear, verbally determinable forms, is represented in the mythic mode, in the imagist fashion peculiar to it, as the opposite between chaos and creation.[70]

The theory of the Logos derived from the biblical account of creation passes, in fact, "the upper limit of verbal expression," for it envisions a Word beyond language. Whitman, on the other hand, expropriates, in the figure of the "yawp," the *topos* of this reaching beyond language, toward the Infinite, to give shape with it to a mostly intuitive perception that is closer to what the creation-myth represents in its pristine version: the emergence of a consciousness "into a world of clear, verbally determinable forms." The biblical Logos of theology is no longer language; the Logos of *Leaves of Grass* is not yet language—only a "yawp." Even so, it *is* creative: "From this indefinite state arises the first determinate existence when the creator god utters his own name, and by virtue of the power dwelling in that word calls himself into being." [71] Cassirer's theory makes it finally clear, then, that the poem conceives mythically of the transformative moment which was found to be its subject, as the uttering forth of the "yawp"—the creator-god protagonist's "let there be 'I'!"

Whitman thus deliberately exploits the biblical myth's idiom of images and gestures to formulate a personal myth. He seems to have known quite well, too, that he was doing so: he might not have taken to the terminology of this conclusion, but his remarks on the peculiarly religious purpose of his undertaking suggest that he would have most likely agreed with its substance. He uses the language of Genesis because his subject is the "greatest poet's" creation of himself—his self-genesis. By drawing the Bible onto "his equal plane" (v) he also gives rank to this self-realization, compelling the listener, too, to recognize it as a mythic event and therefore centrally important in the life of the community. "By a subtle but inevitable implication," writes Dr. Bucke of "Song of Myself," in "the glorification of Walt Whitman . . . every individual, man or woman," is also glorified.[72] Whitman, who said remarkably little about this poem himself, "wrote or revised more than half of [Dr. Bucke's] book and influenced [its] writing from beginning to end," [73] but he let stand the assertion that the "implication," though "subtle," is "inevitable," nor did he tone down the wild hyperbole preceding it: this poem is "the largest and most important that the author produced, and perhaps the most important poem that has so far been written at any time, in any language." [74] Apparently, he assumed—as he had to—that, private though it was, the collective relevance of his personal myth would not be lost on a community that itself came into being through self-genesis.

Just as it is not the "yawp" itself but its "translation," the poem does not constitute its protagonist's self-creative gesture but commemorates it. This is the function implicitly recognized by the suggestion that it is, in fact, an epic poem.[75] Commemorative purpose alone, however, will not an epic make, and there is not much else in the poem to qualify it for the title. "An 'epic' tells a story of heroes or mythic prototypes and tells it objectively," Hyatt H. Waggoner explains in a testy refutation of some "epic" claims. " 'Song of Myself' tells no story, has only the speaker as a 'character,' and is wholly subjective. . . . Whatever epiclike qualities [it] has are not central to its purpose and meaning." [76] As the study of the poem's structure has shown, there are, indeed, no genuine narrative or discursive continuities in it. The particular form through which it commemorates its subject seems to have been sensed most accurately by those readers who have felt that they were responding in it to some manner of drama. Some of Richard Chase's observations are especially suggestive, even if the conclusions he has drawn from them are not always quite convincing. While developing his interpretation of the poem as the "comic drama of the Self," he recognized "something of the spirit of . . . Greek cults" in it, a "ritual submovement" and "a ritual celebration of 'Nature without check with original energy,' " [77] and thus he pointed toward the formal connection between the inner drama which is the substance of the poem's inspiration and the poet's mythic conception of it. Chase's assumptions are based on impressions made by the imagery; his view is reinforced by the incantatory character of the diction and the verse, which is an all but evitable concomitant of a creative idiom thriving on catalogues, parallelism, and an ardent belief that "latent, in a great user of words, must actually be all passions, crimes, trades, animals, stars, God, sex, the past, might, space, metals, and the like— because these *are* the words . . . ." [78] "Whitman . . . at times seems to be engaging in incantation," Gay Wilson Allen has noted, and virtually the entire poem bears him out, especially if one takes into consideration the close and direct link between incantation in its primitive, rather monotonous form and what Allen calls "Biblical cadences" in which "the incremental repetition is not only stylized but even ritualized." [79] In passages like the ones beginning with "This is the grass that grows" (358; 359–65 and 372–80) or "Where the quail is whistling" (731; 731–45) the subject is conjured up rather than told about or explained; the words constitute not an account but a ceremony of the vision or feeling they engage. Such lines are by no means isolated in the poem; they merely bring into clearer focus a quality pervading its style from first to last.

With these motifs of chant and ritual the poem's meaning as a statement in and for a community can be determined at last. Having conceived of its subject as, to borrow Cassirer's phrase, "a mythico-religious protophenomenon," the central event in a personal myth, the poem commemorates it in an essentially dramatic rather than epic or philosophical manner, neither arguing nor recounting but reenacting it. The character of its religious self-awareness, evident in the fabric of mythic allusions and the elements of ritual and incantation, indicates that, within the perspectives of its private myth, this reenactment is of sacral intent and significance. It is the rite through which the truth of the myth it commemorates can become efficient in time: its participants are enabled to recognize themselves as a community. The ceremony of the poet's personal myth of becoming functions, therefore, as an instrument of collective identity.

The awareness that the Preface has projected and made possible is thus realized in the first poem both as "the greatest poet" himself and, at least potentially, as "America," his collective "version." In Leaves of Grass, in its first as well as its subsequent editions, the first poem means the presence of this awareness; it is neither by nor about "the greatest poet" but "the greatest poet" himself. The title it bore from 1860 to 1881 [80]—"Walt Whitman"—supports this reading, for it insists on being radically distinct from all the other poems in the volume as well as from the Walter Whitman who registered the book with the clerk of the district court. "Walter" had to disappear in

"Walt," and the rest of the poems depend on the first for their very existence, much as verse depends on the poet—they are not variants but products of the awareness of which the first poem is the form. The changing of the title, in 1881, to "Song of Myself" works directly against both distinctions. "Walter" reasserts himself by calling "the greatest poet" "myself," and "song" suggests that the poem is just one among many others. It would be fruitless to speculate whether Whitman decided upon this change because he did not understand his own work well enough or because he understood it all too well, but the revision, in any case, is among the least fortunate ones he made.

Whatever the title in the later editions, the poem's meaning and function in the first *Leaves of Grass* should be clear now. Its subject is the mythic instant when the "I" utters forth himself as "the greatest poet" with a primal, indeterminate and "untranslatable" "yawp" sounded over the "fathomless" darkness of his fears and anxieties. The poem is not this mythic act of creation itself but the ceremony of verbal gestures which perpetuates it. The "I," high priest of his own divinity, performs in it the ritual of pronouncing his self-creative Word. The significance of the entire poem is implicit, therefore, in its very first line, just as its complete action is inherent in the protagonist's indolent loafing on the grass. It is the ritual fulfillment of "let there be 'I'!"; not "I am," but its ceremony: "I celebrate myself" (1).

Part Three

THE OTHER POEMS

Chapter Nine

CLOSED STATEMENTS, OPEN STRUCTURE

I

After the first poem, the rest of the book inevitably suffers by comparison; nevertheless, the other eleven poems are essential to the volume's design. They clarify and reinforce the first poem's position by "foiling" it, and they also manage to deal, after a fashion, with the profound and ominous conflict that the first poem could only contain, not resolve.

"The other poems in the 1855 collection," Schyberg conjectured, following Bliss Perry's lead, "are mostly commentaries on or cuttings from 'Song of Myself,' " [1] and Loren K. Davidson claims that "the manuscripts [that is, the scattered fragments, sketches, and tentatively identified notes that survive] make plain such a relationship between the one and the many." [2] At least two likely principles of selection are suggested by the text, and both of them tend to confirm the conclusions reached about the first poem earlier: these poems either spend much more time with "you" than the first one, or they dwell on their subject too long and thus would arrest its "heartbeat."

When the poet's voice is heard again after it trailed off in the unpunctuated farewell concluding his celebration of himself, the reappearance of the title in the same large, bold type which first announced him indicates that a distinct new statement is begun. The text justifies the assumption both here and on the four other occasions on which the title is restated. The poet turns full face to "you" and stays with his listener this time. In the first 30 or so lines of this poem there are more lines consecutively spoken to "you" than in the 1,330 or so lines of the first one. The transition from the first to the second poem, therefore, seems to be deliberately organized around this change in the direction of address. The fact that Whitman eventually discarded the first seven lines,[3] in which this turn to "you" is possibly the most emphatic, confirms this impression.[4] It seems, then, that if the lines that make up this poem are, in fact, "cuttings" from the first one, they were cut because Whitman may have found the dialogue with "you" sustained in them too long for his purposes there.

Thematically, all the "other" poems in the volume elaborate topics that the first one touches upon; the assumption, therefore, that they grew out of segments excised from it is probably correct. Had they been left in the first poem, these lines would sidetrack the "I" in his meditations and thus interrupt the primary rhythm of the "heartbeat" which shapes and sustains his statement, because they dwell on their subjects much too long and much too exclusively. Also, they present self-contained, well-knit arguments, moving from beginning through middle to end, in a clear-cut "sequential" manner incompatible with the first poem's "paratactic" structure.

II

"A Song for Occupations" * elaborates the conviction that "the sum of all known value and respect I add up in you whoever you are" ("A Song for Occupations," 82), and much of it sounds as if it consisted of those parts of the teacher-orator's sermon which

* For the sake of convenience, these "other" poems will be referred to by the titles they bear in Cowley.

began with lines 1052–54 of the first poem but were drowned out by the meditative reflections of the "I." The poem begins and ends with an affirmation of the self's supremacy over its occupations because "the enclosing purport of us here" ("A Song for Occupations," 59) cannot be bound up in matter. The foolish kind of prudence assailed in the Preface is rejected again. About halfway through the poem, after exuberant and impassioned assertions that "all music is what awakens from you when you are reminded by the instruments" ("A Song for Occupations," 94), a diffident and unconvinced voice interjects some rhetorical questions made to be refuted:

> Will the whole come back then?
> Can each see the signs of the best by a look in the
>   looking-glass? Is there nothing greater or more?
> Does all sit there with you and me?
>   ("A Song for Occupations," 97–99)

The speaker's impatient rejoinder, "You foolish child!" ("A Song for Occupations," 100), launches the long and inventive catalogue of tools and instruments which forms the bulk of the poem's substance. It demonstrates that all human activity merely serves to prove the doer superior to whatever can be done:

> In them, not yourself . . . . you and your soul enclose
>   all things, regardless of estimation,
> In them your themes and hints and provokers . . . if not,
>   the whole earth has no themes or hints or provokers,
>   and never had.
>   ("A Song for Occupations," 160–61)

The next poem, "To Think of Time," is Whitman's dance of death. It might have begun as part of the poet's "translation" of the "hints" that he "perceived" in the "grass" about the "dead young men and women" (112), that is, of the lines that, in the first poem, lead the "I" into the crisis that precipitates his transformation into "the greatest poet." Virtually the entire argument would fit between lines 121 and 122, as it moves—again in a neatly sequential fashion—from a morbid preoccupation with the thought that "not a day passes . . . not a minute or second without a corpse" ("To Think of Time," 11) to the assertion that one critic has described as an "outburst of faith in immortality": [5] "I swear I see now that every thing has an eternal soul!" ("To Think of Time," 131). This hypothetical placement is corroborated on every count by Hyatt H. Waggoner's observations that "death is the primary fact here" and that this poem contains "the challenge that produced the unqualified affirmations in 'Song of Myself,' " [6] even though his interpretation of those affirmations themselves is radically different from the one here proposed. The poem's structure is based on a stark contrast between glimpses of life and death or dying, and the gloomy graveyard images predominate:

> Rapid the trot to the cemetery,
> Duly rattles the deathbell . . . . the gate is passed
>   . . . . the grave is halted at . . . . the living
>   alight . . . . the hearse uncloses,
> The coffin is lowered and settled . . . . the whip is
>   laid on the coffin,
> The earth is swiftly shovelled in . . . . a minute . . . .
>   no one moves or speaks . . . . it is done,
> He is decently put away . . . . is there anything more?
>   ("To Think of Time," 37–41)

The eyes linger on every item they perceive because they know that they soon will have to let go of it:

> Thumb extended or finger uplifted,
> Apron, cape, gloves, strap . . . . wetweather clothes
>   . . . . whip carefully chosen . . . . boss, spotter,
>   starter, and hostler,
> Somebody loafing on you, or you loafing on somebody . . . .
>   headway . . . . man before and man behind,
> Good day's work or bad day's work . . . . pet stock or
>   mean stock . . . . first out or last out . . . .
>   turning in at night,
> To think that these are so much and so nigh to other
>   drivers . . . . and he there takes no interest in them.
>   ("To Think of Time," 48–52)

Against this strong, brooding sense of the transience of all only a naive and insistent faith born out of the love of life, more intense because foredoomed, is offered. The argument is as trite as "A Psalm of Life"; the accomplishment is in the sharply elegiac mood realized in the poem. It is an assertion of immortality but a vision of death.

"To Think of Time," like "A Song for Occupations" before it, is a finished, structurally complete poem, but the tension-filled atmosphere created by its anxious striving for reassurance about "the thin, almost imperceptible line between life and death" [7] prepares the reader for the "night journey" [8] that follows. Traditionally, most discussions of this next poem, which in the last edition bore the title of "The Sleepers," begin by remarking that it has not received all the attention it deserves—that it is "a great but insufficiently noticed" poem.[9] The truth is, however, that it has never been really neglected, and at least since Holloway declared that "it gives the clue to the whole poetic mentality of Whitman," [10] it has been frequently analyzed.[11] Among the numerous incisive and highly illuminating commentaries on the poem, Richard Chase's and Edwin H. Miller's conclusions seem particularly useful for the present argument, since very little needs to be added to them to show that the first version of "The Sleepers" corroborates and reinforces the interpretation this study advanced for the volume as a whole.

" 'The Sleepers,' " says Richard Chase, "is a poem about the descent of the as yet unformed and unstable ego into the id, its confrontation there of the dark, human tragedy, its emergence in a new, more stable form." [12] Unlike the rest of the "other" poems, it is not likely to be simply a "cutting" from the first; the relationship between the two is complementary. The process of self-exploration begun in the first poem is concluded in "The Sleepers." The first poem is the constant vigil of the "I" over the conditions of his triumph; in "The Sleepers," instead of waking and thus turning away from the night, he plunges into it. He falls asleep on purpose, so to speak, to avail himself of the freedom of a dream-vision to seek out and confront the source of the horror that the waking self could not possibly look in the face. The poem thus affords a resolution of sorts for the issues that the first poem could only raise and control but had to leave unresolved.

In broad outline the poem's structure is quite clear-cut and simple. After a brief introduction the protagonist falls asleep:

> The earth recedes from me into the night,
> I saw that it was beautiful . . . . and I see that
> what is not the earth is beautiful.
>
> I go from bedside to bedside . . . . I sleep close with
> the other sleepers, each in turn.
> ("The Sleepers," 27–29)

His dreams, confused and indistinct as they are, grow more and more somber. As if to remind himself that he is dreaming, about halfway through the poem the "I"—turning over in his sleep, one might say—mutters:

> I turn but do not extricate myself;
> Confused . . . . a pastreading . . . . another, but with
> darkness yet.
> ("The Sleepers," 92–93)

The sequence culminates in a nightmarish moment of dark, murderous fury ("The Sleepers," 127–34), which then dispels the gloom and yields to serene visions of light and harmony: "A show of the summer softness . . . . a contact of something unseen . . . . an amour of the light and air" ("The Sleepers," 135). From these dreams of healing, reintegration, and joy the "I" wakes up invigorated and enlightened: "I too pass from the night" ("The Sleepers," 195). He has learnt no longer to dread the rhythm of gratification and guilt that defines his consciousness because he has understood that it is but a version of life's cyclic scheme of day and night. Other crises may follow, but he now knows that the night will help him to weather them again:

> I will stop only a time with the night . . . . and rise
> betimes.

236

CLOSED STATEMENTS, OPEN STRUCTURE

I will duly pass the day O my mother and duly return
to you;
("The Sleepers," 201–2)

Two patterns emerge from this sequence. One of them is progressive, from nightfall to dawn, from confusion to reassurance, from fear to trust, or, as a study of the poem's "shades of darkness" has it, from "an empty darkness" to "the softness of a heavenly night that contains all shades of darkness and light." [13] The other, more important pattern is cyclical, leading up to a climactic moment of confrontation with the central mystery and then leading away from it—a going in followed by a coming out, immersion followed by emergence, departure followed by return, search followed by discovery, a quest followed by a homecoming.[14] The sensual nature of the episodes and images that make up the protagonist's dream both before and after its high point indicates that the confrontation has to do with the elemental, unconscious tensions that, manifesting themselves in the interplay of his erotic impulses and inhibitions, determine the distinctive identity of his awareness.

The significance of this confrontation is evident from the pains taken by the "I" to protect his waking self from it with a double barrier of dreams at the same time that he makes strenuous efforts to seek it out. Bucke's statement that "The Sleepers" is simply "a representation of the mind during sleep" [15] stops short of the whole truth on at least two counts. When the poem's speaker announces that he has fallen asleep he does not merely disclaim all moral responsibility for the actions of his mind because, as Holloway put it, "there is in dreaming a moratorium on morality"; [16] he also increases the distance between his conscience and the dreams he would rather not be responsible for by explaining that they are not even his. They are "the dreams of the other dreamers" and while dreaming them he himself is "become the other dreamers" ("The Sleepers," 30–31); therefore, if he incurs blame it is really "theirs," not his. Since on their own the dreams do not quite seem reprehensible enough to justify such intense anxiety about them, one must as-

237

sume that the private significance of what is to follow is much greater than that which meets the casual eye. This impression is confirmed by the strong indications that, in spite of his anxiety or quite possibly because of it, the "I" does not just passively sink into his sleep but brings it on deliberately. As long as he remains awake, he is oppressed by the sights that the night heaps around him; he is "wandering and confused . . . . lost to [himself] . . . . ill-assorted . . . . contradictory" ("The Sleepers," 4). When, in a gesture that is at once "soothing" and self-protecting, he passes his hands "to and fro a few inches from" the wretched sleepers ("The Sleepers," 25), the result is, indeed, "magic," as E. H. Miller remarked,[17] but of a purposeful, intentional kind. The protagonist escapes his anguish by inducing, like a shaman of sorts, his own redemptive and illuminating sleep as if it were a ritual trance: "I am a dance . . . . Play up there! the fit is whirling me fast" ("The Sleepers," 32).

As to the moment of truth at the poem's core, there is not a great deal to add to Richard Chase's reading of it as the culmination of "the more somber moments when we behold the dark motives and characters of the family drama which underlies some of the greatest tragic poems." [18] The scenes leading up to it display considerable variety, and the continuity among them is sometimes not immediately clear, but they all treat of erotic frustration and guilt, and all their participants are identified by some manner of family relationship. Therefore, when the speaker, dreaming that he is Lucifer's "sorrowful terrible heir," exclaims,

> I have been wronged . . . . I am oppressed . . . . I hate
> him that oppresses me,
> I will either destroy him or he shall release me. [. . .]
> Now the vast dusk bulk that is the whale's bulk . . . . it
> seems mine,
> Warily, sportsman! though I lie so sleepy and sluggish,
> my tap is death.
> ("The Sleepers," 127, 128–29, 133–34)

he is, as E. H. Miller has shown, "voicing his oedipal murderous tendencies" and thereby finds "release for pent-up tension and

238

anxiety." [19] What needs to be added is that with his extraordinary "night journey" into the unconscious Whitman's "I" is not merely verifying that he has undergone what might be called the common childhood disease of the psyche. It is certainly no accident that at this point he calls himself by the name of one who, archangel or black slave, must live under the detested sway of a male parental figure—God the Father or Southern "massa," [20]— for throughout the poem "insistently present is the encompassing image of the mother," [21] and to find and possess her and to be possessed by her is his constant purpose, whatever its manifestations. At the same time, he convicts himself with the name "Lucifer," for it places him among those who are morally or—this is 1855—existentially damned forever. He thus acknowledges his offense against the father—the image of the huge, threatening phallic bulk of the whale is, after all, profoundly ambivalent and may suggest the vengeful father as well as it suggests the immense, aggressive spite of the male child—and therefore hates him: this guilty parricidal fury is the intolerable, terrifying bane of the waking self.[22]

Thus, the "I" has finally looked his fears in the face. The central significance of "The Sleepers" in the first *Leaves of Grass* is that under the protection of a dream experienced through surrogate identities the self braves in it the menace of those savage, guilt-haunted regions of the mind that he shrank from in panic terror in the first poem when, enchanted by the "soul," he allowed himself to be lured towards them by the "grass." "The Sleepers" completes, then, what the first poem began, yet it makes clear that the resolution it provides is only temporary. The restorative "night journey" it assures is simply a safety valve against the excessive pressure of the forces that the waking self can control only through the heroic identity which the first poem creates.

The book runs down rather quickly after "The Sleepers." The next poem, "I Sing the Body Electric," is another performance that was probably salvaged from "cuttings" from the first poem—most likely from drafts and variations of the theme of "I

believe in the flesh and appetites" (524); it sounds like a preparation for "the greatest poet's" hymn of praise to his own body
(530 ff.). It has the simplest organization. It begins with a question:

> Was it dreamed whether those who corrupted their
> own live bodies could conceal themselves?
> And whether those who defiled the living were as
> bad as they who defiled the dead?
> ("I Sing the Body Electric," 3–4)

and it concludes with the answer that, indeed, it was not ("I Sing
the Body Electric," [116–19]). This conclusion is reached through
a long and exuberant celebration of the human body and
through it "the divine essence immanent in every material form
and process." [23] By itself, this poem might, perhaps, reveal some
special attractions of its own, but in the neighborhood of "Song
of Myself" and following immediately after "The Sleepers" it is
entirely eclipsed.

On the other hand, "Faces," the next poem, is a fascinating
poetic elaboration of the teacher-orator's expansive declaration
in the first poem that "I acknowledge the duplicates of myself
under all the scrape-lipped and pipe-legged concealments"
(1076). This sentiment becomes the occasion of a virtuoso series
of inventive, vigorous metaphors of faces:

> This face is a haze more chill than the arctic sea,
> Its sleepy and wobbling icebergs crunch as they go. [. . .]
> This face owes to the sexton his dismalest fee,
> An unceasing deathbell tolls there. [. . .]
> This face is a lifeboat; [. . .]
> This face is a flavored fruit ready for eating; [. . .]
> ("Faces," 22–23, 32–33, 52, 54)

As Harold Aspiz has shown, Whitman's perspective is consistently "phreno-physiognomical" in this poem; the two pseudo-
sciences provide him with the theory and terminology out of
which he can develop his report that he has "[descried] man's

240

advancement in time's unending scheme." [24] The list of faces concludes with a portrait which is obviously meant to be the strongest and best proof that the speaker is right not to allow himself to be "tricked" by "haggard and mean disguises" because in the end all faces "show their descent from the Maker himself" ("Faces," 36, 38, 57); no attentive reader of the volume can be surprised by it:

> Behold a woman!
> She looks out from her quaker cap . . . . her face is
>   clearer and more beautiful than the sky. [. . .]
> The melodious character of the earth!
> The finish beyond which philosophy cannot go and does
>   not wish to go!
> The justified mother of men!
>
> ("Faces," 77–78, 83–85)

III

"Faces" is the last poem to be headed by the title "Leaves of Grass" in the volume; the rest of the poems, six shorter pieces in all, are separated from one another only by a continuous double line running across the page. As the preceding pages have shown, each of the five titled poems is a self-contained whole; there are, however, traces of a continuity among them, which bear examining, even if the conclusions they suggest can be only speculative.

These five poems are linked by a motif: the steady, processional movement forward. In "A Song for Occupations" this motif is merely in the cumulative effect of the long catalogue that makes up most of the poem, but in "To Think of Time" it becomes a concrete image in "the burial lines," the "slowmoving and black lines [that] creep over the whole earth" ("To Think of Time," 30, cf. also 90). The motif is continued in the sequence of dreams that leads up to the climactic point in "The Sleepers"; then it modulates into the lovely image of the sleepers as "they flow hand in hand over the whole earth from east to west" ("The Sleepers," 180). "All is a procession," the speaker declares in "I Sing the Body Electric," but then the motif begins to lose intensity as his eyes linger on the "slave at auction" and the "woman at auction" ("I Sing the Body Electric," 78, 83 ff., 104 ff.). Finally, in "Faces" progression is again only an effect in the onrush of the catalogue, and that, too, ceases as the poem comes to a rest with its last, luminous image of "the justified mother of men" ("Faces," 85).

If by virtue of this processional, forward impulse running through them these five poems are viewed not as five separate utterances but as a single, continuous statement, their sequence gives structural prominence to the passages that have been found thematically most relevant to the rest of the volume. At virtually dead center stands the awesome moment in "The Sleepers" which, in a sense, accounts for the entire first poem as the "I" finally lets himself comprehend in it that what fills him with deadly terror is his own oedipal rage. It is logical, then, that the sequence should conclude with the image of the mother, because by reaching it the orphaned sensibility of the "offspring taken out of the mother's lap" (105) has found at last what it was searching for and has no reason to move further.

One must be suspicious, of course, whenever such a neat and symmetrical organization suggests itself in Whitman's work, particularly when it is based on a motif that at times grows very faint indeed and on themes that are nowhere in the volume explicitly started. At any rate, in the remaining six poems, which the lack of the titles sets conspicuously off from the preceding portions of the book, even such tenuous continuity is absent, whether by motif or by theme. They are shorter, plainly limited in scope, and all too uneven in quality.

Holloway thought that "Song of the Answerer" is "in some respects the most harmonious poem in the book," [25] but the reasons that might have prompted his judgment are rather hard to find in it, unless he meant that its unremarkable argument is matched by the undistinguished presentation. It is, as Allen has aptly phrased it, "a weak treatment of one of the themes in the preface, the Messianic role of the 'great poet' "; [26] however, not just the theme but the voice and the manner, too, bring to mind the speaker of the Preface and his stentorian and impersonal declarations:

> Books friendships philosophers priests action
> > pleasure pride beat up and down seeking to
> > give satisfaction;
> He indicates the satisfaction, and indicates them
> > that beat up and down also.
>
> Whichever the sex . . . whatever the season or place he
> > may go freshly and gently and safely by day or
> > by night,
> He has the passkey of hearts . . . . to him the response
> > of the prying of hands on the knobs.
> > > ("Song of the Answerer," 23–26)

Such blandly assertive style had its justification in the Preface, but at this point it is altogether unconvincing and tedious. The less said about the next two poems—"Europe: The 72d and 73d Years of These States" and "A Boston Ballad"—the better. This rapid decline in quality and substance as the book draws near its close is a rather melancholy foreshadowing of what is to come in the years after 1855: none of the subsequent editions of *Leaves of Grass* will ever be free of such annoying flaws. As a matter of fact, they will be even more conspicuous in the later editions than in the first because Whitman's constant expansion and revision of the book strove toward a closed structure, whereas the flexible, open structure of the 1855 volume could admit such liabilities with only the slightest impairment to itself.

The last truly successful piece in the book is "There Was a Child Went Forth." Essentially, it is, as R. W. B. Lewis notes, "Whitman's most unequivocal account of the thrust toward being" [27]—a brief but remarkably complete autobiography of the poetic sensibility that eventually produces *Leaves of Grass*. It has been a favorite with the public from the first, probably because, though vintage Whitman, it seems such a thoroughly un-complicated, simple poem. Many readers have discovered by now all manner of complexity in it,[28] but a remark of the poet himself may afford on it, in the end, the most accurate perspective. Very late in his life, in 1889, he professed surprise, according to Traubel, that his poem found such favor with his readers, adding: "There is really nothing in it at all—nothing at all. . . . It is a mere looking-about at things. . . . Nothing in it except perhaps a suggestion—nothing in it except what is to be credited to the reader himself—except what is stirred up in him." [29] In any case, the hero of this poem is at least as impressive as his story. The child who "went forth" may well be father to "the greatest poet," but he is assuredly twin to the child who said "What is the grass?" (90) and thus launched the "I" toward his fateful encounter with himself.

In the last two poems the creative energy is all but completely exhausted. "Who Learns My Lesson Complete" is an innocuous and trivial reiteration of the poet's "insight" that whatever is, is not so much right as "wonderful"; nowhere else in the volume does Whitman come as close to parodying himself as here:

> And that I grew six feet high. . . . and that I have
>   become a man thirty-six years old in 1855 . . . .
>   and that I am here anyhow—are all equally
>   wonderful; [. . .[
>
> And that I can think such thoughts as these is just
>   as wonderful,
> And that I can remind you, and you think them and know
>   them to be true is just as wonderful,
>   ("Who Learns My Lesson Complete," 22, 24–25)

Finally, with "Great Are the Myths" the first *Leaves of Grass* comes to rest in its own, private Marabar Caves, in which every sound "is entirely devoid of distinction. Whatever is said, the same monotonous noise replies. . . ." In Whitman's poem, the noise is "great," but it is just like Forster's "boum": "utterly dull." [30]

The book thus ends in the hoarse whisper of a man who means to continue shouting but has run out of voice and breath. It is an ending which refuses to be a conclusion. The same principle is at work in it as in most of the catalogues in the volume: even when the words cease, the vision they have induced goes on expanding. It is part of the peculiar excellence of Whitman's achievement that, far from proving a defect, this defiantly inconclusive ending, like the strong fluctuations in quality among various individual pieces, works ultimately to the poet's advantage and reinforces the impression of dynamic completeness that prevails in the book.

As Symonds observed,

> What is most remarkable in the history of this work is the way in which the original conception admitted of infinite extension and adjustment. You feel, on looking through the slender volume of 1855, that the author already contemplated additions, and that the extremely singular style and form of his poems were adapted to this method of treatment. [31]

The secret of this organization is in the first poem's unique capacity to act as the work's indestructible center, fit to harbor for good and bad, splendor and dross, alike. The arrangement of the book suggests that the self-absorption of the first poem's speaker is not an oversight and that he was not exaggerating much when he said that he "[knew his] omnivorous words" (1080). It clearly establishes the special rank and function of the first poem in Whitman's plan. With all the other poems—in all subsequent editions as well as in the first—the first poem, which *is* the self-realized "greatest poet," reaches out into the world around, " [launching them] forth," like the "noiseless patient spider," "filament, filament, filament out of itself." [32] The first edition's structural integrity is due to this dynamic scheme; it makes the book the organic, open affair it is, complete at all times yet capable of accommodating both growth and change.

245

IV

With this last proposition the present attempt to interpret the first edition of *Leaves of Grass* has reached the end of its argument; a brief review of its major conclusions should complete its case.

Even a cursory survey of the book's contents will bear out what its physical design implies: it is not a collection of independent statements but a single poetic argument meant to be read from cover to cover. The arrangement of the volume provides, therefore, the plan appropriate to its study, too. The Preface must be understood before one can make proper sense of the first poem, and the rest of the poems, in their turn, depend squarely on the first for elucidation.

The essay introducing the volume is meant to provide the context which Whitman held indispensable for the proper response to his poems: his audience's intimate familiarity with the poet's person. It is not a conventional preface in which a poetic theory and program are articulated but an oratorical performance in which learning to know the speaker by his distinctive habits of mind and expression is more important than being persuaded by his speech. The essay is organized into five major movements by the alternation of emphasis between its two complementary themes—"America" and "the poet"—and it reflects the "triplicate process," the conceptual pattern of Whitman's thinking. In this process, represented as the universal love-making of opposites, centripetal and centrifugal impulses fuse to create a "bipolar unity" of "pride" and "sympathy," that is, of introversion and extroversion.

Complementary aspects of an envisioned state of mind, "America" and "the poet" project an ambition; the formal realization of the mode of being which fulfills this ambition is what Whitman calls poetry. *Leaves of Grass* is to the ambition that is "the poet" what the United States is to the vision that is "America." The speaker's unwarranted shrillness in discussing politics, sex, and "prudence" reveals that this thematic structure of "triplicate" logic is based on a spontaneous rhythm of association in which elemental impulses of self-assertion are invariably followed by self-denying reactions of compulsive force. In the mentality disclosed by this drama of meaning the reader encounters the person capable of both conceiving and fulfilling the ambition of becoming "the poet."

The first poem realizes this ambition. It begins on a note of emphatic self-assertion, which is particularly loud after the essay's studied impersonality. The poem's language displays a polarity which corresponds to the bipolar unity of "sympathy" and "pride" in the Preface. It is capable of complete rhetorical extroversion in dialogues with "you" and of its opposite in spontaneous, self-absorbed asides or exclamations. This polarity suggests a "triplicate" structure in which the "I" alternately "merges" with the world of the "grass" outside him and the world of the "soul" within. Such a symmetrical arrangement, however, is not supported by the facts. Fewer than a hundred lines are addressed to "you." The poem is almost exclusively self-centered, its bulk being a meditation by a man profoundly alone. This meditation is conducted in three major attitudes: the "contemplative," the "didactic-prophetic," and the "histrionic."

The poem's crucial episode is the passage initiated by the speaker's vision of harmony following his recollection of his metaphoric sexual union with the "soul." The ecstatic vision makes him turn "outward," to the "grass"; that, in turn, precipitates anxiety, then morbid fear of death, which would drive him "inward," toward the "soul" again. The vicious circle would grind him up; to interrupt it, the "I," in desperation, strikes a pose of invincibility—and "the greatest poet" appears! This sequence provides a key to the pattern of rhetorical modulations in the poem. The discourse is gradually drawn by a "centripetal" force through its "prophetic-didactic," "contemplative," and "histrionic" stages toward extreme introversion, but upon reaching this point it is hurled abruptly back toward the opposite end by the "centrifugal" power of the imperative of preserving the "self" through the "other." This pattern, corresponding to the rhythm of association seen in the Preface, is the poem's organizing principle—its "heartbeat." Whitman's comments on his own methods of composition suggest that though not entirely conscious of this "heartbeat," he was not unaware of it, either.

The possibilities of a phasal structure in the poem can be reconciled with this essentially non-phasal rhythm by recognizing that they reflect the reader's perception of the poem, whereas the "heartbeat" formulates its subject: the endless instant in which a single percipient act of the will to become eludes the destructive cycle of horror and ecstasy by embodying the awareness which is "the greatest poet." The poem is the imaginative inventory of that single instant, and as such it can be resolved into a nine-part structure. An introduction which establishes the poetic and conceptual idiom of the protagonist's transformation is followed by the scene of the visionary enactment of his metamorphosis into "the greatest poet," and this scene is reenacted in various contexts of awareness in a pseudo-narrative of seven phases.

As a cultural gesture, the poem is radically new in that it establishes a new, "physiological" mode of self-realization. Implicit in the unembarrassed eclecticism of its methods is its protagonist's categorical demand to be acknowledged as sufficient in and unto himself. The poem is essentially American both by virtue of that demand and because the poet's myth of self-realization coincides with that of the nation. Through his subtle reliance on the idiom of Genesis Whitman expresses his protagonist's transformation as the central event in a personal myth of self-creation. The poem is, ultimately, the rite, the ceremony of verbal gestures, which perpetuates this event; therefore, in the first as well as all later editions of Leaves of Grass it means the presence of the awareness that is "the greatest poet."

The rest of the poems, as this last chapter has shown, round out the volume by providing, in "The Sleepers," at least a temporary resolution of the conflict that precipitates the "greatest

248

poet's" self-creation. They also reveal through their relationship to the first poem the dynamic scheme of organization by which the volume, while complete in itself, proves capable of further expansion and change.

As time went on, that scheme, though admirable to the last, became less and less dynamic, perhaps because Whitman himself was not entirely convinced that he passed the trial that he invited with his first book. It was, to be sure, an all but impossibly demanding test. It would grant the success of *Leaves of Grass* only if "the greatest poet" is "the age transfigured" (xi); therefore, the "age" alone can attest to it by "affectionately absorbing" him. To do so, the "age"—the country—would have to own not just the heroic splendor of his triumph but the fear and trembling as well out of which it is born. Soon enough Whitman himself seems to have found the proposition "interesting, but tough" and, preferring to make more of the triumph and say less about its origins, helped to bury his masterpiece. No edition after the first was to be a "trial" in which private and public significance would have to be realized together or not at all.

He cannot be blamed much for his diffidence and for the element of dissimulation that it introduced into his work, for "the greatest poet" of the first edition has received at best a mirthless and uneasy recognition from his country to this day. He has been "absorbed," indeed, but "affection" has had little to do with it. The text, meanwhile, survives; the trial of the poet, therefore, goes on, only the emphasis has been shifted. The proof of "America" is that it absorbs its "greatest poet" "as affectionately as he has absorbed it" (xii).

NOTES

INTRODUCTION

1. "Song of Myself," lines 12–13, *CRE*, p. 29.

2. Edward Carpenter recorded this remark of the aging Whitman. See Frederik Schyberg, *Walt Whitman*, trans. Evie A. Allen (New York: Columbia University Press, 1951), p. 243.

3. *Putnam's Monthly*, September 1855; rpt. as "Whitman's Leaves of Grass (1855)," in *A Century of Whitman Criticism*, ed. E. H. Miller (Bloomington, Ind.: Indiana University Press, 1969), p. 4.

4. "Some Lines from Whitman," in *Poetry and the Age* (New York: Alfred A. Knopf, 1953), p. 132.

5. *Cowley*, p. x.

6. Quentin Anderson's phrase, in *The Imperial Self* (1971; rpt. New York: Vintage Books, 1972), p. 90.

7. *CRE*, pp. 584–85.

8. The first was published as "Resurgemus," in 1850 (*Early*, pp. 38–41), the second was subtitled "1854" in the later editions (*CRE*, pp. 264–65).

9. *Cowley*, pp. vii–xxvii. *Singer*, pp. 149–69.

10. *Naissance, passim. The Evolution of Walt Whitman: The Creation of a Personality* (Cambridge, Mass.: Harvard University Press, 1960), pp. 47–79.

11. *Cowley*, p. ix.

12. The most recent and by all odds the most complete treatment of the subject is Joseph Jay Rubin's *The Historic Whitman* (University Park, Pa.: The Pennsylvania State University Press, 1973).

NOTES: INTRODUCTION

13. *UPP,* II, 65, 69–70.

14. *UPP,* II, 63*n*1.

15. Cf. R. M. Bucke, "Notes on the Text of *Leaves of Grass,*" *The Conservator,* 7 (May 1896), 40.

16. *UPP,* II, 82.

17. See Rubin, *The Historic Whitman,* p. 307.

18. *WWC,* I, 92.

19. *Historicism Once More* (Princeton: Princeton University Press, 1969), p. 6.

20. Gay Wilson Allen, "Regarding the 'Publication' of the First *Leaves of Grass,*" *American Literature,* 28 (1956), 78–79.

21. The four issues are described by C. J. Furness in *Facs,* pp. [vi]–[vii]; the other data are based on Rubin's account in *The Historic Whitman,* pp. 307–8.

22. For an optimistic report, see "Whitman to Emerson, 1856," *CRE,* p. 730; for a less exuberant account, see *WWC,* III, 115–16.

23. Rubin, *The Historic Whitman,* p. 308.

24. *Facs,* pp. [x]–[xi].

25. *The Historic Whitman,* pp. 306–7.

26. "Poetic Diction and Legal Fiction," in *The Importance of Language,* ed. Max Black (Englewood Cliffs, N.J.: Prentice-Hall, 1962), p. 53.

27. *Die Metamorphose der Pflanzen,* in *Goethes Werke* (Hamburg: Christian Wegner, 1955), XIII, 100–1.

28. Entry dated October 13, 1836, in *The Journals and Miscellaneous Notebooks of Ralph Waldo Emerson,* V, ed. M. Sealts (Cambridge, Mass.: Harvard University Press, 1965), 220.

29. "Humanity of Science," in *The Early Lectures of Emerson,* ed. S. Whicher, R. Spiller, and W. E. Williams (Cambridge, Mass.: Harvard University Press, 1964), II, 23–24. According to the editor's note (*ibid.,* p. 22), Emerson delivered this lecture in a somewhat revised form even after 1840.

30. *Singer,* pp. 52–53.

31. Cf. C. J. Furness' list of some of them in *Facs,* p. [x].

32. Richard Maurice Bucke, M.D., *Walt Whitman* (Philadelphia: David McKay, 1883), p. 137.

33. *Singer,* p. 150.

34. *Cowley,* p. vii.

35. Perry Miller, *The Raven and the Whale* (New York: Harcourt, Brace & World, 1956), p. 107.

36. Thomas Carlyle, *Sartor Resartus* (1833; rpt. New York: Macmillan, 1927), p. 45.

NOTES: WHAT'S IN A TITLE?

CHAPTER ONE / WHAT'S IN A TITLE?

1. *Walt Whitman* (Boston: Houghton Mifflin, 1906), p. 74.

2. *Corr 1868–1875,* pp. 99–100.

3. *Corr 1842–1867,* p. 347.

4. *Corr 1842–1867,* p. 352.

5. *Singer,* p. 386.

6. For some of these second thoughts, see *WWC,* II, 310–11, where Whitman is quoted conceding, in 1888, that he "may have underrated the preface."

7. Cf. Willie T. Weathers, "Whitman's Poetic Translations of His 1855 Preface," *American Literature,* 19 (1947), 21–40.

8. Weathers, p. 33.

9. Weathers, p. 23.

10. Unsigned review in *The New York Tribune,* Monday, July 23, 1855, p. 3. Its author was Charles A. Dana (*Singer,* p. 169).

11. Weathers, pp. 23–24.

12. Jean Catel, *Rythme et langage dans la Ire édition des "Leaves of Grass"* (1855) (Montpellier: Causse, Graille et Castelnau, 1930), p. 15.

13. Emory Holloway, *Whitman: An Interpretation in Narrative* (New York: Knopf, 1926), p. 121.

14. *Workshop,* p. 125.

15. For some representative statements on the Preface, see Holloway, *Whitman,* p. 121; Catel, *Rythme et langage,* pp. 15 ff.; *Singer,* pp. 153 ff.; and Schyberg, *Walt Whitman,* pp. 80–82.

16. "Observations Prefixed to 'Lyrical Ballads,' " in *The Great Critics,* ed. J. H. Smith and E. W. Parks (New York: Norton, 1951), pp. 499–500.

17. Noting these "correspondences," F. O. Matthiessen felt that they were "all the more interesting for being independent reactions" (*American Renaissance* [New York: Oxford University Press, 1941], p. 614), but Roger Asselineau has shown convincing proof that they were not all that independent and therefore not all that miraculous ("Whitman et Wordsworth—Etude d'une influence indirecte," *Revue de Littérature Comparée,* 19 [1955], 505–12).

18. "Egotism—As Manifested in the Works and Lives of Great and Small Men," anonymous article in *Graham's Magazine,* May, 1845; quoted in Asselineau, "Whitman et Wordsworth," p. 509.

19. "Whitman et Wordsworth," p. 509.

20. *Workshop,* pp. 117 ff.

21. *Workshop,* p. 122.

22. *Workshop,* p. 120; also cf. pp. 127, 131, 135, 167, 169, 171, and 174.

23. *Corr 1842–1867,* p. 347.

24. E.g., Holloway, *Whitman,* p. 121, or James E. Miller, Jr., *A Critical Guide to Leaves of Grass* (Chicago: University of Chicago Press, 1957), p. 256.

25. *Walt Whitman,* p. 74.

26. Weathers, p. 23.

27. Anonymous "Advertisement" at the back of *As a Strong Bird on Pinions Free,* Washington, 1872; quoted in *Workshop,* p. 123.

28. "Walt Whitman and His Poems," *United States Review,* September 1855 (anonymously), reprinted in *Walt Whitman, A Critical Anthology,* ed. Francis Murphy (Middlesex, England: Penguin Books, Ltd., 1969), p. 35.

29. *Workshop,* p. 28.

30. *American Renaissance,* (New York: Oxford University Press, 1941), p. 19.

31. *American Renaissance,* p. 20.

32. A boast completely unfounded at this time, made by Fowlers and Wells in an advertisement in *Life Illustrated,* August 16, 1856; quoted in *Singer,* p. 178. Also see *New York Dissected,* ed. E. Holloway and R. Adimari (New York: Rufus Rockwell Wilson, 1936), p. 171.

33. *Workshop,* p. 28.

34. *An American Primer by Walt Whitman,* ed. Horace Traubel (Boston: Small, Maynard Co., 1904), p. vii.

35. *An American Primer,* p. v.

36. *Workshop,* p. 33; also pp. 208–9, n. 45.

37. *Workshop,* p. 36.

38. *Workshop,* p. 49.

39. *Workshop,* p. 34.

40. *WWC,* III, 84.

41. *Workshop,* p. 33.

42. Quoted in *American Renaissance,* p. 553.

43. *Singer,* p. 156.

44. *An American Primer,* p. 20.

45. *Rhythme et langage,* pp. 20–21.

46. Notably by Matthiessen in *American Renaissance,* pp. 22–23 and pp. 549–58.

47. *Workshop,* p. 124.

48. "So Long," lines 53–54, *CRE,* p. 505.

49. *American Renaissance,* p. 557.

50. Cf. Roger Asselineau, *The Evolution of Walt Whitman: The Creation of a Book* (Cambridge: Harvard University Press, 1962), p. 114.

51. Quoted in Catel, *Rythme et langage,* pp. 52–53.

52. For a similar view, see Schyberg, *Whitman,* p. 109.

53. *CRE,* pp. 1–15.

54. See Miller, *Critical Guide to Leaves of Grass,* p. 189.

55. "To You," *CRE,* p. 14.

56. *CRE,* pp. 15–28.

CHAPTER TWO / THE "CURIOUS TRIPLICATE PROCESS"—IN THEORY

1. The distinctions of antiquity that divided all statements into either rhetoric or poetry are clearly useless here. Perhaps Schyberg's observation is the most accurate, even if the conclusions he drew from it are difficult to accept: the Preface is no longer oratory and not yet poetry (*Walt Whitman,* p. 82.).

2. *Essays, First Series,* in *Centenary,* II, 101–2.

3. *Centenary,* II, 68.

4. Perry Miller, *The Raven and the Whale,* p. 111.

5. *The Raven and the Whale,* p. 31.

6. "Language as Gesture," in *Visions and Revisions,* ed. B. S. Oldsey and A. O. Lewis (New York: E. P. Dutton, 1962), p. 204.

7. *Whitman: Explorations in Form* (Chicago: University of Chicago Press, 1966), p. 13.

8. *Studies in Classic American Literature* (1923; rpt. New York: Viking, 1966), p. 165.

9. *Workshop,* p. 49.

10. Waskow, *Explorations,* p. 9.

11. *Explorations,* p. 24.

12. Journal entry dated May 26, 1839, *The Journals and Miscellaneous Notebooks of Ralph Waldo Emerson,* ed. A. W. Plumstead and Harrison Hayford (Cambridge: Harvard University Press, 1969), VII, 200.

13. *Explorations,* pp. 11–12.

14. This list is based on the pairs given in Alfred H. Marks, "Whitman's Triadic Imagery," *American Literature,* 23 (1951), 99–126. Cf. also Emerson's list in "Compensation," *Essays, First Series,* in *Centenary,* II, 96–97.

15. Marks, pp. 99 ff.

16. Marks, p. 109.

17. *Cosmic Optimism: A Study of the Interpretation of Evolution by American Poets from Emerson to Robinson* (Gainesville: University of Florida Press, 1949), p. 107.

18. Marks, pp. 99–100.

19. *Explorations*, p. 23.

20. *The Dialogues of Plato*, trans. B. Jowett (Oxford: Oxford University Press, 1953), III, 153; Stevens's reference is given at the beginning of his essay "The Noble Rider and the Sound of Words," in *The Necessary Angel* (New York: Vintage, 1965), p. 3.

21. *Notes and Fragments Left by Walt Whitman*, ed. R. M. Bucke (London: Talbot, 1899), p. 35. Cf. also Millie D. Jensen, "Whitman and Hegel: The Curious Triplicate Process," *Walt Whitman Review*, 10 (June 1964), 27–34.

22. *Centenary*, I, 10.

23. Herman Melville, *Moby-Dick*, Chapter 35, "The Mast-Head."

24. *Biographia Literaria*, ed. J. Shawcross (1907; rpt. London: Oxford University Press, 1965), I, 74.

25. Melville probably did not know Goethe's remarks. Cf. Henry Pochmann, *German Culture in America* (Madison: University of Wisconsin Press, 1957), pp. 168–69 and p. 756n239.

26. From "The Metamorphosis of Plants," in *Goethe's Botanical Writings*, trans. Bertha Mueller (Honolulu: University of Hawaii Press, 1952); the original text of the passage will be found in *Goethes Werke* (Hamburg: Christian Wagner Verlag, 1955), XIII, 35.

27. *Explorations*, p. 51.

28. *Studies in Classic American Literature*, p. 165.

29. *Workshop*, p. 49.

30. See, for example, the famous note from 1847: "I cannot understand the mystery, but I am always conscious of myself as two—as my soul and I: and I reckon it is the same with all men and women" (*UPP*, II, 66).

31. A well-known passage of *Democratic Vistas* corroborates this interpretation in images and phrasing remarkably similar to Goethe's. The words also suggest at this point an alternative, collective context in which the "triplicate process" of the self's coherence—seen so far only in the context of the "simple separate person"—is possible: "For to democracy, the leveler, the unyielding principle of the average [i.e., the "sympathy" of the figure in the Preface], surely join'd another principle, equally unyielding, closely tracking the first, indispensable to it, opposite (as the sexes are opposite), . . . the counterpart and offset whereby Nature restrains the daily original relentlessness of all her first-class laws [i.e., the laws based on the assumption 'that men, the nation . . . must . . . be placed . . . on one broad, primary, universal, common platform,' p. 380]. This

second principle is individuality, the pride and centripetal isolation of a human being in himself" (PW 1892, II, 391).

32. Naturally this fullness has nothing to do with the concept of *plenitude* Allen discusses as one aspect under which the idea of the Chain of Being is relevant to *Leaves of Grass* (*Handbook*, pp. 278–79). Cf. Coleridge: "*All* is an endlessly fleeting abstraction; the *whole* is a reality" (*Table Talk*, in *Coleridge: Selected Poetry and Prose*, ed. S. Potter [London: Oxford University Press, 1933], p. 506).

33. In this instance, Whitman seems to be following Emerson's lead as he "traces to the root" his word and attempts to resuscitate what may have struck him as its original sense: to do enough, to make sufficient—hence, to fulfill. The full significance of what this meant for Whitman is evident from the parallel he draws in these two lines in the first edition: "I cannot define my satisfaction . . . yet it is so, / I cannot define my life . . . yet it is so" ("To Think of Time," 129–30). In the Preface, the word "satisfy" appears only twice (xi, xii), although both times in this unconventional sense that Whitman uncovered in it. In the poems of the first edition, however, it occurs quite frequently, its power increasing as the odd and initially confusing usage asserts itself. In later editions, Whitman discarded what was, in fact, a surfeit of "satisfaction" in some of these poems.

34. Surveying the representative stands the transcendentalists have taken on "the problems of epistemology," Furness notes that Whitman "eventually adopted the attitude of the older mystics toward perception, embracing the view . . . that 'all knowledge flows out from man into the object,' but that 'the object has a reality in itself, which awakens the knowledge in the spirit' " (*Workshop*, p. 236n138; cf. *Handbook*, p. 254n56).

35. Henry Alonzo Myers, "Whitman's Conception of the Spiritual Democracy, 1855–1856," *American Literature*, 6 (1934–35), 243.

36. There is a similarity between this "poetic quality" in the consciousness and Coleridge's "Inner Sense" (*Biographia Literaria*, I, 172). Both are conceived as faculties that must be cultivated, and there is a degree of refinement to both that each writer considers indispensable for that act of contemplation which I. A. Richards defines as a "realizing intuition" (Myers' "clear vision"): the first, fundamental act in what the one describes as poetry and the other as philosophy. Out of this act follows, in Coleridge's scheme, "the postulate of philosophy and at the same time the test of philosophic capacity . . . the heaven descended KNOW THYSELF" (*Biographia Literaria*, I, 172). The scheme's most provocative statement is that "all knowledge rests on the coincidence of an object with a subject"; taking his cue from it, Richards comments: "Coleridge deliberately makes this postulate seem *arbitrary*. It is an act of the will, a direction of the *inner sense*, a mode of action, or of being, at the same time that it is a mode of knowing. It is that activity of the mind in which knowing and doing and making and being are least to be distinguished" (*Coleridge on Imagination*, [1960; rpt. Bloomington: Indiana University Press, 1965], p. 47.) This account is strikingly close to Charles Feidelson's version of Whitman's concept of poetry: "A poem . . . instead of referring to a completed act of perception, constitutes the act it-

self, both in the author and in the reader; instead of describing reality a poem is a realization" (*Symbolism and American Literature* [Chicago: University of Chicago Press, 1955], p. 18); his words, in turn, may seem just a cautious elaboration of Whitman's own saw: "to be is just as great as to perceive or tell" (viii).

37. *Explorations*, p. 63.

38. *Explorations*, p. 62.

39. Conner, *Cosmic Optimism*, pp. 105 ff.

40. "Whitman's Triadic Imagery," p. 109.

41. *UPP*, II, 69–70. For some other, equally inconclusive, attempts to define the term, see Asselineau, *Walt Whitman: The Creation of a Book*, p. 34; *Handbook*, p. 252; Waskow, *Explorations*, pp. 17–18.

42. E.g., the function of "soul" in such juxtapositions as "If he does not attract his own land body and soul to himself " (xi) or "what is clear to the senses and to the soul" (viii) elucidates the sense of the phrases in which the entire triad is only implied, as in "the soul has never been once fooled and never can be fooled" (ix).

43. Cf. "I too had been struck from the float forever held in solution." ("Crossing Brooklyn Ferry," line 62, *CRE*, p. 162).

44. Cf. R. C. Tuttle's warning: "There is no greater critical absurdity than to attempt to analyze philosophically Whitman's dialectic." (*The Identity of Walt Whitman* [Diss., University of Washington, 1965], p. 24).

45. *Handbook*, pp. 158–59.

46. *Walt Whitman, an American* (Boston: Houghton Mifflin Co., 1943), p. 191.

47. Mary A. Neuman, " 'Song of Myself,' Section 21: An Explication," *Walt Whitman Review*, 13 (September 1967), 98.

48. *Explorations*, p. 30.

49. Key passages in the volume's first poem confirm these hints. The poet's languorous reminiscence of how the soul "reached till you felt my beard, and reached till you held my feet" (81) also recalls that, of the soul's pride and sympathy, "neither can stretch too far while it stretches in company with the other," and the splendid lines about the loving "bedfellow" (52–57) echo the claim that "the inmost secrets of art sleep with the twain" and "the greatest poet has lain close betwixt both."

50. "Plato," in *Representative Men, Centenary*, IV, 55.

51. Whitman himself confirmed the importance of the image of the shoreline in his work (*WWC*, I, 414–15); Paul Fussell, Jr. ("Whitman's Curious Warble," in *The Presence of Walt Whitman*, ed. R. W. B. Lewis [New York: Columbia University Press, 1962] pp. 31–32) and Loren K. Davidson (*Whitman's "Song of Myself "* [Diss., Duke University, 1959], p. 29), among others, have commented upon it at length.

52. Richard V. Chase, *Walt Whitman Reconsidered* (London: Victor Gollancz Ltd., 1955), pp. 64–66.

53. Milton Hindus, "Notes Toward the Definition of a Typical Poetic Line in Whitman," *Walt Whitman Review*, 9 (December 1963), 78.

54. Roy Harvey Pearce, *The Continuity of American Poetry* (Princeton: Princeton University Press, 1961), p. 41.

55. *Singer*, p. 103.

56. Matthiessen notes that Whitman, who does not seem to have been very familiar with Hawthorne's work at all, probably did not have Hawthorne's definition of the romance in mind as he wrote his injunction against it. Nevertheless, Matthiessen goes on, "the poet would have been highly suspicious of Hawthorne's 'neutral territory' ['where the Actual and the Imaginary may meet']" because "it would have struck him as a sign that its author had not completely absorbed and mastered his material" (*American Renaissance*, p. 265). It seems only fair to add that both authors' experimentations with form originated in the same insight. Whitman would have accepted without any reservations any work of art which he found not to "swerve aside from the truth of the human heart." Besides, distrust as he might a self-acknowledged move to "neutral territory," that is, in fact, what he did himself through his language experiment.

57. *American Renaissance*, p. 264.

58. "Whitman's Conception of the Spiritual Democracy, 1855–1856," *American Literature*, 6 (1934–1935), 242.

59. Myers, pp. 246, 244, 243, 245–46, and 251.

CHAPTER THREE / THE "CURIOUS TRIPLICATE PROCESS"—IN PRACTICE

1. *Singer*, pp. 135, 138–39.

2. "Walt Whitman and His Chart of Bumps," *American Literature*, 2 (1931), 350–85.

3. Harold Aspiz, "Educating the Kosmos: 'There Was a Child Went Forth,' " *American Quarterly*, 18 (Winter 1966), 655.

4. Madeleine B. Stern, *Heads and Headlines* (Norman: University of Oklahoma Press, 1971), pp. ix–xv.

5. *Singer*, p. 81.

6. Hungerford, p. 357; *Singer*, p. 81; *Heads and Headlines*, p. 100.

7. Hungerford, p. 364. Cf. also *Singer*, p. 103; *Heads and Headlines*, pp. 102–5.

8. Hungerford, p. 367. Hence the ungainly terms "alimentiveness" and, elsewhere in the essay, "amativeness," and hence the extravagant usage of "comparison" and "causality" as aspects of character. "Alimentiveness" means simply a healthy appetite, and Whitman himself translates, in the very list discussed, "amativeness" as "fondness for women." Hungerford notes that "fondness for children" stands for another resounding phrenological term: "philoprogenitiveness."

9. Hungerford, p. 378.

10. *Whitman* (New York: Macmillan, 1938), p. 90.

11. For his efforts to sell his poems, see, for example, the following letters in *Corr 1842–1867:* Items #9 (p. 38), #15 (p. 47), #20 (p. 51), #24 (p. 57), #162 (p. 260), and #196 (p. 293). Also, his letters to his family show a constant, pathetic, and all too justified concern with money. His only relatively successful financial undertaking was his collection of funds for the wounded during 1862–1865.

12. *Whitman*, p. 107.

13. *Singer*, p. 147.

14. *In Re Walt Whitman,* ed. by his literary executors (Philadelphia: David Mackay, 1893), pp. 33–35; cf. *Singer*, pp. 116–17, 147.

15. *Naissance*, p. 373.

16. *Whitman*, p. 107.

17. "Whitman's Conception of the Spiritual Democracy, 1855–1856," *American Literature,* 6 (1934–35), 243.

18. *American Renaissance*, p. 542.

19. For some of the numerous comments on the Quaker influence on Whitman, see *Singer*, pp. 12–13, 20; Arvin, *Whitman*, p. 106; Matthiessen, *American Renaissance*, pp. 536–41; *Workshop*, pp. 12, 30.

20. "Whitman's Conception of Spiritual Democracy, 1855–1856," p. 246; Cf. also a phrase such as this one from an editorial Whitman wrote for the *Brooklyn Eagle* of June 23, 1847: "For our part, we look on [the] increase of [the] territory and power [of the U.S.] with the faith which the Christian has in God's mystery." *The Gathering of the Forces,* ed. C. Rogers and J. Black (New York: G. P. Putnam's Sons, 1920), I, 23; also *Singer*, pp. 84–85.

21. "Swarmery" is Carlyle's word for democracy in "Shooting Niagara, and After?", *Macmillan's Magazine,* XVI, 322; Whitman's furious response is in "Democracy," *The Galaxy,* IV, 925–26, in *PW 1892,* II, 748–50. See also Gregory Paine, "The Literary Relations of Whitman and Carlyle with Especial Reference to their Contrasting Views on Democracy," *Studies in Philology,* 36 (July 1939), 550–63.

22. *Democratic Vistas*, in *PW 1892,* II, 375.

23. *Singer*, pp. 82–91, 101–5, 146. How persistently the bitterness lingered after can be surmised from the spiteful stubbornness with which Whitman retained in his first volume the lines of invective he first spat onto paper against some politicians of the Democratic party in 1850: "Doughfaces, crawlers, Lice of Humanity, . . . Muck-worms, creeping flat to the ground" ("The House of Friends," in *Early,* pp. 36–37); the phrase is even "embellished": "the swarms of cringers, suckers, doughfaces, lice of politics, planners of sly involutions" (viii), and the same, less than sublime, image-cluster is evoked in one of the poems of the 1855 volume: "This now is too lamentable a face for a man; / Some abject louse ask-

ing leave to be . . . cringing for it, / Some milknosed maggot blessing what lets it wrig to its hole" ("Faces," 17 19).

24. *UPP*, I, 156.

25. Matthiessen, *American Renaissance*, p. 543.

26. In the opinion of Gregory Paine, "Whitman stressed the intelligence, the religion, and the culture of the individual man, and was not especially concerned with reform movements, political parties, labor organizations, or any other form of group action" ("The Literary Relations of Whitman and Carlyle," *Studies in Philology*, 36 [July 1939], 557). Matthiessen, on the other hand, states that Whitman "veered inevitably, though by no very coherent course, from individualism towards socialism" (*American Renaissance*, p. 543). *Libenter credimus quod volumus.* In any case, there is clearly more to understanding Whitman's political attitudes than simply separating his "realistic utterances" from his "romantic" ones, as one critic advised (Leadie M. Clark, *Walt Whitman's Concept of the American Common Man* [New York: Philosophical Library, 1955], p. viii), or forcing into lame "resolutions" either his chronic inconsistencies or his specific contradictions. It has been claimed, for instance, that "Whitman realized . . . the fallacy of Rousseau's conception of the will of the people, and that it must always be checked and held in restraint by constitutional guarantees of the liberty of the individual and for equality between individuals" (Arthur E. Briggs, *Walt Whitman: Thinker and Artist*, [New York: Philosophical Society, 1952], p. 212). There is nothing wrong with this positively idyllic picture of sagacious political moderation, except that it is false.

27. It is rather remarkable that while Paine can—quite accurately, of course—remind his readers that in *Sartor Resartus* "Carlyle first propounded his antidemocratic hero doctrine" ("The Literary Relations of Whitman and Carlyle," p. 552), Fred Manning Smith can argue altogether convincingly that if "Emerson . . . [has] brought [Whitman] to a boil [,] Carlyle"—especially through *Sartor*—"may have started the simmering" ("Whitman's Debt to Carlyle's Sartor Resartus," *Modern Language Quarterly*, 3 [March 1942], 65).

28. *Democratic Vistas*, in *PW 1892*, II, 422.

29. *The Evolution of Walt Whitman: The Creation of a Book*, p. 114.

30. *WWC*, III, 321.

31. Cf. *Handbook*, p. 117; *Naissance*, p. 435; Canby, *Walt Whitman, an American*, p. 202.

32. *Walt Whitman Reconsidered*, p. 50.

33. Wayland Young, *Eros Denied* (New York: Grove Press, 1964), p. 236.

34. *Corr 1842–1867*, pp. 346–47; cf. also *ibid.* n. 31.

35. "Walt Whitman and His Chart of Bumps," pp. 380–81.

36. Orson Squire Fowler, *Amativeness, or Evils and Remedies of Excessive and Perverted Sexuality* (New York: Fowlers and Wells, 1844), p. 22; Hungerford, p. 380.

37. *"Leaves of Grass* and the American Paradox," *Whitman: A Collection of Critical Essays,* ed. Roy Harvey Pearce (Englewood Cliffs, N.J.: Prentice-Hall, 1962), pp. 28–29.

38. Kinnaird, p. 29.

39. The marking is on pp. vii–ix in Whitman's own papercovered copy, now a drab brown but originally probably green, of the second issue of the first edition, in the Oscar Lion Collection in the New York Public Library. For a detailed description of the volume and its curious history, see *Facs,* pp. [xiii], [xvii] and *Workshop,* pp. 115–18.

40. "My prose preface to first Leaves of Grass," Whitman wrote to Peter Dixon in 1870, "was written hastily while the first edition was being printed in 1855 . . ." (*Corr 1868–1875,* pp. 99–100).

CHAPTER FOUR / CONCLUDING REMARKS ON THE PREFACE

1. *Walt Whitman,* p. 81; *American Renaissance,* pp. 541–42; *Singer,* p. 139.

2. Warner Berthoff, *The Example of Melville* (Princeton: Princeton University Press, 1962), p. 128.

3. Allen claims that this is the same as William James's theory of Pluralism (*Handbook,* p. 356n116).

4. Alain Bosquet, *Whitman* (Paris, Gallimard, 1959), pp. 87, 92.

5. *American Renaissance,* p. 531.

6. *The Well-Tempered Critic* (Bloomington: Indiana University Press, 1963), p. 24.

7. *Ibid.,* p. 22.

8. *Ibid.,* p. 20.

9. Cf. Genesis 1:2–4, 6–7, II:25.

10. *The American Adam* (Chicago: The University of Chicago Press, 1955), p. 43.

11. R. B. McElderry, Jr., has drawn attention to an unexpected parallel to this passage in Matthew Arnold's *Essays & Criticism, Second Series* (London, 1888), pp. 3–4 ("Poetry and Religion: A Parallel in Whitman and Arnold," *Walt Whitman Newsletter-Review,* 8 [December 1962], 80–83).

12. Genesis II:24.

13. The most complete list of the major influences and "echoes" in the first edition is probably the one given in *Singer,* pp. 138–45.

14. "Whose Walt Whitman?: French Scholar and American Critics," *English Studies,* 47 (June 1966), 206.

15. *PW 1892,* II, 458.

CHAPTER FIVE / WHITMAN'S LANGUAGE-LESSON AND ITS LIMITATIONS

1. For a similar argument advanced about "Kubla Khan," see Elisabeth Schneider, *Coleridge, Opium, and "Kubla Khan,"* (Chicago: University of Chicago Press, 1953), pp. 22–27.

2. This is, of course, tradition not entirely substantiated by fact. Allen does not mention it in *Singer.* However, Whitman himself claimed it was true in his old age (*WWC,* III, 80), Matthiessen takes it for granted (*American Renaissance,* p. 547, n. 9), and Fredson Bowers argues for it very convincingly (*Whitman's Manuscripts,* p. xxvi). The issue is fully discussed by Loren K. Davidson in an unpublished doctoral dissertation entitled *Whitman's "Song of Myself "* (Duke, 1959), which supports the tradition. Professor Davidson's study is a storehouse of essential data.

3. *Whitman's "Song of Myself,"* p. 146.

4. As patient scholars have ascertained, there are hardly any run-on lines in Whitman's apparently lawless poetry. A. N. Wiley found twenty of them among more than 10,500 lines ("Reiterative Devices in *Leaves of Grass," American Literature,* I [May 1929], 161n2), and according to Lois Ware there are thirty-seven among the 10,376 lines of the Inclusive Edition ("Poetic Conventions in 'Leaves of Grass,' " *Studies in Philology,* 26 [January 1929], 54–56). Ware also notes that commas at the end of lines are often not required (*ibid.,* p. 54); however, she does not document this claim, and subsequent counts fail to substantiate it. E. C. Ross's observation appears more accurate: "The law of [Whitman's] structure is that *the unit of the sense is the measure of the line.* The lines, in sense, are end-stopped. . . . Whitman was composing by lines, not by sentences, and he punctuated accordingly" ("Whitman's Verse," *Modern Language Notes,* 45 [June 1930], 364). Studies of Whitman's prosody are generally in accord with Ross's contention. Cf. Gay Wilson Allen, *American Prosody* (1935; rpt. New York: Octagon Books, 1966), pp. 221–22; Harvey Gross, *Sound and Form in Modern Poetry* (Ann Arbor: University of Michigan Press, 1965), p. 85.

5. *Sound and Form in Modern Poetry,* p. 14.

6. The reader might also have noticed that a double-space separates them from the previous cluster of lines; in this first volume such spacing is Whitman's only device of isolating lines that group together within the same poem. It remains a characteristic feature of his poems throughout his career, although in later editions he often resorts to marking out with numbers the larger, more or less self-contained sections in a poem. The numbering, which often helps in recognizing a poem's structure, sometimes tends to obscure or distort it. This seems to be, unfortunately, the case with the later versions of Whitman's great poem, which he began to divide into numbered sections after 1856; its final arrangement into fifty-two sections or "chants" dates from 1867. The disadvantages of these divisions are not quite set off by the practical advantages of easy reference and the (false) impression of a firm structure.

7. Examples of the hovering accent first noted in Whitman's verse by Sculley Bradley, in "The Fundamental Metrical Principle in Whitman's Poetry," *American Literature,* 10 (1938–1939), 444.

8. George Santayana, "Poetry and Prose," in *Essays in Literary Criticism* (New York: Scribners, 1956), p. 317.

9. Not that this truism does not need to be restated at fairly frequent intervals. Cf. this erudite *cri de coeur:* "Surely, it is impossible, is it not? to look only at the words on the page without modifying them by one's own perceptual matrices— at least, since Bishop Berkeley, we have had trouble talking about fixed realities 'out there' (although it has taken this New Critic, at least, a long time to realize the fact)." (Norman A. Holland, "Toward a Psychoanalysis of Poetic Form," *Literature and Psychology,* 15 [1965], 80n2.) Even critics inclined to accept Whitman's claim at full value begin eventually to hedge. E.g.: "It is literally true that Whitman attempts less to create a 'poem,' as the term is usually understood, than to present the materials of a poem for the reader to use in creating his own work of art. *No doubt in a sense . . . this is the manner in which all esthetic experience takes place"* (italics added). (*Handbook,* p. 378.)

10. *Explorations,* p. 162.

11. Edwin H. Miller, *Walt Whitman's Poetry: A Psychological Journey* (Boston: Houghton Mifflin Co., 1968), p. 88.

12. "A Note on Whitman's Symbolism in 'Song of Myself,' " *Modern Language Notes,* 65 (April 1950), 229–30.

13. Beyond the indirect proof offered by scholarship (Whitman's life-long habit of indiscriminate reading—he was not exactly a voracious reader, but he was a steady nibbler—the countless instances of bits and pieces of "book learning" incorporated into his poetry, etc.), there is the poet's own word that he comes not rejecting but "magnifying and applying" (1020). Recalling the image of stepping into the open with which both the Preface and his first poem begin, he explains that "distilled and "undistilled" knowledge depend on each other to come to life: "The facts are useful and real . . . they are not my dwelling. . . . I enter by them to an area of the dwelling" (484). Cf. also Waskow's commentary on the scene (*Explorations,* p. 160), in which the same thing is argued in a slightly different context.

14. "A Note on Whitman's Symbolism," p. 230.

15. Quoted by W. B. Cairns in "Swinburne's Opinion of Whitman," *American Literature,* 3 (May 1931), 129, from "Under the Microscope" in *Works,* Bonchurch ed., XVI, 411–19.

16. *Explorations,* p. 160.

17. *The New York Tribune,* Monday, July 23, 1855, p. 3.

18. For Whitman's sources in this passage, see note to "Song of Myself," line 899, in *CRE,* pp. 68–69. Whitman apparently relied both on stories heard from his grandmother, who received them from her "father the sailor," and on John Paul

NOTES: WHITMAN'S LANGUAGE-LESSON

Jones's account of the battle between the *Serapis* and the *Bonhomme Richard* in a letter to Benjamin Franklin. See David Goodale "Some of Walt Whitman's Borrowings," *American Literature*, 10 (January 1938), 202–15. For the intriguing though definitely remote possibility that the passage was influenced by Melville's treatment of the story in *Israel Potter*, see Jack Russell, "*Israel Potter* and 'Song of Myself,' " *American Literature*, 40 (March 1968), 72–77.

19. Beginning with the edition of 1867, Whitman makes this passage part of "the story as my grandmother's father, the sailor, told it to me" ("Song of Myself," line 899, *CRE*, p. 69), with the apparent intention to explain somewhat the whole section by making his personal presence in it more explicit. Thus, in the 1867 and 1872 versions the lines are introduced by this exclamation: "O now it is not my grandmother's father there in the fight: / I feel it is I myself" (*Revisions*, p. 237). Although he eventually deleted this aside, in 1881 he added another line: "A few large stars overhead, silent and mournful shining" ("Song of Myself," line 940, *CRE*, p. 71; *Revisions*, p. 239). The pathetic fallacy, which would seem unobtrusive in every setting except this rigorously impersonal one, strikes a soft but distinct personal note. Whitman obviously felt that this sort of clarification improved his poem.

20. *Nature*, in *Centenary*, I, 10.

21. Mary A. Neuman, " 'Song of Myself,' Section 21: An Explication," *Walt Whitman Review*, 13 (September 1967), 98.

22. *Modern Painters*, III, iv, ch. 12.

23. For the most lucid treatment of the critical movements of Romanticism that produced this distinction as well as the many others through which contrasts of the sort found in Whitman were meant to be categorized, see M. H. Abrams, *The Mirror and the Lamp* (New York: Norton, 1953), ch. 9.

24. *Biographia Literaria*, I, 172.

25. Hawthorne, "The Custom House," in *The Scarlet Letter*.

26. Whitman developed this image from the following set of coinages and improvisations, preserved in a manuscript fragment:

"Loveblows. Loveblossoms. Loveapples. Loveleaves. Loveclimbers. Loveverdure. Love Vines. Lovebranches. Loveroot. Climberblossom. Verdure, branch, fruit and vine. Loveroot. Juice Climber. Silk crotch. Crotch bulb and vine. Juicy, climbering mine. Bulb, silkthread crotch and . . . ." (Printed in *Notes and Fragments*, p. 165). This same fragment provides also the basis for line 12 of "Spontaneous Me" (first published in 1856, as "Bunch Poem"): "Love-thoughts, love-juice, love-odor, love-yielding, love-climbers, and the climbing sap" (*CRE*, p. 104). One may also see in it an early record of Whitman's intention to establish the calamus plant as a symbol of male sexuality.

27. The irony is even more forceful against the background of Whitman's whole output, which is all but completely devoid of references to money and always contemptuous of it. Cf. Kenneth Rexroth, "Walt Whitman," *Saturday Review*, September 3, 1966, p. 43.

28. Eric W. Carlson, "Whitman's *Song of Myself*, 59–65," *The Explicator*, 18, No. 2 (November 1959), item 13.

29. E. H. Miller, *Walt Whitman's Poetry*, p. 90. Circumstantial evidence that the two passages are linked may also be seen in the fact, noted in passing by Miller (p. 94), that in 1856, in his first revision of the volume, Whitman exchanged the key words between the two: he emended *bulging* to *swelling* in the first line and *swell* to *bulge* in the second. (*Revisions*, pp. 63, 95.)

30. One of these curious words, "trippers," is cast in a new and fascinating perspective by James A. Kilby's suggestion that besides its primary, general sense it may also mean "[an omnibus] driver employed in the place of another and paid by the trip" ("Walt Whitman's 'Trippers and Askers,' " *American Notes and Queries*, 4 [September 1965], 37–39).

31. "Thou Mother with Thy Equal Brood," line 124, *CRE*, p. 461.

32. Richard Chase, *Walt Whitman Reconsidered*, pp. 60–66, *passim*.

33. *Walt Whitman Reconsidered*, p. 65.

34. Matthiessen, for one, has made a similar observation in *American Renaissance*, p. 548. For a more detailed argument, see T. J. Kallsen, " 'Song of Myself': Logical Unity Through Analogy," *West Virginia University Bulletin*, 9 (1953), 36.

35. *American Renaissance*, p. 548.

36. "The Three Voices of Poetry," in *On Poetry and Poets* (New York: Farrar, Straus & Cudahy, 1957), p. 96.

37. "Structure and Style in the Greater Romantic Lyric," in *From Sensibility to Romanticism*, ed. F. W. Hilles and H. Bloom (New York: Oxford University Press, 1965), pp. 527–60.
   Similar comments have been made by a number of other readers, notably Roy Harvey Pearce, who speaks of the poem as a "hypnagogic meditation" (*Continuity*, p. 77), and E. H. Miller, who describes Whitman's poems in general as "meditations on the anxieties of the search for identity and for a unifying principle in the seeming chaos of existence" and calls "Song of Myself" a "secular meditation . . . originating in deep personal dissatisfactions and cultural inhibitions" (*Walt Whitman's Poetry*, pp. 18–19).

38. *UPP*, II, p. 66; *Handbook*, pp. 250–51. Cf. *Workshop*, p. 200n36.

39. For similar categories applied to Whitman's whole poetry, see Waskow's distinctions among didactic, imagistic, narrative, and "monodramatic" poems (*Explorations, passim*).

40. *American Renaissance*, p. 535.

CHAPTER SIX / "THE VERY HEART-BEAT OF LIFE"

1. *Singer*, p. 159.

2. "Adonais," lines 177, 492, in *The Complete Works of Percy Bysshe Shelley*, ed. Roger Ingpen and Walter E. Peach (New York: Gordian Press, 1965), II, 394–95.

NOTES: "THE VERY HEART-BEAT OF LIFE"

In Whitman's conceit of the grass as the "uncut hair of graves" and the sign that "there is really no death" (117), there is a remarkably close parallel with Stanza 20 of Shelley's poem:

> The leprous corpse, touched by this spirit tender,
> Exhales itself in flowers of gentle breath;
> Like incarnations of the stars, when splendour
> Is changed to fragrance, they illumine death
> And mock the merry worm that wakes beneath;
> Nought we know, dies.
>
> (172–77)

For Shelley's possible influence on Whitman, see also Roland A. Duerksen, "Similarities Between Shelley's 'Defence of Poetry' and Whitman's 1855 'Preface': A Comparison," *Walt Whitman Review*, 10 (September 1964), 51–60, and "Markings by Whitman in His Copy of Shelley's *Works*," *Walt Whitman Review*, 14 (December 1968), 147–51; also Mary K. Sanders, "Shelley's Promethean Shadow on *Leaves of Grass*," *Walt Whitman Review*, 14 (December 1968), 151–59.

3. *The Philosophy of Literary Form* (1941; rpt. New York: Vintage, 1957), pp. 5–6.

4. "Some Lines from Whitman" in *Poetry and the Age* (New York: Knopf, 1953), 131.

5. These are Baudelaire's terms to define the tension that he claimed made up his emotional life from childhood on. See "Journaux intimes," in Baudelaire, *Oeuvres complètes* (Paris: Gallimard, 1961), p. 1296.

6. Cf. Burke's comment: "Though the sex of his lover is not specified in the startling section 5 of *Song of Myself*, the many similarly motivated poems in *Calamus* give reason enough to assume that he is here writing of a male attachement" ("Policy Made Personal," in *Leaves of Grass One Hundred Years After*, ed. M. Hindus [Stanford: Stanford University Press, 1955], p. 85).

7. Cf. Catel: "We are surprised in the passage by an intent to hide the meaning of the words." (*Naissance*, p. 423.)

8. Cf. also Stephen E. Whicher, "Whitman's Awakening to Death: Toward a Biographical Reading of 'Out of the Cradle Endlessly Rocking,' " in *The Presence of Walt Whitman*, ed. R. W. B. Lewis (New York: Columbia University Press, 1962), p. 15.

9. Whicher, pp. 3–7.

10. *Singer*, p. 158.

11. *The Philosophy of Literary Form*, p. 21.

12. "Policy Made Personal," pp. 86–88.

13. *Walt Whitman's Poetry*, pp. 20–22. Some support for Miller's conjecture may be seen in the associations with the image of the "child at the mother's breast" in the line toward the end of the poem, "I reach to the leafy lips. . . . I reach to the polished breasts of melons" (1287), which is a clear echo of "And reached till you felt my beard and reached till you held my feet" (81). For another instance in

the first *Leaves* of the fusion and confusion of oral and sexual gratification, note also the well-known lines in the poem eventually called "The Sleepers":

> The cloth laps a first sweet eating and drinking,
> Laps life-swelling yolks . . . . . laps ear of rose-
> corn, milky and just ripened:
> The white teeth stay, and the boss-tooth advances is
> darkness,
> And liquor is spilled on lips and bosoms by touching
> glasses, and the best liquor afterward.
> (67–70)

14. E.g., Whicher, p. 16; also, Gustav Bychowski, M.D., "Walt Whitman: A Study in Sublimation," in *Psychoanalysis and the Social Sciences* (New York: International Universities Press, Inc., 1951), III, 226.

15. For a similar view, see Stephen A. Black, "Whitman and Psychoanalytic Criticism: A Response to Arthur Golden," *Literature and Psychology*, 20, No. 2 (1970), 81.

16. *King Lear*, IV. vi. 111.

17. *Explorations*, p. 168. Cf. also Stephen A. Black's comments on "the narrator's exceedingly tenuous connection with the people mentioned in the first half of the poem." ("Whitman and the Failure of Mysticism: Identity and Identification in 'Song of Myself,' " *Walt Whitman Review*, 15 [December 1969], 224.)

18. L. K. Davidson, *Whitman's "Song to Myself,"* p. 349; *Notes and Fragments*, p. 38.

19. "Whitman's Awakening to Death," p. 1.

20. *Anatomy of Criticism* (Princeton: Princeton University Press, 1957), p. 39.

21. "The most popular types of *alazon*," Frye states, "are the *miles gloriosus* and the learned crank or obsessed philosopher" (*Anatomy of Criticism*, p. 39). Later he notes that the *alazon* is "normally an object of ridicule in comedy or satire, but often the hero of a tragedy" (*Anatomy of Criticism*, p. 365). Whitman's protagonist will resemble all these versions of the *alazon* in the identity that he begins to assume by striking his pose of self-assurance. He will often sound like a *miles gloriosus* of battles between world and self, and in his persistent yet never quite successful efforts to "explain himself" and to find the "word unsaid" for what "there is" in him (1302, 1299) he will often look like an obsessed philosopher. That his new identity has a richly comic aspect to it and can at times expose him to plain ridicule has been often enough noted by critics and is cheerfully acknowledged by himself. At the same time, as critics have also often enough noted, underneath the optimistic self-confidence of the poem a steady undertow of sadness and foreboding affirms the tragic potentialities in his undertaking.

22. *Anatomy of Criticism*, p. 39.

23. *American Renaissance*, pp. 535–36.

24. Thus, William James himself concludes his discussion of mysticism with this comment: "Mystical states indeed wield no authority due simply to their being mystical states. But . . . the supernaturalism and optimism to which they would persuade us may, interpreted one way or another, be after all the truest of insights into the meaning of this life" (*The Varieties of Religious Experience* [1902; rpt. London: Collier-Macmillan Ltd., 1961], p. 336). See also Matthiessen, who flatly states that the "soul-idyll" (73–89) proves "the poet's belief in divine inspiration" (*American Renaissance*, p. 535). A persuasive and lucid account of the confusion of assumptions which may have led to this confusion in terminology is provided by Yvor Winters' description of Emerson's ideas, from which, he says, "nearly all of Whitman's thought was derived . . . or could easily have been": "God and his creation are one. God is good. Man, as part of the creation, is part of God, and so is good. Man may therefore trust his impulses, which are the voice of God; through trusting them absolutely and acting upon them without reserve, he becomes one with God. Impulse is thus equated with the protestant concept of conscience, as a divine and supra-rational directive; and surrender to impulse, which unites one with God, becomes equivalent in a sense to the traditional and Catholic concept of the mystical experience" (*In Defence of Reason* [Denver: Alan Swallow, 1947], p. 578).

25. Cf. "The Western mind may have ground for concern . . . when men of letters accommodate the traditional terminology and religious implications of Christian mysticism to poetic experiences that are otherwise as fully and more sensibly explicable." (William T. Noon, S. J., *Poetry and Prayer* [New Brunswick, New Jersey: Rutgers University Press, 1967], p. 68.)

26. "Can there be anything more exquisite than this vision in which a charming sensuality countervails the image of decay?" (Catel, *Naissance*, p. 422.)

27. *Walt Whitman's Poetry*, p. 112. E. H. Eby, apparently taking at face value Whitman's assertions and reassurances about immortality, bases on what seem to be the same perceptions a somewhat different interpretation of these lines, in "Walt Whitman's 'Indirections,' " *Walt Whitman Review*, 12 (March 1966), 15. See also Catel, *Naissance*, p. 422 and Robert J. Griffin, "Notes on Structural Devices in Whitman's Poetry," *Tennessee Studies in Literature*, 6 (1961), 15–24.

28. *Whitman's "Song of Myself,"* p. 142.

29. Lucius Daniel Morse, "Dr. Daniel G. Brinton on Walt Whitman," *The Conservator*, 10 (November 1899), 133.

30. *WWC*, III, 149.

31. "Policy Made Personal," p. 83.

32. Christopher Collins, *The Uses of Observation: A Study of Correspondential Vision in the Writing of Emerson, Thoreau, and Whitman.* (Diss., Columbia, 1964), p. 126.

33. "Teaching 'Song of Myself.' " *The Emerson Society Quarterly*, No. 22 (I Quarter 1961), pp. 3, 2.

34. "A Backward Glance O'er Travell'd Roads," *PW 1892*, II, 725.

35. *WWC*, III, 84.

36. *WWC*, II, 25.

37. Quoted by Davidson, *Whitman's "Song of Myself,"* p. 141.

38. John T. Trowbridge, "Reminiscence of Walt Whitman," *The Atlantic Monthly*, 89 (1902), 164–65.

39. Trowbridge, p. 142.

40. *Workshop*, pp. 19, 20–21.

41. "Memoranda," *PW 1892*, II, 683; also, "An Old Man's Rejoinder," *PW 1892*, II, 657.

42. *Singer*, p. 20.

43. *WWC*, II, 19.

44. *Workshop*, p. 20.

45. MS fragment printed by Thomas Donaldson, in *Walt Whitman, the Man* (New York: Francis P. Harper, 1896), p. 73.

46. *PW 1892*, I, 22; cf. also the claim in Dr. Bucke's *Walt Whitman*, p. 137, that Whitman wrote and rewrote the first *Leaves* five times before finding it fit to be published.

47. The evidence familiar from *Notes and Fragments* and from Holloway's edition of the notebooks in *UPP*, II, is substantially expanded and supplemented by the painstaking research of Loren K. Davidson in *Whitman's "Song of Myself,"* who also provides the fullest account of Whitman's life-long practice of collecting fragmentary insights and ideas in an envelope and then eventually working them into a coherent piece (pp. 142 ff.); see also Harrison Smith Morris, *Walt Whitman: A Brief Biography with Reminiscences* (Cambridge, Mass.: Harvard University Press, 1929), pp. 81–82; Asselineau, *The Creation of a Book*, pp. 223–24.

In spite of his own detailed account, Professor Davidson is inclined to believe that Whitman adopted this method only later in his career and that "his early practice was not simply to record emotion recollected in tranquillity but 'to write in the gush, the throb,' " etc., (p. 143), but there is plenty of evidence in his own study (cf. especially its third chapter, on the composition of the poem) to suggest that the first *Leaves*, too, were composed in some version of the envelope-method. As it will be seen shortly, this method does not necessarily mean recording emotion recollected in tranquillity. Similarly, Davidson rejects Bucke's report, presumably received from Whitman himself, that the poet wrote and then threw into the sea the first version of *Leaves of Grass* on a "long, cold, bleak promontory" of Long Island (*Walt Whitman*, pp. 24–26), on the grounds that Whitman did not visit his sister Mary at Greenport between July 1851 (*Singer*, p. 111) and the summer of 1856 (*Singer*, p. 144, n. 9); however, he gives no reason why the first version could not have been written as early as 1851. The

notebooks of 1848 and 1849 alone contain a sufficient number of lines and passages with the mood and intonation of *Leaves of Grass* unmistakably in them to
make such an early effort not only possible but quite plausible.

48. *Explorations*, p. 163.

49. *Whitman: A Study* (1896), in *The Complete Writings of John Burroughs*,
Wake-Robin Edition (New York: Wm. H. Wise & Co., 1924), vol. 18, p. 110.

50. *Naissance*, pp. 383–93.

51. In all fairness one should add that Catel, too, seems to share this view when
he speaks of Whitman's gradual comprehension that "the identity he must realize is no longer to be found between a hostile world and his consciousness but
between his consciousness and his soul, that is, the two parts of his self" (*Naissance*, pp. 398–99).

52. "An Egotistical 'Find'," in *Specimen Days, PW 1892*, I, 210.

53. *Studies in Classic American Literature*, p. 7.

54. Whitman to Traubel, in *WWC*, II, 26, 491.

55. "A Backward Glance O'er Travell'd Roads," *PW 1892*, II, 714.

56. "Preface, 1876, to Volume II of the Centennial Edition, Two Rivulets," *PW
1892*, II, 468.

57. *PW 1892*, II, 396, 398, 394.

58. *CRE*, p. 1, lines 6, 3.

59. Written in 1884, about the "antique." *PW 1892*, II, 770.

60. *ABC of Reading* (1934; rpt. New York: New Directions, 1960), p. 198.

61. *The Continuity of American Poetry*, p. 77.

62. E.g., *Handbook*, p. 117.

63. *Cowley*, p. xvi.

64. *The Uses of Observation*, p. 149.

65. Persuasive as the circumstantial evidence may appear, there is scarcely any
direct proof that Whitman was aware of the specific rhythm of self-assertion and
self-denial in his mental processes which is being proposed here as the source
and guiding force of his creativity, unless one accepts as such his curious and
evidently quite deliberate habit of mind Thomas L. Brasher has noted: having
taken an extreme position on a given issue, Whitman often makes his commitment to it less than complete by backtracking at the last minute, as in his remark
to Traubel, "Be radical—be radical—be not too damned radical" (*WWC*, I, 223).
Citing three such passages, all from Traubel, Brasher adds that the rhetorical figure itself is characteristic of any number of passages in the poetry ("Be—, Be—,
Be Not Too Damned—," *Walt Whitman Review*, 14 [June 1968], 60). Possibly it is
a conscious acknowledgment by "the basic prudential Whitman" of his own
reluctance, if not fear, irrevocably to upset the equilibrium of "opposite equals"

271

and thus an indication, however faint, that he recognizes in his own trains of thought something like the rhythm here ascribed to them.

66. *WWC*, II, 26.

CHAPTER SEVEN / POSSIBILITIES OF A PHASAL STRUCTURE

1. J. Albert Robbins, "The Narrative Form of 'Song of Myself,' " *American Transcendental Quarterly*, No. 12 (Fall 1971), p. 17.

2. *Cowley*, pp. xvi–xvii.

3. *The Continuity of American Poetry*, pp. 77, 83.

4. *Cowley*, p. xvii.

5. For example: Carl F. Strauch, "The Structure of Walt Whitman's 'Song of Myself,' " *The English Journal*, College Edition, 27 (1938), 597–607; *Handbook*, pp. 115–21; *Revisions*, pp. 2–9; Davidson, *Whitman's "Song of Myself,"* pp. 347 ff.; Gay Wilson Allen and Charles T. Davis, *Walt Whitman's Poems: Selections with Critical Aids* (New York: New York University Press, 1955), pp. 127–31; Malcolm Cowley, "Introduction," in *Cowley*, pp. vii–xxvii; James E. Miller, Jr., *A Critical Guide to Leaves of Grass*, pp. 6–35; R. H. Pearce, *The Continuity of American Poetry*, pp. 72–83; Loren K. Davidson, "Whitman's 'Song of Myself': An Analysis," *Litera*, 7 (1960), 49–89 [a recension of Mr. Davidson's unpublished dissertation]; Harry R. Warfel, "A Seminar in *Leaves of Grass*," *The Emerson Society Quarterly*, No. 22 (I Quarter 1961), pp. 27–28; Earl Tannenbaum, "Pattern in Whitman's 'Song of Myself,' " *CLA Journal*, 6 (September 1962), 44–49; Joseph M. DeFalco, "The Narrative Shift in Whitman's 'Song of Myself,' " *Walt Whitman Review*, 9 (December 1963), 82–84; Richard Bridgman, "Whitman's Calendar Leaves," *College English*, 25 (March 1964), 420–25; Waskow, *Explorations*, pp. 157–89; Michael Orth, "Walt Whitman, Metaphysical Teapot: The Structure of 'Song of Myself,' " *Walt Whitman Review*, 14 (March 1968), 16–24; E. F. Carlisle, "Walt Whitman: The Drama of Identity," *Criticism*, 10 (Fall 1968), 271–75; R. W. B. Lewis, *Trials of the Word* (New Haven: Yale University Press, 1965), pp. 11–15; Richard Bridgman, "Introduction," *Leaves of Grass by Walt Whitman: A Facsimile of the First Edition* (San Francisco: Chandler Publishing Co., 1968), pp. xxxv–xxxix; John M. Nagle, "Toward a Theory of Structure in 'Song of Myself,' " *Walt Whitman Review*, 15 (September 1969), 162–71; Ronald Beck, "The Structure of 'Song of Myself' and the Critics," *Walt Whitman Review*, 15 (March 1969), 32–38; J. Albert Robbins, "The Narrative Form of 'Song of Myself,' " *American Transcendental Quarterly*, No. 12 (Fall 1971), pp. 17–20; Bruce R. McElderry, Jr., "Personae in Whitman (1855–1860)," *American Transcendental Quarterly*, No. 12 (Fall 1971), pp. 26–28; F. DeWolfe Miller, "The Partitive Studies of 'Song of Myself,'" *American Transcendental Quarterly*, No. 12 (Fall 1971), pp. 12–14; Todd M. Lieber, *Endless Experiments: Essays on the Heroic Experience in American Romanticism* (Columbus, Ohio: Ohio State University Press, 1973), pp. 76–102; E. Fred Carlisle, *The Uncertain Self : Whitman's Drama of Identity* (n. p.: Michigan State University Press, 1973), pp. 177–204 [an elaboration of the argument in Mr. Carlisle's 1968 article in *Criticism*].

NOTES: POSSIBILITIES OF A PHASAL STRUCTURE

Several studies analyze the poem's coherence without seeking to outline a phasal structure in it. For example: Schyberg, *Walt Whitman*, pp. 83–97; Matthiessen, *American Renaissance*, pp. 534–36, 547–49; Henry S. Canby, *Walt Whitman, an American*, pp. 112–17; T. J. Kallsen, " 'Song of Myself': Logical Unity Through Analogy," *West Virginia University Bulletin*, 9 (1953), 33–40; Chase, *Walt Whitman Reconsidered*, pp. 63–70; Karl Adalbert Preuschen, "Zur Entstehung der neuen Lyrik in Amerika; *Walt Whitman: Song of Myself* (1. Fassung)," *Jahrbuch für Amerikastudien*, 8 (1963), 148–70; V. K. Chari, *Whitman in the Light of Vedantic Mysticism: An Interpretation* (Lincoln, Nebraska: University of Nebraska Press, 1964), pp. 121–27; V. K. Chari, "Structure of Whitman's Catalogue Poems," *Walt Whitman Review*, 18 (March 1972), 10–11; Edwin H. Miller, *Walt Whitman's Poetry*, pp. 85–114.

6. Approximately the same lines are characterized by Carl F. Strauch as expressing "mere presence at a scene," that is, as observing life rather than participating in it. See "The Structure of Walt Whitman's 'Song of Myself,' " *The English Journal*, College Edition, 27 (1938), 604.

7. One of these images, "the marriage of the trapper" (185–88), is actually based on a painting Whitman saw. Cf. Edgeley W. Todd, "Indian Pictures and Two Whitman Poems," *The Huntington Library Quarterly*, 19 (1955/56), 1–11.

8. E.g., Sculley Bradley's excellent prosodic analysis in "The Fundamental Metrical Principle in Whitman's Poetry," *American Literature*, 10 (1938–39), 456–59; Thomas J. Rountree's view that "the woman . . . can symbolize the oneness of the life of being," in "Whitman's Indirect Expression and Its Application to 'Song of Myself,' " *PMLA*, 73 (1958), 554; Barbara Herrnstein Smith's discussion of the first five lines of the passage to show the "obviously subtle and complex" (p. 91) patterns of rhythmic effect in them, in *Poetic Closure: A Study of How Poems End* (Chicago: University of Chicago Press, 1968), pp. 90–92; T. J. Kallsen's argument that the passage "reminds the reader indirectly that sexuality and physicality are only half the answer to what is the Self," in "The Improbabilities in Section 11 of 'Song of Myself,' " *Walt Whitman Review*, 13 (September 1967), 92; James Davidson's suggestion that the twenty-ninth bather is like the twenty-ninth day of February, restricted to "becom[ing] the aggressor, and seek[ing] her mate" every fourth year only, and, in her case, not even then, in "Whitman's Twenty-Eight Young Men," *Walt Whitman Review*, 12 (December 1966), 100–1. The list could go on. . . .

9. The perspective of this image is, of course, based on Whitman's pre-Darwinism notions of evolution. See *Handbook*, p. 315; Asselineau, *The Creation of a Book*, pp. 50–51.

10. Another critic who discerns a marked shift in tone at this point is Bruce R. McElderry, Jr., in "Personae in Whitman (1855–1860)," *American Transcendental Quarterly*, No. 12 (Fall 1971), p. 27.

11. Their first known appearance is in the notebook that has entries supposed to be dating from 1847 (*UPP*, II, 69) or possibly even 1844 (Edward F. Grier, "Walt Whitman's Earliest Known Notebook," *PMLA*, 83 [1968], 1453–56).

NOTES: POSSIBILITIES OF A PHASAL STRUCTURE

12. R. W. Emerson, "The Poet," in *Essays, Second Series; Centenary,* III, 18, 30, 32. Cf. also Hyatt H. Waggoner, *American Poets from the Puritans to the Present* (1968; rpt. New York: Dell, 1970), pp. 150–56.

13. In the 1850s "foofoos" evidently meant "cowardly and affected . . . outsiders . . . [lacking] a certain manliness"; see Kenneth G. Johnston and John O. Rees, Jr., "Whitman and the Foo-foos: An Experiment in Language," *Walt Whitman Review,* 17 (March 1971), 3–10.

14. Each half of this phrase consists of a pair of contrasts; it has, thus, the same structure as the earlier "Hankering, gross, mystical, nude" (388). The paradox not only lends the phrase vigor, it is also highly appropriate, an organic effect. In Whitman's final revision—"Walt Whitman, an American, of Manhattan the son" ("Song of Myself," line 497, *CRE,* p. 52)—the line is reduced to the all but ornamental. Also, Junius H. Browne, who seems to have known whereof he wrote, reported that "a more despicable, dangerous, and detestable character than the New York rough does not exist," in the chapter on "The Roughs" in his *The Great Metropolis: A Mirror of New York,* 1869; quoted by Clarence Gohdes in "Whitman as 'One of the Roughs,'" *Walt Whitman Review,* 8 (March 1962), 18. The comment sharpens Whitman's own perspective, who had this to say even before 1855: "Again the young man of Mannahatta, the celebrated rough, / (The one I love well—let others sing whom they may—him I sing for a thousand years!)," ("Pictures," lines 102–3, *CRE,* p. 647).

15. *Cowley,* p. ix.

16. It has been noted that the elaboration of the "many dumb voices" is a splendid bit of virtuosity, for as it reaches the bottom of degradation it manages also to allude to the highest in the image of "beetles rolling balls of dung" (517), since this is a direct allusion to the ancient Egyptians' sacred scarab rolling the sun across the sky. See T. O. Mabbott, "Whitman's 'Song of Myself,' XXIV, 19," *The Explicator,* 5 (April 1947), item 43.

17. For a somewhat bizarre interpretation of this admittedly bizarre passage as "[the protagonist's] excessively ardent, virtually orgiastic . . . relationship with the horse" see E. H. Miller, *Walt Whitman's Poetry,* p. 102. One should add the suggestion that the stallion may also conceal an allusion to Pegasus, much as the "beetles rolling balls of dung" (517) could carry the association of the sacred scarab (see n. 16, above). The "I" may be recording with it his discovery that poetry of the conventional sort, though within his powers, is scarcely sufficient ambition for him.

18. Cf. Richard Chase's remark in a different context: "Most of 'Song of Myself' has to do not with the self searching for a final identity but with the self escaping a series of identities which threaten to destroy its lively and various spontaneity." (*Walt Whitman Reconsidered,* pp. 65–66.)

19. Not quite all of them, though. The incident of the amputation of the limb (930–31; also, 270–71), for example, may be based, Davidson says, on Whitman's memories of the job he had, at the age of eleven or twelve (1830–31), in the office of a surgeon named Dr. Hunt (Davidson, *Whitman's "Song of Myself,"* p.

76). Allen records the job but mentions neither the physician's name nor the effects the experience may have had on Whitman's poetry (*Singer*, p. 17). On the other hand, the shipwreck (818–27) is clearly based on clippings from the *New York Weekly Tribune* found among Whitman's papers, which reported the sinking of the *S.S.San Francisco* and the rescue of the survivors, on December 23, 1853 (R. M. Bucke, "Notes on the Text of *Leaves of Grass*," *The Conservator*, 7 [May 1896], 40; Davidson, *Whitman's "Song of Myself*," pp. 96 ff.). For discussions of the probable sources of the account of the battle of the *Bonhomme Richard* with the *Serapis* as the "oldfashioned frigate-fight" (890–932), see n. 18 in chapter 5, above. The story "of the jet-black sunrise" is based on the Goliad massacre, an incident of the struggle between Mexico and Texas, in 1836 (Milton Hindus, "The Goliad Massacre in 'Song of Myself,' " *Walt Whitman Review*, 7 [December 1961], 77–78).

20. Robin Magowan, "The House of the Gods: Possession in 'Song of Myself,' " *Walt Whitman Review*, 15 (June 1969), 76.

21. Later on, Whitman apparently decided, anyway, that the line, as it stood, aligned his protagonist too squarely with Christianity: in 1867 he amended "two thousand years" to "thousands of years." (*Revisions*, p. 247.)

22. Thomas Edward Crawley, *The Structure of Leaves of Grass* (Austin: University of Texas Press, 1970), pp. 59, 74.

23. "The Narrative Form of 'Song of Myself,' " *American Transcendental Quarterly*, No. 12 (Fall 1971), p. 18.

24. Whitman's silly habit of flaunting the five or six foreign words that he knew has been, from the first, a matter of so much gratuitous mirth on the part of his readers and therefore has become so tediously familiar that beyond this short note of "acknowledgment" it can be safely ignored.

25. The line opens with four points of suspension. Only once, in line 230, does the same device appear earlier, and then, too, an emphatic shift in intonation is indicated, although it is not more emphatic than in a number of other places, where the four periods do not head the line. If the points of suspension are to underscore here the change in the voice, they perform their function well enough; however, their appearance in this unusual position may be simply due to a typographical error, for Whitman deleted them from both lines by 1856, when he also gave up his idiosyncratic employment of the four-point suspension within the line. See *Revisions*, pp. 102, 264.

26. *Studies in Classic American Literature*, p. 173.

27. According to Clarence Gohdes, the passage simply registers the "unifying intuition" of what Whitman once described as "the absolute balance, in time and space, of the whole of this multifarious, mad chaos . . . we call *the world*" ("Carlyle from American Points of View," in *Specimen Days*, *PW 1892*, I, 258), and thus it "conforms very well with the ineffability and the noetic quality considered to be characteristic of mysticism." ("Section 50 of Whitman's 'Song of Myself,' " *Modern Language Notes*, 75 [December 1960], 654–56). The present interpreta-

tion, which construes the passage as not merely perceiving but actively restoring a balance vital to Whitman's protagonist, rejects Professor Gohdes's view.

28. *Poetic Closure*, p. 172.

29. "Preface 1876—*Leaves of Grass and Two Rivulets*," *CRE*, p. 751.

30. *Handbook*, p. 378.

31. Jon Bracker, "The Conclusion of 'Song of Myself,' " *Walt Whitman Review*, 10 (March 1964), 22.

32. *Poetic Closure*, p. 145.

33. *Walt Whitman Reconsidered*, p. 63.

34. A paraphrase of the title of an article by I. A. Richards: "How Does a Poem Know When It Is Finished?" *Parts and Wholes*, ed. Daniel Lerner (New York: The Free Press of Glencoe, 1963), pp. 163–74.

35. *Poetic Closure*, p. 111.

36. *Ibid.*, pp. 172, 175–76.

37. *Ibid.*, pp. 154, 157, 182.

38. *Ibid.*, p. 92.

39. A number of critics have responded to these echoes, interpreting them in various ways, some of them approximating the one presented here. See, for example, Richard Chase, who contrasts "the delicate precision" of the passage with "the generally grandiose nineteenth-century melodrama of love and death" (*Walt Whitman Reconsidered*, pp. 62–63); Michael Orth, who says that "in the opening lines of Stanza 52 [i.e., lines 1321–26 of the 1855 version] the hawk, a bird of powerful masculinity, but also of death (the Holy Ghost of Whitman's theology?) takes him off on the final voyage" ("Walt Whitman, Metaphysical Teapot: The Structure of 'Song of Myself,' " *Walt Whitman Review*, 14 [March 1968], 23); and R. P. Adams, for whom lines 1329–30 declare "plainly and emphatically . . . that Whitman himself is reborn in his poetry" ("Romanticism and the American Renaissance," *American Literature*, 23 [1952], 428).

40. "How Does a Poem Know When It Is Finished?" *Parts and Wholes*, p. 168.

41. *Handbook*, p. 117; *Singer*, p. 164; *Cowley*, p. xvi; Chase, *Walt Whitman Reconsidered*, p. 66.

42. The first half of line 378 is "histrionic."

43. John B. Mason, "Walt Whitman's Catalogues: Rhetorical Means for Two Journeys in 'Song of Myself,' " *American Literature*, 45 (1973), 34.

44. David Daiches, "Walt Whitman: Impressionist Prophet," in *Leaves of Grass One Hundred Years After*, ed. Milton Hindus (Stanford: Stanford University Press, 1955), pp. 110, 118.

45. Cf. Detlev W. Schumann, "Enumerative Style And Its Significance in Whitman, Rilke, Werfel," *Modern Language Quarterly*, 3 (1942), 172; Catel, *Rythme et langage*, pp. 111, 132–42; and Schyberg, *Walt Whitman*, p. 97.

46. Cf. Lawrence Buell's conclusion: the catalogue is "intended to stir up, not to settle" ("Transcendentalist Catalogue Rhetoric: Vision Versus Form," *American Literature*, 40 [1968], 339).

47. "The Poetry of Barbarism," in *Essays in Literary Criticism* (New York: Scribners, 1956), p. 157.

48. Rene Wellek and Austin Warren, *Theory of Literature* (New York: Harcourt, Brace and Company, 1949), p. 201.

49. Mason, p. 43.

50. Stanley K. Coffman, Jr., " 'Crossing Brooklyn Ferry': A Note on the Catalogue Technique in Whitman's Poetry," *Modern Philology*, 51 (May 1954), 225.

51. Smith, *Poetic Closure*, p. 99.

52. Wellek and Warren, *Theory of Literature*, p. 200.

53. Mason, p. 43.

54. Buell, pp. 333–34.

55. Regrettably little has been made of the suggestion that Whitman's catalogues resemble some techniques of film, in which the purpose is obviously the illusion of simultaneity. See, for example, Emory Holloway, *UPP*, I, lxiii; Muriel Rukeyser, *The Life of Poetry* (New York: A. A. Wynn, 1949), p. 85; Alice Ahlers, "Cinematographic Technique in *Leaves of Grass*," *Walt Whitman Review*, 12 (December 1966), 93–97; and Mason, p. 46.

56. Wellek and Warren, *Theory of Literature*, p. 200.

57. O. W. Firkins, *Ralph Waldo Emerson* (Cambridge, Mass.: Hougton Mifflin Co., 1915), p. 237.

58. "Three Problems of Fictional Form: First-Person Narration in *David Copperfield* and *Huckleberry Finn*," in *Experience in the Novel*, ed. R. H. Pearce (New York: Columbia University Press, 1968), p. 23.

59. Thomas J. Rountree, "Whitman's Indirect Expression and Its Application to 'Song of Myself,' " *PMLA*, 73 (1958), 550; Mason, p. 43; Buell, p. 339.

60. Rountree, p. 549.

61. Wellek and Warren, *Theory of Literature*, p. 146.

62. Cf. Barbara Herrnstein Smith's comments on the paratactic structure of Ralegh's "The Lie": though theoretically interchangeable, "omitting any of the central stanzas would, in a sense, narrow the comprehensiveness of Ralegh's *contemptus mundi* . . . [and] a cumulative effect of the repeated unflinching absolutes makes each succeeding stanza more powerful than the one before" (*Poetic Closure*, p. 105).

63. *Singer*, p. 164.

64. "Structure of Whitman's Catalogue Poems," *Walt Whitman Review*, 18 (March 1972), 10.

65. Mason, p. 49.

66. *Paradise Lost,* V, 580–82, in *The Works of John Milton,* ed. F. A. Patterson and others (New York: Columbia University Press, 1931), II, Part I.

67. Mason, p. 49. See also Catel, *Rythme et langage,* p. 120.

68. "Three Problems of Fictional Form," in *Experience in the Novel,* p. 23.

69. See Mattie Swayne, "Whitman's Catalogue Rhetoric," *University of Texas Studies in English,* 21 (July 1941), 162–78; Thomas J. Rountree, "Whitman's Indirect Expression and Its Application to 'Song of Myself,'" *PMLA,* 73 (1958), 549–55; and *Handbook,* pp. 377–79.

70. "A Backward Glance O'er Travell'd Roads," *PW 1892,* II, 731.

71. *Walt Whitman Reconsidered,* pp. 58–59.

72. *Symbolism and American Literature,* p. 18.

73. "Three Problems of Fictional Form," in *Experience in the Novel,* p. 21.

74. Cf. "For those concerned with literature, the first question to answer is not 'What use is the study of literature?' but, 'What follows from the fact that it is possible?'" (*Anatomy of Criticism,* p. 10.)

75. *Paradise Lost,* VII, 176–79.

76. Although V. K. Chari's concept of the poem's structure as "a prolonged enactment of a single static situation" (*Whitman in the Light of Vedantic Mysticism,* p. 124) seems very nearly identical with the argument presented here, it is developed from the assumption that "Whitman's dynamism is not a compulsive activity arising from an inner necessity, as it is in the dialectical becoming but is a free self-indulgence . . . flowing out of the plentitude of being" (pp. 118–19), and this view fundamentally disagrees with the findings on which the principle of the "heartbeat" and thus the present interpretation are based.

CHAPTER EIGHT / THE METRE-MAKING ARGUMENT

1. "Preface, 1876, to the Centennial Edition," *PW 1892,* II, 473.

2. Oscar Lovell Triggs, "Variorum Readings," in Walt Whitman, *Leaves of Grass, Inclusive Edition,* ed. Emory Holloway (1926; rpt. Garden City, N.Y.: Doubleday, 1954), p. 550.

3. *The Imperial Self,* pp. 95, 114.

4. Newton Arvin, *Herman Melville* (1950; rpt. New York: Viking, 1957), p. 181.

5. *The Imperial Self,* p. 90.

6. "A Backward Glance O'er Travel'd Roads," *PW 1892,* II, 714, 719.

7. See, for example, the chapters on "These States—Egocentrism and Patriotism" and "Democracy—Myself and Man 'En-Masse,'" in Asselineau, *The Creation of a Book,* pp. 129–78; Matthiessen's whole treatment of Whitman in *American Renaissance,* pp. 517–625; Arvin's *Whitman,* written to show "that, from our

recent past, we inherit no fuller or braver anticipatory statement than *Leaves of Grass* of a democratic and fraternal humanism" (p. 290); or Rountree's article on Whitman's "indirections" ("Whitman's Indirect Expression and Its Application to 'Song of Myself,' " *PMLA*, 73 [1958], 549–55), in which the thesis, that the structure of "Song of Myself" consists of one half of the dialogue the poet has initiated with his "reciprocating" reader, posits the "antiphonal," which according to Anderson is missing from Whitman's poetry, as the very backbone of the poem.

8. Only rarely and then only years later, when the particular pressures of the time of his public emergence have largely worn off, does Whitman allow that his "experiment" was also prompted by more private and decidedly less patriotic impulses than "to help the forming of a great aggregate Nation" ("A Backward Glance O'er Travel'd Roads," *PW 1892*, II, 726). See, for example, his remark that the "universal democratic comradeship" consists not only of his "boundless offering of sympathy" but also of his "never-satisfied appetite for sympathy" ("Preface, 1876, to the Centennial Edition," *PW 1892*, II, 471), or the parenthetical comment, ostensibly of George Selwyn but, as Holloway has shown (*UPP*, II, 58n2), actually of Whitman himself that he "never knew a man who . . . seems to be so poised on himself alone" (*UPP*, II, 61).

9. Walt Whitman (anonymously), "Walt Whitman and his Poems," *United States Review*, September 1855; rpt. *Walt Whitman*, ed. Francis Murphy, p. 29; cf. *Singer*, p. 171.

10. From another anonymous review by Whitman, in the Brooklyn *Times*, September 29, 1855, reprinted in the second issue of the first edition; quoted in *Singer*, p. 171.

11. "Whitman to Emerson, 1856," *CRE*, p. 736.

12. One particularly frustrating example, from the 1876 Preface, should suffice: "*Leaves of Grass.*—Namely, a Character, making most of common and normal elements, to the superstructure of which not only the precious accumulations of the learning and experiences of the Old World, and the settled social and municipal necessities and current requirements, so long a-building, shall still faithfully contribute, but which, at its foundations, and carried up thence, and receiving its impetus from the Democratic spirit, and accepting its gauge, in all departments, from the Democratic formulas, shall again directly be vitalized by the perennial influences of Nature at first hand, and the old heroic stamina of Nature, the strong air of prairie and mountain, the dash of the briny sea, the primary antiseptics—of the passions, in all their fullest heat and potency, of courage, rankness, amativeness, and of immense pride. . . ." (*PW 1892*, II, 468.)

13. Anderson, *The Imperial Self*, pp. 201, 95.

14. Seymour Betsky, "Whose Walt Whitman?: French Scholar and American Critics," *English Studies*, 47 (June 1966), 208.

15. Randall Jarrell, "Some Lines from Whitman," in *Poetry and the Age*, p. 114.

16. *Walt Whitman Reconsidered*, pp. 61–62. Stated this baldly, this claim sounds

rather imprecise, in any case. Whitman brought to the treatment of sex a degree of straightforwardness not seen before, but sex is most definitely "a possible subject" in *Wieland* or *Ormond*, for example, or in the works of Poe and, obviously, of Melville; furthermore, Melville knew very well (as Poe perhaps did not) that he was writing about sex.

17. *The Imperial Self*, p. 112.

18. Asselineau, *The Creation of a Book*, p. 218.

19. "Main Drifts in Whitman's Poetry," *American Literature*, 4 (1932), 21.

20. *The Creation of a Book*, pp. 219, 213.

21. Ibid., p. 225.

22. *Specimen Days*, in *PW 1892*, I, 22.

23. *An American Primer*, p. 2.

24. "A Study of Whitman's Diction," *University of Texas Studies in English*, 16 (July 1936), 124. Asselineau's detailed review of the subject (*The Creation of a Book*, pp. 225–38) simply confirms Professor Coy's conclusions.

25. *ABC of Reading*, p. 192.

26. *Revisions*, p. 133.

27. Ibid., p. 148.

28. Ibid., p. 69.

29. "Song of Myself," line 98, *CRE*, p. 33.

30. Harvey Gross's term in *Sound and Form in Modern Poetry*, p. 100 and *passim*.

31. "A Note on Walt Whitman's Prosody," *The Standard of American Speech* (New York: Allyn and Bacon, 1926), p. 292.

32. *American Prosody*, p. 217n1, and p. 220.

33. "The Fundamental Metrical Principle in Whitman's Poetry," *American Literature*, 10 (1938–39), 437–59. Although Professor Bradley's article is now almost forty years old, none of the more recent treatments of the subject seems to have added anything substantially new to his argument. See Harvey Gross, *Sound and Form in Modern Poetry*, pp. 83–88; Asselineau, *The Creation of a Book*, pp. 239–52; Milton Hindus, "Notes Toward the Definition of a Typical Poetic Line in Whitman," *Walt Whitman Review*, 9 (December 1963), 75–81; and Andrew Schiller, "An Approach to Whitman's Metrics," *The Emerson Society Quarterly*, No. 22 (I Quarter 1961), 23–25.

34. Bradley, p. 458.

35. *The Creation of a Book*, p. 226.

36. "Reminiscent of Whitman," *The Conservator*, 8 (May 1897), 38, 40.

37. Matthiessen, *American Renaissance*, p. 531.

38. "Walt Whitman," *Saturday Review,* 3 September 1966, p. 43.

39. *American Renaissance,* pp. 531, 530.

40. *American Renaissance,* p. 532.

41. Sanborn, "Reminiscent of Whitman," p. 38.

42. *Cowley,* p. ix.

43. See *Early,* pp. 3–49.

44. See Bradley, "The Fundamental Metrical Principle in Whitman's Poetry," *passim.* Cf. also Catel's observation: "At its conclusion as well as at its inception Whitman's thought is drawn toward traditional formulation" (*Rythme et langage,* p. 89), which he supports by a detailed though clearly rather forced demonstration that the verse is frequently based on a five-stress "formula" (pp. 84 ff.) and arranged in "regular" strophes or stanzas, primarily quatrains, tercets, and distichs (pp. 133–42).

45. "Observations Prefixed to 'Lyrical Ballads,' " in *The Great Critics,* p. 502.

46. *The Imperial Self,* p. 93.

47. "He is the poet," Henry Alonzo Myers explains, "not of a social and economic period, but of an America that never dies." ("Whitman's Conception of the Spiritual Democracy, 1885–56," *American Literature,* 6 [1934–35], 240.)

48. Cf. Hyatt H. Waggoner's remark: "['Song of Myself'] is 'American' . . . chiefly . . . in the way in which it brings together freely and creatively the most diverse strains from the past to create an image of man facing the future." (*American Poets from the Puritans to the Present,* p. 176.)

49. *The Imperial Self,* p. 108.

50. *Cowley,* p. xvi.

51. "Walt Whitman and his Poems," in *Walt Whitman,* ed. F. Murphy, p. 37.

52. Lionel Trilling, *The Liberal Imagination* (1950; rpt. Garden City, New York: Doubleday, 1953), p. 244.

53. *Studies in Classic American Literature,* p. 8.

54. "Walt Whitman and his Poems," in *Walt Whitman,* ed. F. Murphy, p. 30.

55. *The Dialogues of Plato,* III, 136.

56. Ernst Cassirer, *Language and Myth,* trans. Susanne K. Langer (1946; rpt. New York: Dover Publications, n.d.), pp. 8–9.

57. *Herman Melville,* p. 183.

58. *Anatomy of Criticism,* p. 136.

59. *Language and Myth,* p. 13.

60. Ibid., p. 33.

61. "Preface, 1872, to As a Strong Bird on Pinions Free," *PW 1892,* II, 461.

62. *Handbook*, p. 7.

63. "Preface, 1872, to As a Strong Bird on Pinions Free," *PW 1892*, II, 462.

64. *Workshop*, pp. 39–40.

65. The influence of the Bible on Whitman's versification is admirably discussed in a number of studies by Gay Wilson Allen, e.g., *American Prosody*, pp. 221–38; *Handbook*, pp. 387–409; and *A Reader's Guide to Walt Whitman* (New York: Farrar, Straus and Giroux, 1970), pp. 167–73. Perhaps the most instructive study of the religious and biblical elements in the imagery of the poem is in Thomas E. Crawley, *The Structure of Leaves of Grass*, pp. 88–92 and *passim*.

66. Genesis I: 10, 12, 18, 21, etc.

67. Cf. Genesis II: 7.

68. Paraphrase of a statement in Paton J. Gloag, *Introduction to the Johannine Writings* (London: James Nisbet and Co., 1891), p. 170.

69. Christopher F. Mooney, S. J., *Teilhard de Chardin and the Mystery of Christ* (New York: Harper and Row, 1966), p. 147.

70. *Language and Myth*, p. 81.

71. Ibid., p. 82.

72. *Walt Whitman*, p. 159.

73. Harold Jaffe, "Bucke's *Walt Whitman*: A Collaboration," *Walt Whitman Review*, 15 (September 1969), 191.

74. *Walt Whitman*, p. 159.

75. Whitman himself has contributed to this notion with his remark that there is, among others, "an epic of Democracy" in *Leaves of Grass* ("Preface, 1872 to As a Strong Bird on Pinions Free," *PW 1892*, II, 458); the most elaborate formulation of the idea is in Roy Harvey Pearce's account of the poem as a "proto-epic": "not an epic, but an American equivalent of an epic" (*The Continuity of American Poetry*, p. 83, also pp. 69–83).

76. *American Poets from the Puritans to the Present*, p. 175.

77. *Walt Whitman Reconsidered*, pp. 70–71.

78. *An American Primer*, p. 16. Italics added.

79. *A Reader's Guide to Walt Whitman*, pp. 170, 172–73.

80. Triggs, "Variorum Readings," in *Leaves of Grass*, Inclusive Edition, p. 549; *CRE*, p. 28.

CHAPTER NINE / CLOSED STATEMENTS, OPEN STRUCTURE

1. Schyberg, *Walt Whitman*, p. 123; cf. Perry, *Walt Whitman*, p. 80.

2. *Whitman's "Song of Myself,"* p. 152.

3. Triggs, "Variorum Readings," in *Leaves of Grass*, Inclusive Edition, p. 602.

NOTES: CLOSED STATEMENTS, OPEN STRUCTURE

4. For a similar interpretation of this deletion, see Thomas E. Crawley, *The Structure of Leaves of Grass*, pp. 168–69.

5. Estelle W. Taylor, "Analysis and Comparison of the 1855 and 1891 Versions of Whitman's 'To Think of Time,' " *Walt Whitman Review*, 13 (December 1967), 120.

6. *American Poets from the Puritans to the Present*, p. 166.

7. Taylor, p. 110.

8. R. W. B. Lewis employs this Jungian term to describe "The Sleepers" in *The Trials of the Word*, p. 18.

9. R. H. Pearce, *The Continuity of American Poetry*, p. 168.

10. *Whitman*, p. 123.

11. It should be noted that the difference between the 1855 text of "The Sleepers" and its later revisions is possibly even more significant than in the case of "Song of Myself." See, for example, Howard Waskow's analysis in *Explorations in Form*, pp. 136–56, or James E. Miller, Jr.'s reading in *A Critical Guide to Leaves of Grass*, pp. 130–41, which are based on the final text and therefore can show scarcely any awareness of the tensions that lie at the heart of the first version. See also *Singer*, pp. 166–67; G. W. Allen and C. T. Davis, *Walt Whitman's Poems*, pp. 141–43; Schyberg, *Walt Whitman*, pp. 125–26; R. Chase, *Walt Whitman Reconsidered*, pp. 52–57; and E. H. Miller, *Walt Whitman's Poetry*, pp. 72–84.

12. *Walt Whitman Reconsidered*, p. 54.

13. Sister Eva Mary, O.S.F., "Shades of Darkness in 'The Sleepers,' " *Walt Whitman Review*, 15 (September 1969), 187.

14. For some interpretations of this cyclical view see the argument of E. H. Miller that the poem is "a reenactment of ancient puberty rites" (*Walt Whitman's Poetry*, p. 72 and *passim*) or of R. W. Vince that it embodies a cycle of birth, death, and rebirth ("A Reading of 'The Sleepers,' " *Walt Whitman Review*, 18 [March 1972], 17–28).

15. *Walt Whitman*, p. 171.

16. *Whitman*, p. 123.

17. *Walt Whitman's Poetry*, p. 73.

18. *Walt Whitman Reconsidered*, p. 55.

19. *Walt Whitman's Poetry*, pp. 81, 82.

20. The implication of "The Sleepers," 130–32, that the speaker is a black slave is confirmed by an early manuscript version of the passage, which speaks of "Black Lucifer" (*Notes and Fragments*, Item 40). For evidence that Lucifer in this passage is kin to Apollyon, the king of "the scorpion-locusts of God's revenge upon the wicked" in Revelations ix. 4, 5, 11, see Francis E. Skipp, "Whitman's 'Lucifer': A Footnote to 'The Sleepers,' " *Walt Whitman Review*, 11 (June 1965), 52–53; for an argument that Whitman's Lucifer can be, unlike Milton's, "sorrowful" because

he was probably suggested by the Lucifer of Bailey's "Festus," see Sholom J. Kahn, "Whitman's 'Black Lucifer': Some Possible Sources," *PMLA*, 71 (1956), 932–44.

21. Chase, *Walt Whitman Reconsidered*, p. 55.

22. Perhaps it is not entirely irrelevant to recall at this point that Walter Whitman, Sr., who had been a near-helpless invalid for some time, died on July 11, 1855, less than a week after the first *Leaves of Grass* was published, but what his poet son, speaking many years later to Dr. Bucke about this period, found worth recording was that "I went off to the east end of Long Island, and spent the late summer and all the fall—*the happiest of my life*—around Shelter Island and Peconic Bay" (italics added; Bucke, *Walt Whitman*, p. 26).

23. Stuart C. Woodruff, "Whitman: Poet or Prophet?" *Walt Whitman Review*, 14 (June 1968), 35.

24. "A Reading of Whitman's 'Faces,' " *Walt Whitman Review*, 19 (June 1973), 39.

25. *Whitman*, p. 128.

26. *Singer*, p. 168.

27. *The Trials of the Word*, p. 15.

28. Thus, Howard Waskow has argued, for example, that "the story of the child is about merging and particularity, but wholly within the context of organicism. . . . [It] begins with quiet and orderly lines . . . but . . . slides into a style . . . in which subjects and objects, speaker and action spoken of . . . blend until they are sometimes indistinguishable" (*Whitman: Explorations in Form*, p. 132; also pp. 129–35); E. H. Miller has demonstrated at length that the poem is "one of the most astute diagnoses of the emergent self" (*Walt Whitman's Poetry*, p. 28; also pp. 24–40); Harold Aspiz has shown Whitman's debt to the conceptual idiom of phrenology in the poem ("Educating the Kosmos: 'There Was a Child Went Forth,' " *American Quarterly*, 18 [Winter 1966], 655–66); Hyatt H. Waggoner has called it "an epitome of Whitman's . . . Transcendentalism" and interpreted it as "[moving] toward and through the birth of consciousness, with the alienation this brings, and beyond pure conscious rationality to reunion and reintegration" (*American Poets from the Puritans to the Present*, p. 170); and Sister Margaret Patrice Slattery has noted complementary patterns of cyclic and contrasting imagery in the poem's progression through "the cycle of life, death, and life in death" ("Patterns of Imagery in Whitman's 'There Was a Child Went Forth,' " *Walt Whitman Review*, 15 [June 1969], 112, also 112–14).

29. *WWC*, V, 310.

30. E. M. Forster, *A Passage to India* (New York: Harcourt, Brace & World, 1924), p. 147.

31. John Addington Symonds, *Walt Whitman, A Study* (London: George Rutledge & Sons, 1893), pp. 21–22.

32. "A Noiseless Patient Spider," line 4, *CRE*, p. 450.

SELECTED BIBLIOGRAPHY

Abrams, M. H. "Structure and Style in the Greater Romantic Lyric," *From Sensibility to Romanticism*. Ed. F. W. Hilles and H. Bloom. New York: Oxford University Press, 1965, pp. 527–60.

Adams, R. P. "Romanticism and the American Renaissance." *American Literature*, 23 (1952), 419–32.

Ahlers, Alice. "Cinematographic Technique in *Leaves of Grass*." *Walt Whitman Review*, 12 (December 1966), 93–97.

Allen, Gay Wilson. "Regarding the 'Publication' of the First *Leaves of Grass*." *American Literature, 28 (1956)*, 78–79.

—— *American Prosody*. 1935; rpt. New York: Octagon Books, 1966.

—— *A Reader's Guide to Walt Whitman*. New York: Farrar, Straus & Giroux, 1970.

—— *The Solitary Singer: A Critical Biography of Walt Whitman*. New York: Grove Press, 1955.

—— *Walt Whitman Handbook*. Chicago: Packard and Co., 1946.

Allen, Gay Wilson, and Davis, Charles T. *Walt Whitman's Poems: Selections with Critical Aids*. New York: New York University Press, 1955.

Anderson, Quentin. *The Imperial Self: An Essay in American Literary and Cultural History*. 1971; rpt. New York: Vintage-Knopf, 1972.

Arvin, Newton. *Herman Melville: A Critical Biography*. 1950; rpt. New York: Viking, 1957.

—— *Whitman*. New York: Macmillan, 1938.

Aspiz, Harold. "Educating the Kosmos: 'There Was a Child Went Forth.' " *American Quarterly*, 18 (Winter 1966), 655–66.

—— "A Reading of Whitman's 'Faces.' " *Walt Whitman Review*, 19 (June 1973), 37–48.

SELECTED BIBLIOGRAPHY

Asselineau, Roger. *The Evolution of Walt Whitman: The Creation of a Personality*. Cambridge, Mass.: Harvard University Press, 1960.

—— *The Evolution of Walt Whitman: The Creation of a Book*. Cambridge, Mass.: Harvard University Press, 1962.

—— "Whitman et Wordsworth—Etude d'une influence indirecte." *Revue de Littérature Comparée*, 19 (1955), 505–12.

Barfield, Owen. "Poetic Diction and Legal Fiction." *The Importance of Language*. Ed. Max Block. Englewood Cliffs, N.J.: Prentice-Hall, 1962, pp. 51–71.

Beck, Ronald. "The Structure of 'Song of Myself' and the Critics." *Walt Whitman Review*, 15 (March 1969), 32–38.

Berthoff, Warner. *The Example of Melville*. Princeton: Princeton University Press, 1962.

Betsky, Seymour. "Whose Walt Whitman?: French Scholar and American Critics." *English Studies*, 47 (June 1966), 199–208.

Black, Stephen A. "Whitman and Psychoanalytic Criticism: A Response to Arthur Golden." *Literature and Psychology*, 20 (1970), 79–81.

—— "Whitman and the Failure of Mysticism: Identity and Identification in 'Song of Myself.' " *Walt Whitman Review*, 15 (December 1969), 223–30.

Blackmur, R. P. "Language as Gesture." *Visions and Revisions*. Ed. B. S. Oldsey and A. O. Lewis. New York: E. P. Dutton, 1962, pp. 204–26.

Blodgett, Harold W. "Teaching 'Song of Myself.' " *The Emerson Society Quarterly*, No. 22 (I Quarter 1961), pp. 2–3.

Bosquet, Alain. *Whitman*. Paris: Gallimard, 1959.

Bracker, Jon. "The Conclusion of 'Song of Myself.' " *Walt Whitman Review*, 10 (March 1964), 22.

Bradley, Sculley. "The Fundamental Metrical Principle in Whitman's Poetry." *American Literature*, 10 (1938–39), 437–59.

Brady, Sister Mary William. *Whitman's Revisions of the "Song of Myself."* Diss., University of Chicago, 1947.

Brasher, Thomas L. "Be—, Be—, Be Not Too Damned—." *Walt Whitman Review*, 14 (June 1968), 60.

Bridgman, Richard. "Whitman's Calendar Leaves." *College English*, 25 (March 1964), 420–25.

Briggs, Arthur E. *Walt Whitman, Thinker and Artist*. New York: Philosophical Library, 1952.

Bucke, Richard Maurice. "Notes on the Text of *Leaves of Grass*." *The Conservator*, 7 (May 1896), 40.

—— *Walt Whitman*. Philadelphia: David McKay, 1883.

Buell, Lawrence. "Transcendentalist Catalogue Rhetoric: Vision Versus Form." *American Literature*, 40 (1968–69), 325–39.

Burke, Kenneth. *The Philosophy of Literary Form.* 1941; rpt. New York: Vintage-Knopf, 1957.

—— "Policy Made Personal: Whitman's Verse and Prose—Salient Traits." Leaves of Grass *One Hundred Years After.* Ed. with and Introduction by Milton Hindus. Stanford: Stanford University Press, 1955, pp. 74–108.

Burroughs, John. *Whitman: A Study.* 1906; rpt. in *The Complete Writings of John Burroughs,* Wake-Robin Edition. New York: Wm. H. Wise & Co., 1924, Vol. 18.

Bychowski, Gustav, M.D. "Walt Whitman: A Study in Sublimation." *Psychoanalysis and the Social Sciences.* New York: International Universities Press, 1951, III, 223–61.

Canby, Henry Seidel. *Walt Whitman, an American.* Boston: Houghton Mifflin, 1943.

Carlisle, E. Fred. *The Uncertain Self: Whitman's Drama of Identity.* N.p.: Michigan State University Press, 1973.

—— "Walt Whitman: The Drama of Identity." *Criticism,* 10 (Fall 1968), 271–75.

Carlson, Eric W. "Whitman's Song of Myself, 59–65." *The Explicator,* 18 (November 1949), item 13.

Cassirer, Ernst. *Language and Myth,* trans. Susanne K. Langer. 1946; rpt. New York: Dover Publications, n.d.

Catel, Jean. *Walt Whitman: La Naissance du Poète.* Paris: Rieder, 1929.

—— *Rythme et langage dans la Ire édition des "Leaves of Grass" (1855).* Montpellier: Causse, Graille et Castelnau, 1930.

Chari, V. K. "Structure of Whitman's Catalogue Poems." *Walt Whitman Review,* 18 (March 1972), 3–17.

—— *Whitman in the Light of Vedantic Mysticism: An Interpretation.* Lincoln, Neb.: University of Nebraska Press, 1964.

Chase, Richard V. *Walt Whitman Reconsidered.* London: Gollancz, 1955.

Clark, Leadie Mae. *Walt Whitman's Concept of the American Common Man.* New York: Philosophical Library, 1955.

Coffman, Stanley K., Jr. " 'Crossing Brooklyn Ferry': A Note on the Catalogue Technique in Whitman's Poetry." *Modern Philology,* 51 (May 1954), 225–32.

Coleridge, Samuel Taylor. *Biographia Literaria.* 2 volumes. Ed. J. Shawcross. 1907; rpt. London: Oxford University Press, 1965.

Collins, Christopher. *The Uses of Observation: A Study of Correspondential Vision in the Writing of Emerson, Thoreau, and Whitman.* Diss., Columbia University, 1964.

Conner, Frederic William. *Cosmic Optimism: A Study of the Interpreta-*

SELECTED BIBLIOGRAPHY

tion of Evolution by American Poets from Emerson to Robinson. Gainesville: University of Florida Press, 1949.

Cooke, Alice L. "A Note on Whitman's Symbolism in 'Song of Myself.' " *Modern Language Notes,* 65 (1950), 228–32.

Coy, Rebecca. "A Study of Whitman's Diction." *University of Texas Studies in English,* 16 (July 1936), 115–24.

Crawley, Thomas Edward. *The Structure of Leaves of Grass.* Austin: University of Texas Press, 1970.

Daiches, David. "Walt Whitman: Impressionist Prophet." *Leaves of Grass One Hundred Years After.* Ed. with and Introduction by Milton Hindus. Stanford: Stanford University Press, 1955, pp. 109–22.

[Dana, Charles A.] Review of *Leaves of Grass* in *The New York Tribune,* July 23, 1855, p. 3.

Davidson, James. "Whitman's Twenty-Eight Young Men." *Walt Whitman Review,* 12 (December 1966), 100–1.

Davidson, Loren K. *Whitman's "Song of Myself."* Diss., Duke Uinversity, 1959.

—— "Whitman's 'Song of Myself': An Analysis." *Litera,* 7 (1960), 49–89.

DeFalco, Joseph M. "The Narrative Shift in Whitman's 'Song of Myself.' " *Walt Whitman Review,* 9 (December 1963), 82–84.

Donaldson, Thomas. *Walt Whitman, the Man.* New York: Francis P. Harper, 1896.

Duerksen, Roland A. "Similarities Between Shelley's 'Defence of Poetry' and Whitman's 1855 'Preface': A Comparison." *Walt Whitman Review,* 10 (September 1964), 51–60.

—— "Markings by Whitman in His Copy of Shelley's Works." *Walt Whitman Review,* 14 (December 1968) 147–51.

Eby, E. H. "Walt Whitman's 'Indirections.' " *Walt Whitman Review,* 12 (March 1966), 5–16.

Eliot, T. S. "The Three Voices of Poetry." *On Poetry and Poets.* New York: Farrar, Straus & Cudahy, 1957, pp. 96–112.

Emerson, Ralph Waldo. *The Complete Works of Ralph Waldo Emerson.* Ed. with and Introduction by E. W. Emerson. Boston: Houghton Mifflin, 1903. Volumes 1–4.

—— "Humanity of Science." *The Early Lectures of Emerson,* Volume II: 1836–1838. Ed. S. Whicher, R. Spiller, and E. Williams. Cambridge, Mass.": Harvard University Press, 1966, pp. 22–40.

—— *The Journals and Miscellaneous Notebooks of Ralph Waldo Emerson.* Volume 5, ed. M. Sealts. Cambridge, Mass.: Harvard University Press, 1965; Volume 7, ed. A. W. Plumstead and H. Hayford. Cambridge, Mass.: Harvard University Press, 1969.

Sister Eva Mary, O.S.F. "Shades of Darkness in 'The Sleepers.' " *Walt Whitman Review,* 15 (September 1969), 187–90.

SELECTED BIBLIOGRAPHY

Feidelson, Charles. *Symbolism and American Literature.* Chicago: University of Chicago Press, 1955.

Fowler, Orson Squire. *Amativeness, or Evils and Remedies of Excessive and Perverted Sexuality.* New York: Fowlers and Wells, 1844.

Frye, Northrop. *Anatomy of Criticism: Four Essays.* Princeton: Princeton University Press, 1957.

—— *The Well-Tempered Critic.* Bloomington, Ind.: Indiana University Press, 1963.

Fussell, Paul, Jr. "Whitman's Curious Warble: Reminiscence and Reconciliation." *The Presence of Walt Whitman.* Ed. R. W. B. Lewis. New York: Columbia University Press, 1962, pp. 28–51.

Gloag, Paton J. *Introduction to the Johannine Writings.* London: James Nisbet & Co., 1893.

Goethe, Johann Wolfgang. "The Metamorphosis of Plants." *Goethe's Botanical Writings,* trans. Bertha Mueller. Honolulu: University of Hawaii Press, 1952.

Gohdes, Clarence. "Section 50 of Whitman's 'Song of Myself.'" *Modern Language Notes,* 75 (December 1960), 654–56.

—— "Whitman as 'One of the Roughs.'" *Walt Whitman Review,* 8 (March 1962), 18.

Goodale, David. "Some of Walt Whitman's Borrowings." *American Literature,* 10 (1938–39), 202–15.

Grier, Edward F. "Walt Whitman's Earliest Known Notebook." *PMLA,* 83 (1968), 1453–56.

Griffin, Robert J. "Notes on Structural Devices in Whitman's Poetry." *Tennessee Studies in Literature,* 6 (1961), 15–24.

Gross, Harvey. *Sound and Form in Modern Poetry.* Ann Arbor: University of Michigan Press, 1964.

Hindus, Milton. "Notes Toward the Definition of a Typical Poetic Line in Whitman," *Walt Whitman Review,* 9 (December 1963), 75–81.

Holland, Norman A. "Toward a Psychoanalysis of Poetic Form: Some Mixed Metaphors Unmixed." *Literature and Psychology,* 15 (1965), 79–91.

Holloway, Emory. *Whitman: An Interpretation in Narrative.* New York: Knopf, 1926.

Hungerford, Edward. "Walt Whitman and His Chart of Bumps." *American Literature,* 2 (1930–31), 350–84.

Jaffe, Harold. "Bucke's *Walt Whitman:* A Collaboration." *Walt Whitman Review,* 15 (September 1969), 190–94.

James, William. *The Varieties of Religious Experience.* 1902; rpt. London: Collier-Macmillan, 1961.

Jarrell, Randall. "Some Lines from Whitman." *Poetry and the Age.* New York: Knopf, 1953, pp. 112–32.

SELECTED BIBLIOGRAPHY

Jensen, Millie D. "Whitman and Hegel: The 'Curious Triplicate Process.' " *Walt Whitman Review,* 10 (June 1964), 27–34.

Johnston, Kenneth G., and Rees, John O., Jr. "Whitman and the Foofoos: An Experiment in Language." *Walt Whitman Review,* 17 (March 1971), 3–10.

Kahn, Sholom J. "Whitman's 'Black Lucifer': Some Possible Sources." *PMLA,* 17 ('1956), 932–44.

Kallsen, T. J. "The Improbabilities in Section 11 of 'Song of Myself.' " *Walt Whitman Review,* 13 (September 1967), 87–92.

—— " 'Song of Myself': Logical Unity Through Analogy." *West Virginia University Bulletin,* 9 (1953), 33–40.

Kilby, James A. "Walt Whitman's 'Trippers and Askers.' " *American Notes and Queries,* 4 (September 1965), 37–39.

Kinnaird, John. "Leaves of Grass and the American Paradox." *Whitman: A Collection of Critical Essays.* Ed. R. H. Pearce. Englewood Cliffs, N.J.: Prentice-Hall, 1962, pp. 24–36.

Lasser, Michael L. "Sex and Sentimentality in Whitman's Poetry." *The Emerson Society Quarterly,* No. 43 (II Quarter 1966), 94–97.

Lawrence, D. H. *Studies in Classic American Literature.* 1923; rpt. Garden City, N.Y.: Anchor-Doubleday, 1951.

Lewis, R. W. B. *The American Adam: Innocence, Tragedy, and Tradition in the Nineteenth Century.* Chicago: University of Chicago Press, 1955.

—— *The Trials of the Word: Essays in American Literature and the Humanistic Tradition.* New Haven: Yale University Press, 1965.

Lieber, Todd. *Endless Experiments: Essays on the Heroic Experience in American Romanticism.* Columbus, O.: Ohio State University Press, 1973.

Mabbott, T. O. "Whitman's 'Song of Myself,' XXIV, 19." *The Explicator,* 5 (April 1947), item 43.

Magowan, Robin. "The Horse of the Gods: Possession in 'Song of Myself.' " *Walt Whitman Review,* 15 (June 1969), 67–76.

Marks, Alfred H. "Whitman's Triadic Imagery." *American Literature,* 23 (1951–52), 99–126.

Mason, John B. "Walt Whitman's Catalogues: Rhetorical Means for Two Journeys in 'Song of Myself.' " *American Literature,* 45 (1973–74), 34–49.

Matthiessen, F. O. *American Renaissance.* New York: Oxford University Press, 1941.

McElderry, Bruce, Jr. "Personae in Whitman (1855–1860)." *American Transcendental Quarterly,* No. 12 (Fall 1971), 26–28.

—— "Poetry and Religion: A Parallel in Whitman and Arnold." *Walt Whitman Review,* 8 (December 1962), 80–83.

SELECTED BIBLIOGRAPHY

Miller, Edwin H. *Walt Whitman's Poetry: A Psychological Journey*. Boston: Houghton Mifflin, 1968.

Miller, F. DeWolfe. "The Partitive Studies of 'Song of Myself.' " *American Transcendental Quarterly*, No. 12 (Fall 1971), 12–14.

Miller, J. Hillis. "Three Problems of Fictional Form: First-Person Narration in *David Copperfield* and *Huckleberry Finn*." *Experience in the Novel: Selected Papers from the English Institute*. Ed. R. H. Pearce. New York: Columbia University Press, 1968, pp. 21–48.

Miller, James E., Jr. *A Critical Guide to Leaves of Grass*. Chicago: University of Chicago Press, 1957.

Miller, Perry. *The Raven and the Whale: The War of Words and Wits in the Era of Poe and Melville*. New York: Harcourt, Brace & World, 1956.

Morris, Harrison Smith. *Walt Whitman: A Brief Biography with Reminiscences*. Cambridge, Mass.: Harvard University Press, 1929.

Morse, Lucius Daniel. "Dr. Daniel G. Brinton on Walt Whitman." *The Conservator*, 10 (November 1899), 132–35.

Myers, Henry Alonzo. "Whitman's Conception of the Spiritual Democracy, 1855–1856." *American Literature*, 6 (1934–35), 239–53.

Nagle, John M. "Toward a Theory of Structure in 'Song of Myself.' " *Walt Whitman Review*, 15 (September 1969), 162–71.

Neuman, Mary A. " 'Song of Myself,' Section 21: An Explication." *Walt Whitman Review*, 13 (September 1967), 98–99.

Noon, William T., S.J. *Poetry and Prayer*. New Brunswick, N.J.: Rutgers University Press, 1967.

[Norton, Charles Eliot.] Anon. review of *Leaves of Grass* in *Putnam's Monthly*, September 1855; rpt. as "Whitman's *Leaves of Grass* (1855)" in *A Century of Whitman Criticism*. Ed. E. H. Miller. Bloomington, Ind.: Indiana University Press, 1969, pp. 2–4.

Orth, Michael. "Walt Whitman, Metaphysical Teapot: The Structure of 'Song of Myself.' " *Walt Whitman Review*, 14 (March 1968), 16–24.

Paine, Gregory. "The Literary Relations of Whitman and Carlyle with Especial Reference to Their Contrasting Views on Democracy." *Studies in Philology*, 36 (1939), 550–63.

Pearce, Roy Harvey. *The Continuity of American Poetry*. Princeton: Princeton University Press, 1961.

Perry, Bliss. *Walt Whitman*. Boston: Houghton Mifflin, 1906.

Pochmann, Henry. *German Culture in America*. Madison: University of Wisconsin Press, 1957.

Pound, Ezra. *ABC of Reading*. 1934; rpt. New York: New Directions, 1960.

Preuschen, Karl Adalbert. "Zur Entstehung der neuen Lyrik in Amerika;

SELECTED BIBLIOGRAPHY

Walt Whitman: *Song of Myself* (1. Fassung)." *Jahrbuch für Ameri-kastudien,* 8 (1963), 148–70.

Rexroth, Kenneth. "Walt Whitman." *Saturday Review,* September 3, 1966, p. 43.

Richards, Ivor Armstrong. *Coleridge on Imagination.* 1960; rpt. Bloomington, Ind.: Indiana University Press, 1965.

—— "How Does a Poem Know When It Is Finished?" *Parts and Wholes.* Ed. Daniel Lerner. New York: The Free Press of Glencoe, 1963, pp. 163–74.

Robbins, J. Albert. "The Narrative Form of 'Song of Myself.' " *American Transcendental Quarterly,* No. 12 (Fall 1971), 17–20.

Ross, E. C. "Whitman's Verse." *Modern Language Notes,* 45 (1930), 363–64.

Rountree, Thomas J. "Whitman's Indirect Expresssion and Its Application to 'Song of Myself.' " *PMLA,* 73 (1958), 549–55.

Rubin, Joseph Jay. *The Historic Whitman.* University Park, Pa.: The Pennsylvania State University Press, 1973.

Rukeyser, Muriel. *The Life of Poetry.* New York: A. A. Wynn, 1949.

Russell, Jack. "*Israel Potter* and 'Song of Myself.' " *American Literature,* 40 (1968–69), 72–77.

Sanborn, Frank B. "Reminiscent of Whitman." *The Conservator,* 8 (May 1897), 37–40.

Sanders, Mary K. "Shelley's Promethean Shadow on *Leaves of Grass.*" *Walt Whitman Review,* 14 (December 1968), 151–59.

Santayana, George. *Essays in Literary Criticism.* New York: Scribner's, 1956.

Schiller, Andrew. "An Approach to Whitman's Metrics," *The Emerson Society Quarterly,* No. 22 (I Quarter 1961), 23–25.

Schneider, Elisabeth. *Coleridge, Opium, and Kubla Khan.* Chicago: University of Chicago Press, 1953.

Schumann, Detlev W. "Enumerative Style and Its Significance in Whitman, Rilke, Werfel." *Modern Language Quarterly,* 3 (1942), 171–204.

Schyberg, Frederik. *Walt Whitman,* trans. E. A. Allen. New York: Columbia University Press, 1951.

Scott, Fred Newton. "A Note on Walt Whitman's Prosody." *The Standard of American Speech.* New York: Allyn and Bacon, 1926, pp. 285–311.

Skipp, Francis E. "Whitman's 'Lucifer': A Footnote to 'The Sleepers.' " *Walt Whitman Review,* 11 (June 1965), 52–53.

Slattery, Sister Margaret Patrice. "Patterns of Imagery in Whitman's 'There Was a Child Went Forth.' " *Walt Whitman Review,* 15 (June 1969), 112–14.

SELECTED BIBLIOGRAPHY

Smith, Barbara Herrnstein. *Poetic Closure: A Study of How Poems End.* Chicago: University of Chicago Press, 1968.

Stern, Madeleine B. *Heads and Headlines.* Norman, Okla.: University of Oklahoma Press, 1971.

Stovall, Floyd. "Main Drifts in Whitman's Poetry." *American Literature,* 4 (1932–33), 3–21.

Strauch, Carl F. "The Structure of 'Song of Myself.' " *The English Journal,* College Edition, 27 (1938), 597–607.

Swayne, Mattie. "Whitman's Catalogue Rhetoric." *University of Texas Studies in English,* 21 (July 1941), 162–78.

Symonds, John Addington. *Walt Whitman, A Study.* London: George Rutledge & Sons, 1893.

Tannenbaum, Earl. "Pattern in Whitman's 'Song of Myself.' " *CLA Journal,* 6 (September 1962), 44–49.

Taylor, Estelle W. "Analysis and Comparison of the 1855 and 1891 Versions of Whitman's 'To Think of Time.' " *Walt Whitman Review,* 13 (December 1967), 107–22.

Todd, Edgeley W. "Indian Pictures and Two Whitman Poems." *The Huntington Library Quarterly,* 19 (1955–56), 1–11.

Traubel, Horace. *With Walt Whitman in Camden.* 5 vols. Vol. 1, Boston: Small, Maynard, and Co., 1906. Vol. 2, New York: D. Appleton and Co., 1908. Vol. 3, New York: M. Kennedy, 1914. Vol. 4, ed. Sculley Bradley, Philadelphia: University of Pennsylvania Press, 1953. Vol. 5, ed. Gertrude Traubel, Carbondale, Ill.: Southern Illinois University Press, 1964.

Trowbridge, John T. "Reminiscence of Walt Whitman." *The Atlantic Monthly,* 89 (1902), 163–75.

Tuttle, R. C. *The Identity of Walt Whitman.* Diss., University of Washington, 1965.

Vince, R. W. "A Reading of 'The Sleepers.' " *Walt Whitman Review,* 18 (March 1972), 17–28.

Waggoner, Hyatt H. *American Poets from the Puritans to the Present.* 1968; rpt. New York: Dell, 1970.

Ware, Lois. "Poetic Conventions in 'Leaves of Grass.' " *Studies in Philology,* 26 (1929), 47–57.

Warfel, Harry R. "A Seminar in Leaves of Grass." *The Emerson Society Quarterly,* No. 22 (I Quarter 1961), 27–28.

Waskow, Howard J. *Whitman: Explorations in Form.* Chicago: University of Chicago Press, 1966.

Weathers, Willie T. "Whitman's Poetic Translations of His 1855 Preface." *American Literature,* 19 (1947–48), 2–40.

Wellek, Rene, and Warren, Austin. *Theory of Literature.* New York: Harcourt, Brace, and Co., 1949.

SELECTED BIBLIOGRAPHY

Whicher, Stephen E. "Whitman's Awakening to Death: Toward a Biographical Reading of 'Out of the Cradle Endlessly Rocking.' " *The Presence of Walt Whitman: Selected Papers from the English Institute.* Ed. with a Foreword by R. W. B. Lewis. New York: Columbia University Press, 1962, pp. 1–27.

Whitman, Walt. Gay Wilson Allen and Sculley Bradley, eds. *The Collected Writings of Walt Whitman.* New York: New York University Press, 1961– .

　　The Correspondence. Ed. Edwin H. Miller. Vol. I, 1846–1867 (New York, 1961); Vol. II, 1868–1875 (New York, 1961).

　　The Early Poems and the Fiction. Ed. Thomas L. Brasher. New York, 1963.

　　Leaves of Grass: Comprehensive Reader's Edition. Ed. Harold W. Blodgett and Sculley Bradley. New York, 1965.

　　Prose Works 1892. Ed. Floyd Stovall. Vol. I, *Specimen Days.* (New York, 1963); Vol. II, *Collect and Other Prose* (New York, 1963).

—— *Leaves of Grass: Fascimile of the 1855 Edition.* With an Introduction by C. J. Furness. Facsimile Text Society Publication No. 47. New York: Columbia University Press, 1939.

—— *Leaves of Grass: A Facsimile of the First Edition.* Ed. with an Introduction by Richard Bridgman. San Francisco: Chandler Publishing Co., 1968.

—— *Leaves of Grass: The First (1855) Edition.* Ed. with an Introduction by Malcolm Cowley. New York: Viking, 1959.

—— *Leaves of Grass,* Inclusive Edition. Ed. Emory Holloway. 1926; rpt. Garden City, N.Y.: Doubleday, 1954.

[Whitman, Walt.] *An American Primer.* Ed. Horace Traubel. Boston: Maynard, 1904.

—— *The Gathering of the Forces.* Ed. C. Rogers and J. Black. 2 volumes. New York: Putnam's Sons, 1920.

—— *In Re Walt Whitman.* Ed. by his literary executors. Philadelphia: David McKay, 1893.

—— *New York Dissected.* Ed. E. Holloway and R. Adimari. New York: Rufus Rockwell Wilson, 1936.

—— *Notes and Fragments Left by Walt Whitman.* Ed. R. M. Bucke. London: Talbot, 1899.

—— *The Uncollected Poetry and Prose of Walt Whitman: Much of Which Has Been But Recently Discovered with Various Early Manuscripts Now First Published.* Ed. Emory Holloway. 2 volumes. Garden City, N.Y.: Doubleday, Page & Co., 1921.

—— *Walt Whitman's Workshop: A Collection of Unpublished Manuscripts.* Ed. with an Introduction and Notes by C. J. Furness. Cambridge, Mass.: Harvard University Press, 1928.

SELECTED BIBLIOGRAPHY

Wiley, Autrey Nell. "Reiterative Devices in *Leaves of Grass.*" *American Literature*, 1 (1929–30), 161–70.

Winters, Yvor. *In Defence of Reason*. Denver: Alan Swallow, 1947.

Woodruff, Stuart C. "Whitman: Poet or Prophet?" *Walt Whitman Review*, 14 (June 1968), 35–40.

INDEX

INDEX

INDEX

Matthiessen, F. O., 19, 23, 57, 65, 79-80, 114, 214, 259, 261, 269, 278
McElderry, Bruce R., Jr., 273
Melville, Herman, 40-41, 79, 92, 133, 256, 280
"Merge," the, as metaphor of the triplicate process, 50-52, 77, 103-6, 109, 112, 125, 133, 158-64, 222, 247
Mill, John Stuart, 20, 22
Miller, Edwin H., 100, 110, 129-31, 139, 235, 238, 274, 284
Miller, J. Hillis, 197, 201, 204
Miller, Perry, 9, 32
Milton, John, 200, 205
Myers, Henry Alonzo, 45, 57-58, 64, 281
Mysticism, 135-36, 170
Myth, 218-20, 222-27, 248

"Noiseless Patient Spider, A," 245
Noon, William, S. J., 269
Norton, Charles Eliot, 2

O'Connor, William D., 220
Organicism, 8, 30, 36, 46, 284
Orth, Michael, 276
"Out of the Cradle Endlessly Rocking," 105

Paine, Gregory, 261
Parataxis, paratactic structure, 196-97, 199, 219, 232, 277
Parton, Mrs. Sara Payson Willis, 7-8
Pearce, Roy Harvey, 6, 55, 148, 151, 282
Perry, Bliss, 13, 18, 26, 231
Phrenology, 61-62, 72, 240
Physiology, 146-47
"Pictures," 274
Plato, 40-41, 85
Plenitude, 257
Poe, Edgar Allan, 280
Pound, Ezra, 2, 147, 211
"Preface 1855," 4, *13-87*, 91-5, 100, 104, 108-11, 118-19, 122-23, 125, 128, 149, 159-60, 195, 202, 207, 211, 216, 218, 221, 226, 233, 243, 246-47, 257; Whitman's views of, 13-14; Whitman's revisions, 14, 86; viewed

as a poetic theory and program, 15-16, 18, 23; title, 16-18; theme of "America," 30-32, 35, 47, 52-55, 57, 67, 69, 74, 76, 84, 86, 100, 218, 226, 246, 249; theme of the "greatest poet," 31-33, 35-38, 42, 44-47, 49, 52-57, 68-69, 74, 76, 78-80, 83-84, 86, 91, 100, 104, 110, 119, 125, 136, 160, 202, 205, 210-11, 214, 216-18, 223-24, 226-27, 233, 240, 246, 249; structure, 31-32, 52-54, 69, 248; Whitman's principal intentions with, 76

Quakers, 65, 142-43, 214

Rexroth, Kenneth, 214
Richards, I. A., 190, 257
Rites, ritual, 225-27, 238, 248
Robbins, J. Albert, 171
Rome, Andrew and James, 6-7
Ross, E. C., 263
Rossetti, William, 14, 71
Rountree, Thomas J., 198, 279
Rubin, Joseph Jay, 8
Ruskin, John, 103

Sanborn, Frank B., 214
Santayana, George, 97-98, 195
Schyberg, Frederik, 79-80, 231
Scott, Fred Newton, 213
Self, 2, 40, 48, 55, 74, 97-98, 100-3, 111-13, 115, 117-18, 135-36, 140, 146, 160, 164-67, 169-71, 175, 177-78, 182, 189, 203, 217, 223, 225, 233, 235, 237, 239, 248
Shelley, Percy Bysshe, 37, 85, 124, 267
Skipp, Francis E., 283
Slattery, Sister Margaret Patrice, 284
"Sleepers, The," 3-4, 71, 94, 235-42, 248, 268, 283
Smith, Barbara Herrnstein, 184, 187-88, 273, 277
Smith, Fred Manning, 261
"Song for Occupations, A," 3, 220, 232-33, 235, 241
"Song of Myself," 3-4, 25, 74-76, *91-227*, 233-36, 239-40, 242, 245-48; rhetorical

INDEX